OBJECTIVE ECONOMICS

How Ayn Rand's Philosophy
Changes Everything about Economics

M. Northrup Buechner

University Press of America,® Inc.
Lanham · Boulder · New York · Toronto · Plymouth, UK

University Press of America,® Inc.
4501 Forbes Boulevard
Suite 200
Lanham, Maryland 20706
UPA Acquisitions Department (301) 459-3366

Estover Road
Plymouth PL6 7PY
United Kingdom

Library of Congress Control Number: 2011921825
ISBN: 978-0-7618-5481-4 (paperback : alk. paper)
eISBN: 978-0-7618-5482-1

To Ayn Rand

Who changed my life

Who will change the world

TABLE OF CONTENTS

PREFACE

This book is the product of forty-eight years spent studying Ayn Rand's philosophy of Objectivism and the science of economics. When I read *Atlas Shrugged* in 1962, I was stunned that Ayn Rand rejected everything I had been taught in two economics courses. Like most of economics in 1962, the purpose of those courses was to justify government intervention in the economy. Ayn Rand advocated laissez-faire capitalism, that is, an economy with no government intervention. I set out to find the truth. Forty-eight years later, I have learned a lot about what is wrong with modern economics and where much of the truth lies. In particular, I have figured out some of the implications for economics of Ayn Rand's concept of *objective*. The purpose of this book is to communicate that knowledge.

To the best of my knowledge, this book represents the first attempt to rewrite economics in the light of Ayn Rand's philosophy of Objectivism. As such, it is an application of Objectivism to the theory of how a free economy works, that is, to the theory of how men's independent, self-interested actions to produce and exchange economic values are integrated into an *economic system*. Ayn Rand did not leave us a new economics, but something much more important—a philosophical foundation for all the special sciences. My purpose is not to present the Objectivist philosophy, but to apply Objectivism to economics. For an authoritative account of Objectivism, there is no substitute for Ayn Rand's own writings.

This book is written for any man who wants to know how a free economy works and/or some of the implications of Ayn Rand's philosophy for economics. In the body of the book, I have done my best to pre-suppose no knowledge of economics or Objectivism. I have confined my critique of modern economics to four appendices. Particularly in the appendices, I refer frequently to modern economics and modern economists, by which I mean academic economists, that is, economists employed in colleges and universities. By "modern," I mean roughly the last fifty years. Undergraduates are taught essentially the same economic principles today that I was taught in 1960.

This is not a disinterested study. If one wants to live on earth, what is required to sustain man's life on earth is of urgent interest. The subject matter of economics is how the members of an economic system obtain the material values of man's life, such as food, clothing, and shelter. These things do not fall from heaven. They are the result of a specific and, in the history of the human race on earth, an unprecedented economic system.

In principle, the fundamental choice of economic systems is between laissez-faire capitalism and government controls. In politics, the equivalent choice is the choice between freedom and tyranny. In terms of concrete results, this is the choice between life and death. If one chooses life, then one chooses freedom, which includes economic freedom, and economic freedom, if it means anything, means laissez-faire capitalism. Unfortunately, economic freedom has no definite meaning to most people. They take it as meaning today's mixed economy, which is not free, which is far from laissez-faire, and which has been sliding haltingly, but inexorably, toward complete state control for over a hundred years. In the concept "laissez-faire capitalism," laissez-faire is redundant. In principle, anything other than laissez-faire is not capitalism and is not free. Consequently, throughout this book, I use the terms free enterprise, free economy, free markets, market economy, and capitalism interchangeably, to mean the same thing, that is, laissez-faire capitalism.

In the slide from freedom toward tyranny, modern economics has played a not inconsequential role. For a hundred years, all of its esoteric theories have carried a single message that the general public has absorbed and that they now take as self-evident—the message that laissez-faire capitalism is *impractical*.

The practicality of capitalism is my general thesis; Ayn Rand's concept of *objective* is my starting point. The general reader may be surprised to hear that philosophy has implications for economics, but I promise that if this seems unlikely here, at the beginning of the book, it will seem inescapable by the end.

The philosophical overview of my book is this: Modern economics is the product of modern philosophy. Since on every important issue, Objectivism is the opposite of modern philosophy, Objectivism changes everything about economics. This includes economics' method, the conception of the economy, the meaning of competition, the conception of price, the principle of gains from trade, the nature of business costs, the concepts of supply and demand, the theory of price, the role of scarcity, and the theory of aggregate production. Overall, as the result of all the preceding, Objectivism confirms the practicality of capitalism.

Economics is a positive science, not a normative science; that is, economics is descriptive, not prescriptive. Economics can tell us what the effect of a minimum wage law is on employment, but economics cannot tell us whether that effect is good or bad. Good and bad are concepts of evaluation. They presuppose a standard and ultimately a system of morality. Economics is not ethics. Nevertheless, economics is not cut off from ethics. Ayn Rand defined ethics as "a code of values to guide men's choices and actions" (1964, 2), and some such code, explicit or implicit, underlies everything men do. This includes the work of economists in analyzing an economic system.

Ayn Rand's ethics of rational self-interest is an ethics of egoism, the view that selfishness is a virtue and the individual should be the beneficiary of his own actions. Her ethics is my ethics. By contrast, for the last hundred years, economists have presupposed the opposite ethics as the base for both generating and evaluating theories: that ethics is altruism, the morality of selflessness and self-sacrifice—the morality of the Judeo-Christian tradition—the morality that dominates our age and that has dominated Western civilization for two thousand years.

The clash between altruism and capitalism is irremediable. Capitalism is *the* economic system of self-interest. Capitalism depends on self-interest, it encourages self-interest, it sanctions self-interest. At every level and in every detail, the motivation of self-interest is the motivation of capitalism. Consequently, the altruists have loathed capitalism from its beginning in the Industrial Revolution. This loathing is the fundamental cause of "the sweeping market reforms that economists have long advocated" (Mandler 1999, 151).

The primary purpose of economics is to identify, interpret, and explain how a capitalist economy works. Altruism assured economists that capitalism is evil in advance of that knowledge. The evil consequences of this belief permeate all of economics, damning capitalism in both theory and practice. In theory, capitalism never had a chance. Since an evil system cannot work, capitalism was convicted *a priori*. As for capitalism's practice, economists' commitment to the immorality of capitalism blinded them to the facts. Every datum, every event, every phenomenon, every result, every aspect of capitalism was twisted and distorted out of any resemblance to reality in order to make it conform to the altruist agenda. Ayn Rand's refutation of altruism makes it possible for the first time in history to present the theory and practice of capitalism objectively, untouched by moral distortion. This is the first study of economics to take advantage of that fact, and in the end, an objective perspective is the primary value I have to offer.

A note to the businessmen in my audience: Qua businessman, a man does not need to know economics. If he does know it, his knowledge does not affect his strictly business decisions, such as whether or not to raise his price when his costs increase. But each businessman does need to understand economics if he wants to defend his business against those who want to seize it or shut it down or confiscate his profits. A businessman does not need to understand economics in order to run his business successfully—just in order to keep it. That is the understanding I am offering here.

I would like to suggest to those who know something about economics that they begin by reading the first three appendices. My theory departs radically from standard economics and I have found that people with some background in economics often do not understand me, particularly the fact that I have abandoned supply and demand curves. Appendices A, B, and C present my critique of modern economics and explain why I have taken the direction I have.

I also call the reader's attention to the Exegesis and Glossary (pp. 333–35). This overview of the various meanings of the concept of value can help one to keep these meanings straight as one reads the text.

The modern context requires that I mention that throughout this book, as well as in this preface, I use the terms "man," "he," and "his" in the generic sense, meaning human beings in general. I am unalterably opposed to the current fad of pretending that, after a thousand years of absolute clarity on the subject, the generic use of man somehow excludes women.

I am indebted to many friends and colleagues for helpful comments on this project at various stages over the twenty years of its development. Some of them have forgotten helping me, but I remember. They include Robert W. B. Love, Jr., Young Back Choy, Charles Clark, Daniel Drake, Israel M. Kirzner, Walter J. Primeaux, Jr., Warren Samuels, Gary

Schuld, Gordon Tullock, Harry Binswanger, Peter Schwartz, and Mike Berliner. Mary Ann Sures, persuaded me to direct my book to the general reader. Anthem Foundation's grant to St. John's University reduced my course load from three to two in the fall 2005 semester. John Ridpath gave me line-by-line comments on many chapters. Marlene Podritske greatly improved an early version of the manuscript. Donna Montrezza contributed important grammatical points. Finally, the lion's share of the line editing fell to Darcy Lorin, who meticulously copyedited most of the present version and saved me from many errors.

My special thanks go to those who read the entire manuscript: to my brothers Robert and Donald who responded as noneconomists to a book written for noneconomists; to Leland B. Yeager, who gave me his usual thoughtful comments; and especially to my most dedicated and relentless editor, M. Kathryn Eickhoff, who read everything and many chapters more than once, who gave me detailed editorial comments on the entire book, and on many chapters more than once, and who brought the invaluable perspective of a business economist to my book and kept me from insulting that venerable group. Finally, my most reliable supporter has been Shrikant Rangnekar, who changed the book's structure with his observations, who formatted the book for publication, whose enthusiasm for my project has never lagged, and who has been the main force behind its appearance in its present form. I am grateful to all these people, and all of them are innocent of any errors that may remain.

M. Northrup Buechner
New York, NY
November 2010

INTRODUCTION

What facts of reality gave rise to the science of economics? This is Ayn Rand's unique method of grasping the meaning of a concept—to identify the facts of reality that are its cause (1979 51). I will be using this approach throughout.

The answer is the creation of wealth. Economics appeared in England during the Industrial Revolution when wealth had increased to the point that thinking men grasped that there was something new that needed to be explained. The definition of economics is the science that identifies the principles governing the origin and growth of wealth.[1] Economics discovers these principles by studying the exchange of wealth, that is, the purchase and sale of goods and services, and all the phenomena that arise out of such exchange. The fundamental economic activity is exchange—buying and selling. All other economic phenomena can be traced to exchange. Economics deals with the principles governing production only in so far as the producer intends to sell his product. Price is the condition of exchange, what one gives or receives in order to buy or sell.

An economy consists of the total means of production and exchange (including people) in a geographical area, integrated by prices into a system. The science of economics identifies the principles governing an economy; it shows how producing, selling, and buying by men are tied together by prices into a consistent, integrated, and harmonious whole. In other words, the function of economics is to explain how an economy works, and thus results in the accumulation of wealth.

As that science, economics solves an enormous puzzle. In their economic actions, in their purchases and sales, in the jobs they take and the products they produce and the prices they charge and pay, in every economic action of their lives, millions upon millions of men are motivated primarily by their desire for their own material welfare. They are trying to increase their personal wealth and/or the goods and services at their disposal and/or the material well-being of themselves and those they love. In their economic actions, not one of them is primarily concerned with the overall functioning of the economy or with the general welfare of their fellow men. Yet somehow, all these actions of all these millions of human beings are made consistent with one another and put together into what is normally a smoothly functioning unit. The result is that every man who wants to work can find a job, every businessman can sell his output, and every man willing to pay the price can buy anything he wants, as much as he wants, whenever he wants it.

Considered abstractly, this is an amazing phenomenon. Prior to Adam Smith (economics' founding father), men believed that it was impossible, that if the state allowed people to do whatever they wanted, the economy would collapse into chaos. Almost nobody believes that today. Those who are willing to look can see, around the world, that the freer economies are the most productive and the controlled economies have collapsed into chaos.

But how is it possible? How can everybody go his own way, follow his own star, pursue his own interests, take any job he wants, produce whatever he wants, sell whatever he wants, buy whatever he wants, and in so doing, participate in a system where what he chooses to produce and buy and sell is consistent with what everyone else chooses to produce and buy and sell? Why is the result not chaos? That is the puzzle economics solves—the question economics answers—the phenomenon I will explain. Many answers have been offered, many of them partially correct. But a full answer was not possible until Ayn Rand's creation of Objectivism and her concept of objective value. I stand on her shoulders.

Ayn Rand is best known to the general public as the author of *The Fountainhead* (1943) and *Atlas Shrugged* (1957), and for the morality of rational self-interest she advanced in those two novels. However, for the last twenty-five years of her life, she published only nonfiction in which she developed the details, implications, and applications of her philosophical system.

One of her seminal identifications was that there are two themes running through the history of men's philosophical ideas. She called those themes intrinsicism and subjectivism. Intrinsicism is the premise that our ideas originate in reality alone and that we passively receive what reality writes on our minds (for example, the ideas of Plato, Augustine, and religious thought in general). Subjectivism is the premise that our ideas originate within us, that our minds create ideas out of our own internal resources (for example, the ideas of Hume, Kant, and virtually all of contemporary philosophy). Ayn Rand held that intrinsicism and subjectivism constitute a false alternative. The answer to both of them, she argued, is the viewpoint she called Objectivism—that our ideas originate in a voluntary relationship between our minds and reality in which we are able to grasp the facts if we follow the right method. She considered Aristotle her primary predecessor and, to a much lesser extent, the nonreligious half of Thomas Aquinas.

When we apply this tripartite division of thought to economics, the effects are revolutionary. The most important and fundamental of those effects is on the meaning of *economic value*. Economic value is the fundamental concept of economic thought, the concept at the base of all the other concepts, problems, and phenomena that are distinctively economic. Economics has never had a generally accepted definition of value. Economists have always used that concept with the feeling Ayn Rand called "I kinda know what I mean" (Rand 1990, 21). What have they meant?

Two antagonistic and largely implicit concepts of economic value have dominated the history of economics. The first is an expression of intrinsicism; the second is an instance of subjectivism. (1) value as a phenomenon of external reality, existing *in* goods, determining prices, and causing men's evaluations of goods, and (2) value as a phenomenon of man's mind, residing in men and their subjective feelings. The first of these concepts dominated the British classical school and Marxist economics; commentators frequently have called it *intrinsic value*, and that is what I will call it. At the end of the nineteenth century, the concept of intrinsic value came under attack and eventually was replaced by (2), the modern concept of *subjective value*.

I will argue that both of these concepts of value are invalid, that economic value does not exist in the form described by either of them, and that as the foundation of economic thought, economics needs a new concept of value, a concept derived from Ayn Rand's concept of *objective value*. Objective value is a concept of value neither as residing in reality alone nor in man's mind alone, but as the product of a relationship between the facts of reality and man's mind. Unqualified, consistent adherence to objective value transforms economic thought.

The solution to the puzzle I posed in the second paragraph lies in the price system that characterizes every capitalist or semi-capitalist economy. Consequently, the theory of price is the basis for understanding how a free economy works and the key theory for all of economic thought. This book presents the foundation, derivation, explanation and proof of a new theory of price and then uses that theory to show how a capitalist economy works.

This book is divided into thirteen chapters. Chapters 1 through 4 present the foundations on which my theory depends. In chapters 5 through 9, I derive my theory of objective prices and show that every price is a measure of objective economic value. Chapters 10 and 11 show how a free economy responds to changes in economic conditions. Chapter 12 shows how prices distribute an economy's productive resources among the economy's business enterprises in order to maximize total output and economic growth. Chapter 13 applies the theory of objective prices to the measurement of the economy's total output and to the conception of total spending.

Let us begin.

CHAPTER ONE

METHOD AND CONTEXT

This chapter identifies and defends the method that I will follow and the context in which my theory applies. Logically, both these issues must be settled before anything else can be taken up.

I. The Method of Economics

This section makes the case for induction as the basic means to knowledge in economics. Consequently, we have to deal with fundamental issues of epistemology, issues that have been subjects of intense controversy by philosophers over centuries. As a result, critics may regard my treatment of these issues as absurdly short. Its length is justified by my intent, which is not to resolve these issues, but to identify my method and indicate the direction in which its justification lies. See Peikoff (1991, 4– 17) for a complete explanation of the Objectivist position.

Method gives the steps by which men create the content of their science. Consequently, a science's method has a major impact on what that content is. For example, the model-building approach of modern economics has given us a science that consists almost exclusively of mathematical models (see appendices A and B). It is important, therefore, to state at the beginning of a work the method one intends to use in reaching one's conclusions. Since my science is economics, I must state how I think a properly grounded economics should proceed.

The method of economics presupposes the law of cause and effect. In the Western world, since the Renaissance, thinkers have interpreted the law of causality as a link between *actions*, one action causing another; for example, a rolling billiard ball hits a stationary billiard ball causing it to roll (Peikoff 1991, 16). David Hume used this interpretation to invalidate causality (1739; see, for example, 151–2). In fact, causality as a link between actions cannot be proved and Ayn Rand rejected that interpretation.

Ayn Rand held that causality is a link between entities and their actions. The law of causality says that what a thing can do depends on what it is; how an entity can act depends on its identity.

> The law of causality is the law of identity applied to action. All actions are caused by entities. The nature of an action is caused and determined by the nature of the entities that act; a thing cannot act in contradiction to its nature (Rand 1961, 188).

The law of identity says that a thing is what it is. A is A.

> Whatever you choose to consider, be it an object, an attribute or an action, the law of identity remains the same. A leaf cannot be a stone at the same time, it cannot be all red and all green at the same time, it cannot freeze and burn at the same time (Rand 1961, 153).

An entity's identity consists of its attributes; its attributes make the entity the kind of thing it is. One grasps a causal connection by grasping the attributes of the entity that cause the entity's action. For example, when one billiard ball strikes another billiard ball, the struck ball rolls. The attributes of the struck ball that cause that effect include its roundness, its hardness, its weight, and so forth (Peikoff 1991, 16). Causality also requires that we take account of the surrounding conditions (the context), which consist of other entities and their identity. For the struck ball to roll, the conditions include that it lie on a flat, smooth surface and that its movement be unimpeded. For nonhuman entities, when the conditions are the same, the entity's action is the same.

Since the subject matter of economics is man acting to gain economic values (goods and services), economic laws depend on man's nature, and as such, are instances of the law of cause and effect. As every other entity, what a man can do depends on what he is. Man's defining characteristic—the essence of his identity—is the faculty of reason. How he acts depends on what he thinks, which is the product of his use or misuse of reason. Every economic law, theory, or principle depends on man's rational nature.

Objectivism holds that the exercise of man's rational faculty is volitional—that man's nature is such that he must choose—he cannot avoid choosing. At root, volition consists of the choice to use reason or not—to think or not—to focus on reality or make oneself blind to it. (Rand 1961, 146–48; 1964, 11–14). In every minute of his life, in every activity he undertakes, every man has to choose to think or to evade that effort. The fact that he must make that choice is not subject to his choice. Man's volition is an expression of causal law; that he must choose is necessitated by what he is.

Because man has the choice to think or not, he does not always take the same action under the same conditions. This is the fundamental difference between economics and the physical sciences. For example, after considering his income and his expenses, a man may decide that he cannot afford to buy a new car (the cause is his thought; the effect is his decision not to buy). The same man under the same conditions can evade that knowledge and buy the new car (the cause is his evasion; the effect is his purchase).

The fact that man does not always do the same thing under the same conditions does not mean that the conditions surrounding a theory about human beings are irrelevant. In presenting a theory, one has to identify the context in which it applies. The surrounding conditions constitute the context. Absent that context, one cannot know where or how to apply a theory.

We can gain knowledge of nonhuman entities by observation because we know in principle that they act the same when the conditions are the same. (This does not mean that acquiring such knowledge is easy or automatic.) But how are we to gain knowledge by observing the economic actions of human beings when they do *not* necessarily do the same thing under the same conditions? This book constitutes my answer to that question. At this point, I can say only that, (1) explicitly or implicitly, the proviso "if they are rational" precedes almost every proposition I make and (2) introspection is essential.

A. Induction

Induction is the fundamental method by which man gains knowledge. Induction consists of reaching principles or theories or laws by generalizing from individual instances. When one induces, one looks at reality—at the facts—as the basis for both originating and proving theories. For ex-

ample, the origin of our knowledge that all men are mortal is our knowledge that throughout history, every man ever born has died. To prove
man's mortality, we make additional observations. One is that throughout history, not just every man, but every living thing also has died. Still
another observation is that as living things age, they all become increa-
singly frail and vulnerable to disease and internal breakdown. We conclude that the aging process, and death as the end, is inherent in life.

The base of induction is the law of cause and effect. Since what an
entity can do depends on what it is, the actions we observe express the
nature of the entity. When we repeatedly observe the same action by the
same entities under the same conditions (for example, living things die),
we can infer a generalization regarding all entities of that kind, and state
that generalization as a law or theory (for example, all men are mortal).[1]

Deduction consists of moving from the general to the particular, of
applying theories and laws to individual instances. Deduction is the method by which we integrate our knowledge into a noncontradictory
whole, the method by which we determine to what subjects a theory applies and to what it does not. For example, the general proposition that
all men are mortal in conjunction with the observation that Socrates is a
man allows us to deduce that Socrates will die. When we deduce the application of a principle to a new subject, we acquire new knowledge.

The importance of Aristotle's validation of deduction and his identification of the valid forms of deduction cannot be exaggerated. But it is
induction, not deduction, that is the fundamental means to human knowledge.[2] Before we can deduce from a theory, we have to have the theory.
Induction is how we get the theory. Induction precedes deduction and is
the means to it. Without induction, there can be no deduction and no
conceptual knowledge of any kind.

The process of inducing involves questions that vary from case to
case and that are answered on a case-by-case basis. These are questions
such as: What constitutes evidence in this case? How do we know when
we have enough evidence to reach a generalization? What are the relevant conditions? How can we tell when the conditions are the same? And
so forth. Answering these questions can be difficult, but they can be
answered, have been answered, and are being answered—as evidenced
by the scientific and technological knowledge that is the foundation of
modern industrial civilization. If men had not answered these questions
in case after case, New York City would not exist.

Summing up, there are three aspects to the use of induction in reaching economic laws: (1) Economic laws are instances of the law of cause

and effect. Economic laws describe the actions of men that are caused by their use of reason. (2) The conditions where the theory applies establish the context for the theory. (3) Induction is the means to reach the theory; we generalize from concrete instances to reach general laws or principles.

B. Other Things Equal

Ceteris paribus is the traditional name for the method of economics. A Latin phrase, it is translated "other things equal." It means the assumption that "other things do not change." This assumption is at the base of most economic theories.

The standard argument for assuming other things equal is that the world is very complicated, everything in it is constantly changing, and it is impossible to reach knowledge if we cannot hold some things constant. In the physical sciences, scientists hold other things constant in material reality with their scientific tools. A simple example is a vacuum jar; empty out the air, hold the air friction constant at zero, and a feather falls like a stone.

Economists cannot hold other things unchanging in material reality because the reality they deal with consists primarily of human beings. Instead, they hold things unchanging in their imagination. For example, consider how economists prove the law of demand. The law of demand says that an increase in price reduces the quantity people want to buy. Therefore, if the price of chicken rises, the housewife buys less. However, if at the same time, she hears that chicken is better for one's health, or her husband gets a big raise, or the price of beef also rises, then instead of buying less chicken at the higher price, she may buy more. To prove the law of demand, economists assume that none of these other things happen; that is, they assume that things other than the price of the product (chicken) and the quantity of it sold do not change.

I have a different concept of demand and a different proof of the law of demand, but my proof also depends on the assumption that other things do not change. Nevertheless, the absence of an explicit statement of "other things equal" cannot invalidate a theory. If we can identify a causal connection on the assumption that other things do *not* change, then that causal connection exists when other things *do* change. If that were not true, the theory would be valid only in an unchanging world. Since the world that exists is characterized by continuous change, the theory would be false, as the law of demand would be if it did not hold when "other things" change.

All this is small potatoes, however. The wider significance of other things equal is the necessity of identifying the surrounding conditions that characterize any instance of induction. The surrounding conditions establish the context in which the theory applies. Properly understood, the ceteris paribus assumption is a shorthand expression for identifying and holding constant the context in which the theory is true. From that perspective, other things equal is always implicit in the background of every economic theory. There can be no theory without it.

C. How to Evaluate This Book

Induction requires that one look at reality and take into account all the relevant facts and only the relevant facts; that one distinguish scrupulously between that for which one has evidence and that for which one does not; that one gauge carefully and conscientiously what conclusion the evidence supports and with what degree of certainty. When one infers facts from existing facts, one has to look at reality and be sure that the "existing facts" exist. If knowledge is the goal, one may not simply make up convenient facts or ignore facts that are inconsistent with one's theory.

In light of the forgoing, let me state unequivocally the standard of knowledge for this book—the standard on which the theory presented here should be judged. Unless indicated otherwise, everything that follows here is a description of the actions of individuals and businesses in a real economy. My theory consists of identifying what men do when they pursue economic values and the principles they follow in setting the prices at which they sell those values. If at any point in my exposition, men do not act as I say they do or the consequences are not what I say they are, then on that point I am wrong and my theory is wrong. My purpose throughout has been to insure that there are no such points.

II. Laissez-Faire Capitalism

The general context in which my theory applies is laissez-faire capitalism. In the widest, all-embracing sense, this political-economic system (capitalism, for short) defines the surrounding conditions (the context) discussed above (pp. 12–16).

The ideological root of capitalism is man's rights. The Declaration of Independence names the relationship of government to man's rights which Thomas Jefferson learned from John Locke:

> We hold these truths to be self-evident, that all men are created
> equal, that they are endowed by their creator with certain unalienable
> rights, that among these are life, liberty and the pursuit of happiness.
> That to secure these rights, governments are instituted among men, . . .

Men need the institution of government to secure their rights, and in capitalism, the government is limited to that function. The concept of rights draws a line between each man and all other men, a line that neither society nor the state nor any man, group, collective, or association may morally cross. When the line is crossed, a man's rights are violated. On his side of the line, every individual is free to do anything as long as he does not violate another man's rights. This condition defines political freedom.

What principle defines the violation of man's rights (Rand 2009, 213)? Locke did not name this principle, and the Founding Fathers did not know more on this subject than what they had learned from Locke. In part for this reason (more fundamentally, due to the rise of collectivism in the 19th century), the next generation of intellectuals rejected the concept of man's rights as meaningless. "Nonsense on stilts" was Bentham's famous epithet for man's rights, an epithet that accurately reflected the 19th-century intellectuals' hostility to America's founding idea—and their intellectual superficiality. The American people held on to the concept of rights as best they could in the face of the intellectuals' opposition, but the original meaning eventually was lost. Today, everyone feels free to claim a "right" to anything they feel strongly about while simultaneously they have no idea of what they have a right to and of what they do not.

It remained for Ayn Rand to rescue man's rights from the abyss, to make clear what rights are, what their foundation is, when they are violated, and what are the proper functions of a government limited to the protection of man's rights (Rand 1964, 123–34). Her crucial identification is that rights are violated by the initiation of physical force.

In gross contradiction of this principle, governments have initiated every form of physical force, including mass murder. A government that initiates the use of force is a worse scourge than all the criminals in the world put together. This includes all the modern, semicivilized welfare states who initiate physical force against their own people without compunction. Men who have initiated force against no one are sent to jail, threatened with jail, fined or have their property seized by countless government agencies. In principle, the laws enforced by the initiation of force against innocent men violate all men's rights and reverse the proper function of government "to secure these rights."

Under laissez-faire capitalism, the government exercises force only in retaliation against those who initiate its use (criminals). This is what it means to protect men's rights. A proper government threatens the initiators of force with jail or financial penalties and puts them in jail or imposes fines on them when they are caught. The economic system in which the government is limited to this function is capitalism: "a social system based on the recognition of individual rights, including property rights, in which all property is privately owned" (Rand 1966, 11).

Capitalism is the context in which my theory applies. I will assume that all property is privately owned and the government does nothing but protect men's rights, including their property rights—that the government never initiates force in any form against its own citizens—that there is complete separation between the economy and the state in the same way that traditionally there has been separation between church and state. Unless stated otherwise, I assume that there is no government intervention in the economy, that there are no government laws, regulations, rules, directives, or edicts restricting the private, voluntary economic relations of individual human beings.[3]

In fact, the study of economics has to begin, and always has begun, with the assumption, more or less fuzzy, that men are free to act on their best rational judgment. It is not possible to begin with a system in which the government initiates physical force, intervening, regulating, controlling, and usurping countless details of economic activity and then ask a question such as "Why do prices rise?" It is impossible in such a system to distinguish the effects of the government's controls from the effects of men's independent, noncoerced choices. Maybe the government imposes a tax on corporate profits. Is that the reason prices rise? There is no way to answer that without a theory of how prices would be set in the absence of the tax.

One has to begin by seeing how capitalism would work when there are no government controls or regulations. Once that is clear, it is possible to project a government action or regulation and consider how it changes the free market result. But first one has to have the free market result. That is what I provide in this book.

In the preceding discussion, I have made no attempt to give the moral justification for laissez-faire capitalism. In particular, I have not defined man's rights nor explained why men have rights. I have not explained what is wrong with the initiation of physical force and why it is only such force that violates men's rights. I have not tried to argue that capitalism is the ideal social system, though I believe it is. Proving these things is the responsibility of political philosophy, not economics. Here, I have been concerned only to identify *what* laissez faire is. That it should exist is another subject.

Money

The existence of money is a prerequisite for the existence of an economy. When there is no money, one cannot count on being able to trade for something one needs, no matter how desperately. Consequently, if something is required for survival, everyone must produce it himself.

For example, suppose you need additional wheat to get through the winter and you take a cow to market to trade for wheat. But suppose everyone has had a poor harvest and no one has brought wheat to trade. Or, suppose someone has brought wheat to trade, but he does not want your cow. Maybe a three- or four- or five-way exchange can be worked out whereby each party gets what he wants. But maybe not.

Europe during the Dark Ages shows us the result when there is no money. Economically, it consisted of little, self-sufficient settlements spread over the landscape, the inhabitants meeting occasionally to trade by barter. There was almost no division of labor and nothing that could be called an economy. Consequently, I deny that barter economies are part of the subject matter of economics. There are no barter economies.[4]

Under laissez-faire capitalism, the base of the money supply would be something durable, readily acceptable, and with a history of maintaining its value. Paper does not have these characteristics. Gold does. That is why since the Renaissance, in the Western world, when men were free to choose the money they would accept, they chose gold. Gold is durable, has sufficient value per ounce to be easily carried, can be divided up or combined to reach any desired value, and all units can be produced to the same grade of purity (for example, 18-karat gold). If someone invented an inexpensive way to produce gold so that gold's value per ounce fell to the value of lead, people would choose some other durable metal of high value as money. The important point about money under laissez faire is that individuals voluntarily choose to accept it in exchange. *It is not chosen or enforced or controlled by the government.*

In laissez-faire capitalism, the government has no function to perform with regard to money. There is no central bank. The supply of money is entirely in the hands of private, profit-making banks and mints. An explanation of how this system would work is outside the scope of this book,[5] but there is no question that it would work.[6] This is essentially the monetary system that the United States had between the Civil War and the establishment of the Federal Reserve in 1913. Under that system, the United States had an average annual rate of economic growth (over 5 percent a year) higher than any country has ever had over a similar period of time in the history of the world. That growth rate lifted the United States from an economically insignificant participant in world trade to the leading industrial power of the globe.

For this book, my assumption regarding money is that money exists. My theory of price does not depend on money being gold. It does depend on the monetary unit being reasonably stable in value, that is, explosive growth in the quantity of money does not cause high rates of price inflation, and steep declines in the quantity of money do not cause depressions. In other words, I assume monetary conditions essentially equivalent to those experienced by the United States between 1982 and 2007. The only thing a central bank can do for an economy is not cause inflation, and for twenty-five years, that is what the Federal Reserve System did for the United States. The result for that quarter century was the essential monetary environment that people require for rational economic action, that is, they did not have to guess the rate of price inflation in making their long-range plans to save and invest.

The United States' monetary regime between 1982 and 2007 was not laissez-faire. The salutary monetary conditions of that era were essentially the achievement of two men: first, Paul Volcker (1979–1987) and then Alan Greenspan (1987–2007), the two chairmen of the Federal Reserve System during that period. The achievement of Volcker and Greenspan indicates the fatal flaw of central banking. It effectively puts control of the nation's money supply in the hands of a single man and requires him to be a paragon of integrity, courage, independence, intelligence, and rationality—and to know something about economics. When his character and/or his knowledge is lacking, a country pays a terrible price, as the United States did during the Great Depression of the 1930s, the Great Inflation of 1965 to 1982, and what is currently being called the Great Recession of 2007–2009. There is nothing about the way a central bank functions that rules out much worse consequences. The value of money can be destroyed, all forms of savings wiped out, all retirees ruined, production crippled, and exchange reduced to barter—for example, Germany in 1923 (Peikoff 1982, 185–88) and countless third world countries. Only laissez faire and the gold standard rule out such horrors. However, my subject is the theory of price, not the theory of money.

Now we can take up the conceptual foundation of my theory, objective economic value.

CHAPTER TWO

OBJECTIVE ECONOMIC VALUE

I. The Modern Meaning of Value

[F]rom no source do so many errors, and so much difference of opinion in [political economy] proceed, as from the vague ideas which are attached to the word value. (Ricardo 1821, 13)

[T]he question of value is fundamental. Almost every speculation respecting the economical interests of a society . . . implies some theory of value: the smallest error on that subject infects with corresponding error all our other conclusions; and anything vague or misty in our conception of it creates confusion and uncertainty in everything else. (Mill 1848, 436)

As Ricardo half-grasped and Mill clearly understood, the fundamental concept of economic thought is economic value. This concept is the root of everything in economics; indeed, the subject matter of economic theory consists of practically nothing else. The theory of gross national product is the theory of variations in the total value of the all the goods and services produced in a year. Price theory is the theory of the economic value of individual goods and services. Even an unemployment rate has meaning only in the context of a market economy where businessmen pay workers their economic value. Outside of that context, the term "unemployed" does not apply because such men are not looking for work. Instead, they are the hoards of beggars, thieves, and robber gangs of medieval Europe, of India a hundred years ago, and of many third world countries today.

Economic value is central. As a first approximation, economic values are values that are bought and sold—they are the objects of trade and exchange—they are "goods and services." Values that are produced but not sold, such as the family dinner cooked by a homemaker, are not *economic* values.[1]

Ricardo and Mill thought nothing was more important to economic theory than clarity on the meaning of value. One cannot say that modern economic theorists dispute their viewpoint, because it has simply vanished. There is little interest in the concept of value today (Sraffa 1926, 535) because the old controversies over its meaning have been buried by equating value with price or market value. The error in this practice is indicated by the fact that market value is a particular kind of value, a subdivision of value in general. Consequently, one cannot grasp the meaning of market value without first grasping, at least implicitly, the meaning of value (and market).[2]

A further consequence of the vagueness of value's meaning in modern economics is that value continues to have the effects ascribed to it by Ricardo and Mill. What economists mean by value today is not just vague, it is a contradictory hodgepodge of the concepts of intrinsic, subjective, and objective value presented in the introduction. The same economists hold all three concepts of value at the same time, and they switch from one concept to another without notice to either themselves or others, depending on their subject matter. For example, intrinsic value underlies the measurement of gross national product (chapter 13). Subjective value is the base on which economists have erected their theory of price, (this chapter and appendices A and B). Sometimes, not often, economists' implicit concept of value is objective value—for example, when the subject is businessmen's costs of production.

The Role of Philosophy

The distinctions among the intrinsic, the subjective, and the objective are philosophical distinctions. Philosophy is the foundation of human knowledge; philosophy establishes the fundamental premises on which all of man's other intellectual endeavors proceed. An error in the philosophical foundation eventually infects every idea that men hold. That is what has happened in economics. In all their thinking and theorizing, economists have been caught between the intrinsic and the subjective, between the idea that knowledge is injected directly from reality into men's minds and the idea that men create knowledge out of their internal resources, according to their feelings, unaffected by reality.

Since this chapter analyzes the philosophical foundations of economic value, let us begin by indicating the effect of philosophy on economics: Briefly, one's philosophy determines how one expects free men to behave, and therefore, how one expects a free economy to function, and therefore, what content one expects of economic knowledge, and therefore, what one will accept as economic knowledge.

The intrinsicist, for example, expects men to behave as passive reactors to imprinting from reality. Hence, he expects economic activity to proceed in rigid conformity to external forces and he expects economic theory to consist of laws cataloguing those forces. Marxist economics is the most thoroughgoing and unqualified intrinsicist system in the history of economics, and it takes exactly that form. Marxist economics includes, for example, the law of the falling rate of profit, the law of crises and depressions, the law of the reserve army of the unemployed, the law of the increasing misery of the proletariat, and so forth. To the uninitiated, these so-called laws sound like jargon, but Marx holds that they are inherent in material reality and therefore inevitable, unavoidable facts.

The subjectivist expects people to behave as autonomous, emotion-driven beings who act independent of reality. Therefore, he expects economic activity to be chaotic and unintelligible and he expects economic knowledge to consist of abstractions cut off from reality (for example, modern model building). In an unusually explicit statement of this viewpoint, Buchanan says "Subjective economics [is] a means of imposing an intellectual order on apparent chaos" (1982, 16).[3]

The advocate of objective value expects men's actions to be guided by reason and, therefore, to be consistent with the facts. Consequently, he expects economic activity to be orderly and intelligible, and economic theory to describe men's rational responses to the facts of their economic lives. That is what I expect and that is what this book presents.

II. The Objective versus the Intrinsic and the Subjective

This section develops further the intrinsic-subjective-objective distinction, focusing on the different methods of knowledge implied by each. My purpose is to explain the tripartite division sufficiently for my readers to grasp my theoretical premises because I am going to use that tripartite division immediately to illuminate the concept of economic value, and then throughout the book.

Ayn Rand's distinction between the intrinsic, the subjective, and the objective identifies three different theories of how man's ideas relate to the external world (Rand 1966, 14–15). *Intrinsicism* holds that man's ideas are inherent in reality independent of his mind; *subjectivism* holds that man's ideas are the product of his mind independent of reality; *objectivism* holds that man's ideas are the product of his choice to think about reality.

The adherents of "intrinsicism" (a term coined by Rand) hold that the active source and determinant of man's ideas is reality itself. They hold that two plus two equals four because reality makes that truth unavoidable. The subjectivists hold that consciousness is the active source and creator of our ideas, apart from and independent of external reality. They hold that two plus two equals four because we have arbitrarily assigned definitions to "two," "plus," "equals," and "four" which necessitate that result. Ayn Rand holds that our ideas are the result of self-directed, volitional processing by our minds of the evidence of reality given by our senses. Every child has to choose to do conceptual work in order to grasp (as opposed to parroting) that two plus two equals four.

Now consider what each of these three approaches implies about the method men must use in order to reach knowledge.

A. The Intrinsic

Intrinsicism has a long and influential past. Historically, it was the first view adopted by men in trying to explain their ideas about the world. It is probably still the dominant viewpoint of the man-in-the-street.

The intrinsic view of conceptual knowledge implies that no specific method of acquiring knowledge is necessary. The intrinsicist thinks that if you are honest, if you open yourself up to reality, knowledge is infallibly given in direct communication from reality. The intrinsicist takes vision as the model for all human awareness. You open your eyes, and there it is. One does not need a method in order to see, and that which one sees is unquestionable.

The most popular version of the intrinsicist view of knowledge is the idea that God communicates his truths directly to us in the form of divine revelation. In contemporary philosophy, the leading intrinsicists are the Marxists. Marx held that "the material forces of production" determine all our ideas, which he called "the ideological superstructure." The notion that material objects determine ideas is a version of intrinsicism.

B. The Subjective

Subjectivism appeared on the scene when thinkers began to grasp that man's mind has a nature that affects his knowledge, and that men can choose what method to follow in the pursuit of knowledge. Moreover, we can observe that they choose all kinds of methods. Some people pray for God's help, some try to enlist the help of the dead, some study their horoscopes, some go by what others think, some follow their fancy, some are wedded to their feelings, some use reason to study the object. The subjectivists hold that there are no revelations from God, reality does not write on our minds, and that therefore one method is as good as another. We can believe whatever we want to believe; the conclusions reached by a drugged witchdoctor in the jungle are as valid as the conclusions of a scientist in a laboratory.

While intrinsicism implies that no method is necessary to reach knowledge, subjectivism implies that no method is possible—that method is the disqualifying element in the pursuit of knowledge. A method is a process followed by a mind, and subjectivists share the intrinsicist premise that only unprocessed knowledge is true knowledge. Real knowledge has to be projected directly into our minds by reality, untouched by any attribute of consciousness. There is no such knowledge, the subjectivists hold; all knowledge is processed, and distorted, by the actions of consciousness. Hence, they conclude that knowledge consists of any idea one happens to have.

The subjectivists deny that there is any objective, conceptual standard to distinguish knowledge from fantasy. This leaves them with only one logical possibility as a standard, that is, emotions. Subjectivists treat emotions as causal primaries, as the bedrock on which everything else is built. Knowledge consists of whatever we feel strongly about. Whatever your emotions, or your group's emotions, tell you is true *is* true for you or your group, regardless of the method by which that "knowledge" was reached.

C. The Objective

Ayn Rand denied that conceptual knowledge is either passively received from reality or the subjective creation of the mind independent of reality. Rather, she held that conceptual knowledge is the grasp, by choice, of a conceptual consciousness of the nature of something that exists. Ayn Rand discovered a new theory of what it means to be objective, a theory that makes *objective* diametrically opposed to *intrinsic*, with which it has always been confused.

Ayn Rand held that all our conceptual knowledge results from our minds processing the facts of reality. The faculty that does the processing is reason,[4] the processing is called cognition; knowledge is the product. Ayn Rand defined knowledge as "a mental grasp of the facts of reality, reached either by perceptual observation or by a process of reason based on perceptual observation" (1967, 35). Note that in contrast to intrinsicism and subjectivism, method is a major part of this definition. In answer to the intrinsicists, the mind is not passive in the acquisition of knowledge; one must identify the method that differentiates and integrates the facts and then carefully, conscientiously, follow that method. In answer to the subjectivists, use of the proper method is what enables man's mind to grasp reality; it is the means, not the obstacle, to knowledge. However, the mind *grasps* reality; it does not *create* reality.

To sum up the three alternatives in the most elemental terms, the intrinsic is *the out there*, the subjective is *the in here*, and the objective is *the out there as processed by the in here*.

Now we can analyze the three concepts of value that correspond to these philosophical alternatives. The following explanation does not present the viewpoint of any specific economist. Although these three concepts have affected the thought of every economist, it is doubtful that any of them has held any of these conceptions of value in the full, logically consistent form described below. Reduced to their essential meaning, they cannot be combined; there is no middle ground between or among them; there is no fourth alternative.

III. Intrinsic Value versus Subjective Value

On the premise of intrinsic value, the economists of the early 19th century thought that a good's economic value was caused by how hard it was to produce. On the premise of subjective value, most modern economists think that value reflects men's individual emotions. Implicit in the viewpoint of the early economists was the idea that value was an aspect of external reality. Implicit in the viewpoint of most modern economists is the idea that value is in man and his subjective feelings.

A. Intrinsic Value

The definition of value implied by the intrinsicist view is *an autonomous aspect of existence that imprints itself on consciousness and determines the values held by consciousness.* There have been two variations of the intrinsic view of value. Let us call them the naïve view and the less naïve view.

The naïve conception is that value is literally contained within goods as a kind of essence. The economists who believe this think of value as inhering in goods as part of their nature—an attribute of a good like its other attributes (size, weight, shape, color, and so forth).[5] In barter exchange, the naïve view is that if one bushel of wheat trades for one gallon of milk, it is because a bushel of wheat contains the same quantity of value as a gallon of milk. In a money economy, the naïve intrinsicist thinks that the relative prices of all goods reflect the amount of value contained in them. If one bushel of wheat costs two dollars and one gallon of milk costs one dollar, it is because one bushel of wheat contains twice as much value as one gallon of milk.

The less naïve intrinsicists do not think that value exists in goods as a kind of stuffing. Rather, their view is that value is created and fixed by some external thing, usually labor.[6] If one gallon of milk trades for one bushel of wheat, the less naïve intrinsicists say it is because they are both the product of the same quantity of labor. This is called the labor theory of value.

The naïve intrinsicist thinks that the value of a good is determined by how much value is *in* that good. The less naïve intrinsicist thinks that the value of a good is determined by how much labor was required to produce it. The two views merge in what was probably the dominant idea of the 19th century—that the value in goods is put there by labor. Thus, both views think of *value as originating in material reality prior to and independent of human evaluation.*

Classical economics inherited the concept of intrinsic value from medieval religious philosophy (Pribram 1983, 13). In its religious form, a thing's intrinsic value was determined by the order in which it was created by God, as described in Genesis. In the eighteenth century, however, in the Age of Reason, the idea of intrinsic value required some nonmystical, semirational explanation. The labor theory of value was that explanation. The labor theory holds that men value goods according to the quantity of labor "embodied" in them. How do they know how much labor that is? How does that quantity determine human valuation? The essential failing of the labor theory is that its only answer to those questions is "somehow."

B. Subjective Value

Subjective value is the dominant concept of value in the modern era. The basic premise of subjective value is that value exists in man's mind or feelings, not in things; that value is *in* the valuing human being, not *in* the valued object. Mises (1966, 96) expressed this view unequivocally: "Value is not intrinsic, it is not in things. It is within us."

We saw in part II (p. 27) that the subjectivists take emotions as causal primaries. This premise leads them directly to the view that value exists and motivates human action in the form of emotions. This implies a definition of value as *the intensity of the positive feeling with which one regards a good or service.*

In opposition to the intrinsicists, the subjectivists hold that no facts of reality cause value. Nothing in reality requires a man to value a house more than an ashtray. Because no facts of reality cause value, whatever people happen to value is arbitrary, and therefore beyond rational analysis or investigation—a view that often is held explicitly. Again, Mises (1966, 95) made the clearest statement: "the ultimate ends of human action are not open to examination from any absolute standard. Ultimate ends are ultimately given, they are purely subjective . . . ." In a survey article on ethics in economics, Hausman and Mcpherson (1993, 680) observed that "Economists typically take preferences as givens and not themselves subject to rational appraisal."

What is the emotion residing in consciousness that constitutes value? Subjectivists have given a variety of answers to this question, for example, needs, wants, desires, pleasure, utility, preference. For a long time, the almost universal answer was utility, where utility was equated with the satisfaction of one's preferences. "[T]he greater the number, and strength, of a person's preferences that are satisfied, the greater the person's utility" (Haslett 1990, 69). As this quotation indicates, in the context of economic values and evaluation, the fundamental concept in economics today is preference, not utility (Mandler 1999, 78–82).

What does preference mean? Economists give very little, if any, attention to this question, but the way they use the word suggests that preference is a desire with most of the emotion squeezed out of it. Thus, the substance of a preference is the emotion that has *not* been squeezed out.

Modern economists take preferences as what they call "primitives" (Mandler 1999, 78). A primitive is a causal primary for which no explanation is required or can be offered. "We have to take human preferences as given" is the standard expression that sums up this viewpoint.[7] The consistent subjectivist view is that one's preference for a specific good or service is a simple, unanalyzable fact—an elemental starting point (Jevons 1871, pp. 45 and 65–66). Conceived in this way, preference has the fundamental characteristic of subjective value, that is, value as an emotion, and emotion as a phenomenon of consciousness independent of existence.

IV. Objective Value

A. Introduction

As an indication of the need for a new concept of value, consider what is probably the original economic action—economizing. To economize means to reduce one's use of a good or service by using it more carefully or by substituting an alternative. Why would someone do this? The intrinsicist would say that it is forced on the individual by reality, by something outside his control, perhaps by a crop failure. The subjectivist would say that it is his choice, that there is nothing to say beyond the fact that he chooses to use less, perhaps because he has lost his taste for the good.

Economics needs a theory of values—a theory of how economic values come into being and of what they consist—as grounding for its subject matter—so that we can understand economic actions such as economizing. Intrinsic value implies that no grounding is necessary, that value inheres in reality independent of man. Subjective value implies that no grounding is possible, that there is no way to explain why men value what they value. Both of these alternatives are false. Equally damning, each represents a dead end for economic knowledge.

A third concept of value—objective value—has received no explicit recognition in economics. This section explains the meaning of objective value and presents a theory of values based on objective value. It concludes with an explanation of why people economize.

B. The Standard of Objective Economic Value

Economic values may be good for people or bad; they may support men's lives or be harmful to them; they may nourish people or make them sick. As the science that studies wealth creation and exchange, economics has nothing to say about the objective merit of goods and services. They are all economic values. Ayn Rand's definition of value that encompasses all economic values is "that which one acts to gain and/or keep" (Rand 1961, 147). By this definition, a value is any object of ac-

tion—any goal, end, or purpose that a living being acts to reach. This is
the widest possible concept of value. It subsumes the values pursued by
every form of life, including plants and animals. It subsumes all the values pursued by human beings, including all economic values.

The consequence of wealth creation and exchange is the material
support of man's life on earth. This is why economics is important and
why we have to distinguish the economic values that contribute to man's
life from those that do not. The theory of *objective* economic value defines a subset of all economic values. Identification of that subset depends on an objective standard of value, that is, a standard based on the
facts of reality and independent of anyone's feelings.

Ayn Rand established "man's life" as the standard for her theory of
objective *moral* values. Thus, "All that which is proper to the life of a
rational being is the good; all that which destroys it is the evil" (Rand
1961, 149). This book evaluates economic values as objective or nonobjective by the same standard. Since we will rely on this standard
throughout, let us briefly summarize Ayn Rand's argument for man's life
as the standard of objective moral value. Her argument applies equally to
objective economic values.

Human values are not primaries, as the intrinsicists and subjectivists
suppose. The existence of values presupposes answers to the questions
"To whom?" and "For what?" A value presupposes someone to whom it
is a value and an end to which the value is a means. The fact that values
presuppose an end implies that some value must be an end in itself. An
infinite series of means to ends is impossible and would make values impossible (Rand 1964, 17). In addition, values require "the necessity of
action in the face of an alternative. Where there are no alternatives, no
values are possible" (Rand 1961, 147).

The fundamental alternative faced by all living beings, the alternative that is the root of every other alternative, is life or death. The fact
that one can die is what makes action necessary to gain and keep the values that support life. The point is *not* that one has to be alive in order to
pursue values. The point is that one must pursue and obtain values in order to *remain* alive. Life is the end in itself that causes the phenomenon
of values. The alternative of life or death is *the* value-generating alternative (Peikoff 1991, 211).

This is the answer to the subjectivist view that all values—ends and
means—are arbitrary. Man's life is not an arbitrary end. It is the cause of
human values. To reject this end is the equivalent of rejecting values as
such, and thus of ejecting oneself from the discussion (and from life).

The standard of man's life removes economic values from the realm of arbitrary feeling.

Objective *economic* values arise out of a relationship between men and what they require for their material survival.[8] Value is not *in* reality independent of man (intrinsicism); human values exist because, as a living being, man needs values in order to survive. But neither is value *in* man independent of reality (subjectivism), because *what* man needs depends on the facts—the facts of man's nature and the nature of the things in reality that will support his life. It is man's nature that he needs sustenance to live, and it is the nature of chicken eggs, for example, that they can provide that sustenance. The two together make eggs a value to man when he has *knowledge* of that relationship. Knowledge is a precondition of objective economic values.

C. Knowledge and Objective Economic Value

An item can be an objective value to a man only when he has grasped the relationship between the item and his life. A car or a toothbrush or a savings account or property rights or a free society can be a value to an individual only when he understands how it can help him get what he wants.[9]

Knowledge of any specific value depends on the choice to process the facts of existence, and depends equally on the processing mind and the processed facts. Objective values are processed values—values processed by reason. This is what defines objective value and distinguishes it fundamentally from both subjective value and intrinsic value. Both subjectivists and intrinsicists agree that to be valid, knowledge must be unprocessed (p. 27 above).

Cognition and evaluation are the two ways in which reason processes facts. Objective value originates in, and depends on, both. With respect to cognition, a specific item can be a value to someone only if he knows many things, including the nature of the item,[10] the nature of the end for which he wants it, and the relationship between the item and the end. For example, a necessary condition for people to regard a new food as a value is that they believe it will taste good and not make them sick. *Objective value depends on a relationship between consciousness and the facts, on a connection in reality that is grasped by reason.*

A man's knowledge of the relevant facts is a precondition of an objective value. His evaluation of those facts makes the value objective when the standard is man's life. Evaluation is a form of cognition. "To evaluate" means "to establish a graded relationship of means to end," with the end serving as the standard (Rand 1990, 33; Mises 1949, 96).

For example, if a man wants a dog to guard his junkyard, this end constitutes his standard for judging dogs, and he looks for mean, aggressive,
barking dogs in the dog pound. If he wants a pet for his children, that end
constitutes his standard and he evaluates the same dogs differently.

Evaluation is the process of ranking things in terms of whether they
cohere with the standard or contradict it, and to what extent. The value
that results from evaluation is the joint product of existence and consciousness. This is Ayn Rand's conception of *the objective*. The facts of
the case (the dog's nature) are identified and evaluated by one's mind
(consciousness).

Three Meanings of Value

The result of evaluation is that one identifies something (like a dog) as a
value, and at the same time, the thing is given a positive value (ranking)
in consciousness. In English, and in other languages as well, the word
value has three meanings reflecting three different perspectives on this
joint product.

(1) Value means the thing in reality one acts to gain and/or keep; the
object ranked by the evaluation. For example, water is a *value* to a thirsty
man means that water is one of his *values*; that he has identified water as
a means to furthering his life. The dog a man chooses as a pet for his
children also is a value, something he has identified as a source of pleasure. All goods and services are values—economic values.

(2) Value means the positive ranking in one's mind of the thing in
reality; value is the consequence of evaluating something as a value. For
example, water has a high *value* to a thirsty man means that a thirsty man
ranks water high. "After considering all the dogs in the pound, I value
this one the most," means I rank this dog highest.[11]

(3) A third meaning of value is the attributes or consequences of an
item that make it the means to an end and therefore the object of action.
For example, the *value* of water to a thirsty man is that it quenches his
thirst. The value of this dog as a pet is its good-tempered, friendly nature.

The subject of this chapter is primarily (1) values as things in reality
"one acts to gain and/or keep." Our main purpose has been to identify the
standards by which values are objective. Subsequent chapters will be
primarily concerned with value as ranking in a hierarchy of values—
which is the form value takes in our minds and in the economy as prices.
When we deal with the value of money in the next chapter, the third
meaning will be relevant. But clearly, there can be no values without all
three aspects: the valued object, the human mind which ranks the value,

and the particular attributes of the object which are the basis for the ranking.

D. Optional Values Are Objective Values

Optional values represent a different perspective on objective values. Consider some examples of things one might buy: a 16-ounce box of Cheerios; one pound of 93 percent lean ground beef; a 1997 used Oldsmobile, driven 46,366 miles, with a dent in the back-right quarter-panel; a 10-room, two-bath, ranch-style house, built in 1990, at 16 Orchard Drive. Because only specific concrete things exist, we buy specific concrete things. Those things are almost all optional values.

Optional values are optional on the standard of the survival requirements of a rational being. Optional values are not required to live, but they do objectively support man's life. Indeed, mandatory values on the standard of man's life are unusual. They seem to be limited to medical treatments that are necessary to ameliorate a life-threatening disease or physical defect.

Optional values take two forms: (1) the concrete form in which we choose to gain objective values, for example, the four concretes with which this section begins. Most of the specific choices that we make are optional selections (such as an eight-ounce sirloin steak) within a wider category of objective values (such as food). (2) the relative proportions in which we choose to gain objective values. Some people allocate more of their income for meals at restaurants while others prefer to be well-dressed—but both food and clothing are objective values.

Optional values are not subjective; they are not arbitrary creations of man's mind. They reflect the rule of reason, that is, man knows his optional values are optional by reason—that in reason, either steak or chicken (but not arsenic) will satisfy his need for food.

E. Nonobjective Values Are Objective Disvalues

Nonobjective values are values that contradict either or both of the two foundations of objective value: (1) man's life as the standard and (2) reason as the faculty for grasping the means to that end.

Nonobjective values are values based on something other than man's life (for example, unconsciousness, the environment, global warming, self-sacrifice, being green, the needs of others, God's will, nirvana, death), and/or values that originate in something other than a rational grasp of the facts (for example, faith, hope, fear, self-hatred, fantasy, the opinion of others, arbitrary commitment). As an example of the former, the end in itself for an alcoholic is unconsciousness (and thus, not life), but he has grasped reality correctly to the extent that alcohol is a means to that end. For the latter, the wafer a man eats in church does not threaten his life, but its consumption is inconsistent with man's life on earth where reason is his means of survival.

Nonobjective values are not subjective in the philosophic sense. They are not phenomena of consciousness independent of existence. Even nonobjective values proceed from an evaluation by consciousness, of something, according to some standard. They are nonobjective because the evaluation is not based on reason and/or the standard is something other than man's life.

However, nonobjective values *are* subjective in the sense that the valuer does not know or care about the value's relation to reality (Rand 1964, 14). Nonobjective values do not spring causelessly into consciousness, but they might as well, since the standard and/or method by which a man selects such values does not allow him to know whether they are good or bad for his life. In this fundamental sense, nonobjective values are not optional; that is, there is nothing in the selection process that insures such values will not destroy one's life—and most nonobjective values do just that (self-sacrifice is the most obvious example). Thus, nonobjective values are also objective disvalues.

The phenomenon of subjective value as proclaimed by the subjectivists does not exist. Nonobjective values are as close as men can come to pure subjectivity in their value choices. If subjective value means anything in reality, it means nonobjective value.

F. Objective Value versus Subjective Value

The modern concept of subjective value developed, in large part, as a reaction against and in answer to intrinsic value—a reaction that intrinsic value deserved. However, the early advocates of subjective value had no concept of objective value, and therefore made no distinction between subjective value and objective value. Consequently, their view of value often was a mishmash of both concepts, while the valid points they sometimes made depended on the objective part of the mishmash. To a lesser extent, this is still true of contemporary economic theory, which is self-consciously, avowedly subjectivist (without a clear understanding of what that means [Buchanan 1982, Vaughn 1982]), but still combined with some objective elements.

Nevertheless, in the way that counts, modern economics is fully subjectivist. What makes it so is its explicit foundation in the idea that all economic activity flows out of consumer preferences. Modern economists regard facts as relevant only insofar as consumer preferences make them relevant. The ultimate standard ruling the economy, they believe, the key to understanding its nature and functioning, is subjective preferences—and preferences, that is tastes, that is *values*, economists view as arbitrary and independent of the facts.[12]

The choice between objective value and subjective value is fundamental. It is the choice between an economics cut off from reality and an economics rooted in the facts.

G. Objective Economic Values

Economic values are values that are bought and sold. Hence, economic values have prices in money and are subject to rational monetary calculation in production, use, and exchange. A businessman can add up the prices of all the men, materials, and machines used in production to measure his total cost. He can add up the prices for each unit of output he sells and calculate his total revenue. He can subtract his total cost from his total revenue and learn whether he is gaining or losing. He can estimate the future revenues a new machine will make possible and compare the value of those revenues with the machine's cost. A mother can weigh the cost of a nanny for her child against other household expenses and the money available to pay for them. The ability to perform such calculations transforms the way men deal with their means of survival. It is the cause of all the phenomena of an economic system.

Not all economic values are objective. Some are nonobjective—they do not support human life and/or do not originate in a rational grasp of the facts, for example, charms, love potions, divining rods, religious articles—the things Menger called "imaginary goods" (1871, 53). Economic theory does not distinguish between objective values and nonobjective values because almost every objective value can be used in nonobjective ways (for example, the way the morbidly obese use food). More important, both objective and nonobjective values are equally subject to economic law. Nevertheless, broadly speaking, nonobjective values are the exception in a free economy. If they were not—if nonobjective values were the rule—people's grasp of reason and concern for life on earth would be insufficient to support an economic system. We would still be in the Dark Ages—or entering a new one.

Objective *economic* values are *objective* values that are bought and sold. Such values dominate a free economy in part because the free market teaches rationality to everyone who is willing to learn. In a free economy, irrationality is penalized by the loss of income, wealth, and welfare. Rationality is rewarded by the gain or retention of income, wealth, and welfare. Functioning rationally means bringing oneself into mental contact with reality and acting accordingly, which means acting to attain objective values that are within one's means. Thinking is reinforced and encouraged by freedom.

Why do people economize? When the price of a good rises, people use less or switch to less expensive alternatives as a means of conserving their money for other things. Economizing is a means of protecting one's economic welfare, of defending one's standard of living, of preserving one's business, and more generally, of preserving one's life. Economizing makes no sense unless there is an end at stake, and the only end consistent with the existence of an economy is man's life.

Most economic values are objective; they have an inextricable, positive connection to human survival. That connection is what motivates most of the actions of most of the participants in a free economy. One has not understood the nature of such an economy unless one has grasped that it consists of people acting to gain and keep objective economic values in order to support their lives.

CHAPTER THREE

FUNDAMENTAL ECONOMIC CONCEPTS

This chapter defines and explains the concepts (the individual words) on which the remainder of this book depends.

I. Supply and Demand

This section explains the importance of a theory of price to the survival of civilization and the role that the law of supply and demand has played in protecting this one. I define the concepts of supply and demand so that they can continue to play that role. These definitions play an integral part in the theory of price that I will build on objective value.

A. The Importance of a Theory of Price

Why do we need a theory of price?

In a capitalist economy, prices are the subject of intense and continuing interest to virtually everyone. People spend time thinking about prices, they worry about prices, they talk about prices, they complain about prices and, much less often, they praise prices. Why do people care so much about prices?

The answer is that prices determine how well people live. They do this in two interrelated forms: (1) In the form of wages and salaries, prices determine most incomes; and (2) The prices of consumer goods and services determine what men can afford to buy with their incomes. Together these two sets of prices determine the goods and services each individual is able to purchase, use, and enjoy—which constitutes his standard of living.

All adults understand this. Consequently, people spend much time and effort on trying to alter prices in their favor. There are essentially two opposite ways to accomplish that:

(1) By individual effort: On the one hand, a man can raise the price an employer will pay him by getting more education or special training. He can work hard and put in extra hours in order to earn promotions and raises in pay. On the other hand, he can affect the prices he pays for consumer goods and services by shopping carefully and sometimes bargaining with sellers for lower prices.

(2) By government force: Many people try to raise their incomes through the power of the state—by supporting legislation to establish minimum wage laws, wages and hours legislation, and price supports for their products. They support the use of government force to lower prices through programs such as the regulation of insurance and utility rates, and rent controls.

Resorting to force to raise or lower prices contradicts a prerequisite of capitalism: respect for property rights. People express this respect by acting on the principle that one can acquire values from others only with their consent—that all exchange has to be voluntary. A country that has never found this principle or that has abandoned it, is either a dictatorship or, worse, not a country but a collection of rival gangs in a state of permanent war.

B. The Historical Role of the Law of Supply and Demand

Historically, one of the ideas supporting the principle of property rights has been the law of supply and demand. The law of supply and demand says that *prices and wages are caused by facts—the facts of supply and demand.*

If people do not believe that prices and wages are caused by facts, then they must believe prices and wages are arbitrary. If people believe that prices are arbitrary, then they will think that prices and wages can be manipulated against them, that a seller or employer can set any price he wants, that prices reflect only the wishes and cunning of the price- and wage-setters who hold an inexorable and unfair advantage over them. Then people come to resent prices, the price-setters, and property rights; they feel justified in stealing and looting. In urban riots, interviews with self-righteous, guilt-free looters appear on our television screens.

If people think that prices and wages are arbitrary, then they think that the government can decree lower prices and higher wages with impunity. In an economic emergency, such as a serious price inflation or a financial crisis, people will demand that the government abandon the principle of property rights and resort to force (for example, Nixon's wage-price freeze of 1971 and Bush's nationalization of AIG in 2008). Disrespect for prices goes hand in hand with disrespect for property rights.[1]

The law of supply and demand is by far the most widespread economic theory held by the general public. The consequence has been the prevention (or at least the mitigation) of the above scenarios. People who know little of economics and nothing of the modern interpretation of the law, use these words, "the law of supply and demand," to stand for the rule of facts in the determination of prices. Hence, the widespread acceptance of the law's message that even the government cannot violate the law of supply and demand without dire consequences.

Originating with Adam Smith, the principle of "supply and demand" spread rapidly through economic thought in the early years of the 19th century, in part due to the efforts of Malthus, who called it the "great principle" (Thweatt 1983). From the British classical school of that era, the idea spread to the general public, and over the last two centuries, has been the basis for the belief that prices reflect the facts of supply and demand. Today, virtually every adult in the English-speaking world has heard of the law of supply and demand, whether they accept the law's message or not. The fact that many do accept that message is the primary positive contribution of economic thought to Western civilization.

Despite the enormous importance of the law of supply and demand, it plays almost no role in modern price theory. Some advanced price theory texts do not even include the law (for example, Mas-Colell, Whinston, and Green 1995), and those which do give it at most one chapter out of twenty.[2] The law of supply and demand has been essentially abolished from modern economics.

C. The Meaning of Supply and Demand

To save the concepts of supply and demand, we have to define them the way Adam Smith and the classical economists thought of them, and the

way businessmen and intelligent laymen think of them: as simple concrete quantities—as the quantity demanded and the quantity supplied
over a specific time period (a month, unless indicated otherwise).[3]

Because this meaning flies in the face of one hundred years of entrenched terminology in economics, I have to be absolutely clear on what
I am suggesting. I define demand as the quantity of a product that the
customers want to buy—meaning that the customers have the necessary
money and they are ready to spend it on this product.

An example of demand would be the quantity of Lexus cars that
Lexus customers buy each month. Many different facts may affect that
quantity: the current price of Lexus cars, the prices of competing cars in
the luxury car market, the current and expected price of gasoline, quality
differences between Lexus and other luxury automobiles, the current and
expected income of Lexus customers, the anger customers feel at Japan
over a recent international incident, the feel of the leather on the Lexus
seats, the colors of cars available from Lexus and from competing car
companies, and many other facts. Some of these facts will be relevant for
some potential buyers and irrelevant for others. But taken altogether,
these facts determine the quantity of Lexus cars Lexus customers want to
buy each month. That is the demand for Lexus cars.

Contrary to the practice of modern economics, I reject any distinction between demand and quantity demanded.[4] The demand for a product
is the quantity demanded. A change in demand *is* a change in the quantity demanded. Demand for a product may be changed by a change in the
price of the product or in the price of a competing product or in the price
of a complementary product or in the income of the business's customers
or in their tastes, or in anything else that changes the quantity people
want to buy.

Defined as the quantity people want to buy, this concept of demand
applies to every business in a market economy. People purchase a specific quantity per month from every business.[5] The quantity sold is the
quantity people are buying, and by definition, that quantity is the current
demand for the product.

The definition of supply parallels the definition of demand. Supply is
the quantity a business or an industry makes available for sale over a
month. Normally, a businessman tries to supply the same quantity that
his customers want to buy. This is not a coincidence. The businessman
selects prices for his products at which he expects to make a profit and
then produces and/or sells as much as his customers demand. If the quantity his customers want to buy goes up, the businessman increases the

quantity he produces and/or offers for sale. If the quantity his customers want to buy goes down, the businessman offers that much less for sale. Usually there is no specific quantity the businessman *wants* to sell. He wants to sell as much as he can sell at the prices he has set.

Defined as a concrete quantity, the concept of supply applies to every business in a market economy. Each one is offering for sale some definite quantity over some period of time. That is the business's supply. An increase in supply is an increase in that quantity and a decrease in supply is a decrease in that quantity.

The definition of demand as the quantity customers *want* to buy has a special significance. Sometimes businessmen misjudge demand and offer to sell less than their customers want. That condition is called a *shortage*. A shortage is defined as the excess of the quantity demanded over the quantity available at the current price. If Kyocera is offering for sale 1000 cell phones a week for $50 each, and at that price consumers want to buy 1200 a week, there is a shortage of 200. When there is a shortage, some people willing to pay the price are unable to find the product. For example, some years ago a breakfast cereal was introduced that tasted like oatmeal cookies. It vanished from grocery stores and was unavailable for weeks. The quantity people wanted to buy (their demand) exceeded the quantity businessmen were offering for sale (their supply).

In a free market, businessmen increase output to meet a shortage as quickly as possible. Since they are making a profit on each unit sold at the current price, selling more increases their profits. Usually businessmen do not raise their prices under these conditions because they do not want to undermine the blessing of an unexpectedly high demand.

Businessmen also may offer more for sale than their customers want to buy at the price they have set. That condition is called a *surplus*. A surplus is defined as the excess of the quantity supplied over the quantity demanded at the current price. If Kyocera is offering for sale 1000 cell phones a week for $50 each, and at that price consumers want to buy only 900 a week, there is a surplus of 100. For example, at the beginning of a recession, the demand for products falls and businessmen often accumulate some unwanted inventory before they realize that demand has decreased. But when they realize it, they reduce their output to meet the reduced level of demand and eliminate the surplus.

Even absent conditions that could be called a shortage or a surplus, the demand for products fluctuates over time. Consequently, demand does not equal supply from instant to instant. But if we allow time for businessmen to adjust their supply to transitory changes in demand, then the supply of most goods and services is approximately equal to the demand over a time period such as a month or a quarter.

In fact, the law of supply and demand has been widely interpreted to mean that the quantity supplied *always* equals the quantity demanded at the current price. That interpretation is wrong. The most important exception is workers, who routinely spend weeks, sometimes months, looking for jobs. Other exceptions include products such as hotel rooms, new and used housing, apartment rentals, retail and commercial office space, and land, where supply and demand are seldom, and in some cases *never*, equal at the going price. Retail establishments, such as drugstores, shoe stores, grocery stores, and so forth, typically have large stocks of goods on their shelves, only a portion of which they sell each month. They offer for sale their inventory at the beginning of the month plus whatever additions they make during the month—the total of which greatly exceeds the quantity they sell. Retail service outlets, such as restaurants, nail salons, barbershops, and so forth, usually have the ability to serve many more customers than they do. By their nature, retail businesses normally have an excess of supply over demand. Finally, utilities, such as electric power and phone companies, always maintain excess capacity in order to meet peak load demand.[6]

In the light of these facts, I reject the interpretation of the law of supply and demand as meaning that supply equals demand *always*.

D. The Law of Supply and Demand

Defined as quantities, both supply and demand are real phenomena for every business in a market economy. This means that we can apply the law of supply and demand to the whole economy. What is that law? Its essence is that wages and prices are determined by *facts*—the facts of supply and demand (p. 40).

Properly understood, the law of supply and demand is not a theory of price. It says prices are caused by the facts of supply and demand, but it does not tell us *how* these facts cause the price; it does not give us a chain of cause and effect that results in a price. In addition, we will see that there are facts other than supply and demand that affect prices. Consequently, the law's place in economics is as a subdivision of the theory of price that subsequent chapters will develop. The law of supply and demand is not to be scorned. It was the first great theoretical step in the direction of grasping that prices are objective. But it was not the last step.

II. Goods and Services

All the output and all the inputs of the economy are commonly included under these two terms, goods and services. The primary purpose of this section is to establish a rational meaning for the term service, which modern economics does not have.

What facts of reality give rise to the concept of a service? Some examples of services are an orchestra playing a symphony, a bank clearing checks, an insurance company promising to pay in the event of a loss, a doctor performing surgery, a teacher teaching a class, a secretary writing a letter for her boss, a cashier ringing up a sale in a retail store, a janitor cleaning an office, a man on an assembly line installing car doors, a CEO planning strategy.

All these services have in common that they are actions by human beings creating values that other men want. The pleasure of listening to a symphony is an end in itself to the audience,[7] while the bank, by clearing your checks, helps you pay your bills and maintain your financial solvency. The insurance company promises to pay money in the future if necessary and in the meantime gives you peace of mind. The doctor's surgery restores your health. The teacher communicates knowledge. All the activities of a business's employees (secretaries, janitors, salesmen, assembly line workers, cashiers, the CEO) create values which are means to the end of producing and selling the business's product. The fundamental fact about services is that men do things which create values for which other men are willing to pay. *A service is an action a man is paid to perform because it creates an economic value.*[8]

Now let us consider a number of concrete goods; for example, a suit, a dress, a carrot, a roast beef, a car, a machine tool, a screw driver, a factory (an integrated collection of goods), an office building, a ton of iron ore, a bridge, a house, an airplane, a computer, a toothbrush. These are all economic values. They are distinguished from services by the fact that they are physical things, three dimensional objects—whereas services are human actions.

In short, goods are entities; services are actions. Both are economic values; that is, both are bought and sold.

All goods are the product of men performing services, and simultaneously, men cannot perform services without goods[9], without the machines, tools, and equipment that are the output of other men performing services, who also require goods to do their work. This chain of men performing services with the use of tools which were produced by other men performing services with the use of other tools produced by other men, and so forth, is not an infinite regression, but it is close. It goes back to the first caveman who used one rock to chip pieces off another rock to make a tool.

Now look again at the definition of service as an action a man is paid to perform because it creates an economic value. That definition names the essence of economic production. All economic actions are taken by human beings, and in the process of production, all those actions create economic values. The total output produced in an economy over a year is all the result of services performed by men using goods.

There is an intimate relation between the concept of service and the concept of production. The widest definition of production is the creation of a value. *Economic* production is the creation of a value for sale. Both economic production and service subsume the same actions, the creation of economic values. The difference between the two concepts is one of emphasis. The concept of production focuses on the values that are created. The concept of service focuses on the human action that does the creating.

A modern business enterprise typically consists of many people performing services to create values, all of which are necessary to the production and sale of the business's products, whether those products are goods or services or both. The employees of a company act as an integrated unit under the direction of the head of the company and, properly understood, all of them together produce the company's output.

When a business produces goods, the modern economic theory of production implies that they are produced by the workers on the assembly line. In fact, those workers perform services. If a man installs doors on an automobile, that is the service he performs, and installed doors is the value he produces for every car he works on every day. The automobile ready for delivery to a dealer is the product of not just those workers on the factory floor, but also of every other employee of the company, each of whose services are necessary to the successful functioning of the business. The workers on the assembly line could not perform their services without the rest of the company's employees performing theirs.

Depending on one's perspective, the value created by a service-provider may be a good, a service, or the product of a service. The first perspective is to look at the service-provider as part of a business, in which case his product is the good or the service the business produces. The second perspective is to look at the service-provider's value within the business and for which the business hires him. From that perspective, there are again two alternative ways to look at it: (1) the service he performs and (2) the product he creates. These are different perspectives on the same value. For example, the service performed by a janitor is cleaning the floors; clean floors are the product of his service. Similarly, the service performed by a bookkeeper is keeping accurate records; accurate records are the product of that service. Consumer services performed by individuals, such as housekeepers, plumbers, and painters, usually are subject to this same dual perspective on the same value—the service performed and the value created.

III. Market

The original meaning of market was a place where people brought their wares to trade or exchange. For example, "farmers' markets" still exist as physical locations in many cities. Consequently, the idea of "a place" is built into the concept of a market. Perhaps because of that idea, there is a widespread tendency to reify the concept of market, to treat markets as if they were independently existing things with actions and ideas of their own. Businessmen are said to put their goods "on the market." Supply and demand are said to rule "the market." "The market" is said to determine which businessmen succeed and which fail. When the opening price of a new stock falls, the price is said to have been unacceptable "to the market." And stock investors talk incessantly about what the market "wants to do."

Whether or not any of these propositions can be given a rational interpretation, a market does not exist independently of human beings and their products. A market can have no effects, causes, or consequences apart from effects, causes, or consequences initiated by men. Nor can the actions of men have any effect on the market apart from their effect on other men and their property.

The concept of market is built on the concepts of place,[10] of economic goods, and of buyers and sellers. Consequently, the meaning of market that I will use is *all the people who buy and sell a particular product in a particular geographical area or place*. For example, the shoe market in a neighborhood is everybody who buys and sells shoes in the shoe stores of that neighborhood. The market price of shoes is the average price the sellers are charging and the buyers are paying in those shoe stores.[11] There is no market apart from the people who compose it; there is no market price apart from the people who charge it and pay it.

IV. Capital and Wealth

Capital goods are the nonhuman means of production. They consist of land, machines, equipment, factories, plants, structures of all kinds, as well as farm animals, materials, parts and ingredients.

Capital is an abstraction from capital goods. It means the monetary value of capital goods. The capital invested in a business is the sum of money for which all the capital goods owned by the business could be sold.

At a still higher level of abstraction, capital means a sum of money intended for the purchase of capital goods. When economists or businessmen talk about flows of capital, usually they mean that an investor sells capital goods in one place for money which he can spend on capital goods in another place. Around the world, capital flows out of failing industries and into growing industries when businessmen sell their factories and equipment for money to invest somewhere else.

Wealth is the durable, nonhuman means of production and consumption which can be sold. Some forms of underwear are highly durable, yet they are not part of anyone's wealth because in a modern economy no one will buy them. The wealth of a business is the money value for which everything the business owns can be sold. This often includes what is called "good will," which stands for the reputation the business has created over time and which is part of its value. The wealth of an individual consists of the sale value of everything which he owns, including stocks, bonds, money, and debts owed to him by others (which he can sell), minus the value of any debts he owes to others.

An individual's or a business's wealth includes money. Income is derived from wealth. For example, the wealth of employers is used to pay their employees' wages and salaries. The money the employees receive constitutes wealth until they spend it. If they invest part of their wealth, they receive interest or dividends, which are forms of income.

A country's wealth differs from the wealth of an individual primarily in that a country's wealth does not include money. Imagine two countries with equal amounts of material wealth, one of which has twice as much money. The only difference between them would be that the country with twice as much money would have prices twice as high. A country cannot increase its wealth or raise the standard of living of its citizens by creating more money. If it could, every citizen of every country in the world would be rich.

The difference between capital and wealth is that capital subsumes only capital goods while wealth includes everything included in capital, plus anything else that can be sold.

V. Price

A price is *the sum of money required in exchange for an economic value.* A price consists of a sum of money, such as $1.59 for a can of tomatoes. What is the meaning of that sum of money to the buyer and the seller? Please note this question is entirely separate from the question of what determines or causes the price to be what it is.

To the best of my knowledge, Adam Smith was the first to give this subject serious attention. He stated the question as "what is the real measure of exchangeable value; or wherein consists the real price of all commodities?" (1776, 46). Contemporary economists ask, "What is the real cost of a good or service?"—a slightly different question, because a price is a cost only to the buyer. I will put it this way: "When one has understood a price, what has one understood?" If one hears or says or thinks, "$1.59 for a can of tomatoes," $1.59 has a definite meaning in one's mind. What is that meaning? The answer depends on the relation of $1.59 to all the other prices in the economy. The idea that names that relation is the doctrine of relative prices.

A. The Doctrine of Relative Prices

There is general agreement among modern economists on this doctrine. It says that the meaning of any individual price depends on its relation to other prices. All prices are relative prices. No price stands alone. This doctrine is true. Let us see what it means.

The significance of the idea of relative prices is best conveyed by an historical example. During the 1970s, there were price controls in the United States on the energy industry, particularly on oil and gas. Consequently, there were periodic shortages of gasoline. In 1974 and again in 1979, long lines of cars waited at gas stations until the stations' supplies of gas ran out. There were also many other inconveniences and irrationalities which together became known as "the energy crisis." Advocates of the free market said that these troubles could be eliminated by repealing the price controls. Absent the controls, they said, the price of gasoline would rise until the quantity people wanted to buy equaled the quantity supplied by the oil companies, thus ending the shortage.

The politicians, intellectuals, and bureaucrats who favored controls responded that under the controls, gasoline prices had been rising over four percent a year (from 1975 through 1978) while the quantity purchased had been rising at the same time. "Gasoline is a necessity," they said. "People must have it for essential purposes, like driving to work. Consequently, increases in price do not reduce the quantity of gasoline people want to buy. Removing the controls would allow the oil companies to reap huge profits while doing nothing to remedy the gasoline shortage."

This argument in favor of controls was wrong on every count, not the least of which was the moral premise that the state owns the economy and has the right to expropriate the property and profits of its citizens. However, for the doctrine of relative prices, the important fact was this: over the same years that the price of gasoline was rising four percent a year, the annual increase in the Consumer Price Index was averaging over seven percent. That is, relative to prices in general, gasoline prices had been falling, and the rising sales of gasoline over this period were absolutely consistent with the principle that rising prices reduce the quantity people want to buy.

This is the significance of the doctrine of relative prices: every price exists in a network of other prices. Each price gets its meaning from its relation to this network. Prices are high and low, increase and decrease, only in relation to other prices. If a price increases less than the average increase in prices, that is a fall in relative price, with the economic consequences of a fall in price. If a price increases more than the average rise in prices, that is an increase in relative price, with the economic consequences of an increase in price. An economy in which the average price increases over time is an economy inflicted with price inflation, and prices increase or decrease only relative to the average increase in all prices. (The American economy has had price inflation since the mid-1930s.)

The doctrine of relative prices is both true and important. However, modern economists make an error when they distinguish between the nominal price and the real price. This is their idea: The *nominal* price is the *absolute* price—the price in money, for example, $1.59 for a can of tomatoes. *The real price is the relative price.* The *real* price, they allege, is the nominal price adjusted for the changing value of money—that is, adjusted for the general rate of price inflation. Whether the nominal price rises or falls is inconsequential, economists hold. Changes in the real price are what affect economic decisions. For example, if the nominal price of a product increased from $100 to $106 while the inflation rate was 6%, the real price of the product would be unchanged and demand would be unaffected. If instead the inflation rate were 15%, then the increase in the nominal price from $100 to $106 would represent a decrease in the real price and demand would increase.

The only meaning that this interpretation of real prices has in practice is in the statistics of price indices. Changes are calculated for the index of the general price level by averaging the changes in the prices of thousands of different goods and services over some time period. Then the change in this general price index is compared with the changes in price indices for narrow categories of goods and services, such as medical care, college tuition, and gasoline. If the general index has risen more than the index for, let us say gasoline, then it is said that the real price (the relative price) of gasoline has fallen. If the general index has risen less than the index for gasoline, then it is said that the real price (the relative price) of gasoline has risen.

These statistical calculations are not invalid. They are the only way to answer the question of which prices really have risen over a period of time, such as a year or a decade. Certainly calculations of this kind contributed to the end of price controls in 1979. But such calculations, *and the distinction between nominal and real prices*, are relevant only to price changes averaged over some time period and reported as a statistic. It is bizarre to tell people that the real price is not the nominal price they pay; that the real price is the nominal price they pay *adjusted for the inflation rate*, when no buyer—businessman or consumer—ever pays anything but nominal, unadjusted, prices.

People do not choose what to buy and what not to buy by reference to price indices. But then what is the relevance of relative prices for human choices based on prices? What *is* the real price?

B. The Objective Price

The essence of the answer is this: All prices are relative prices. An increase in price is an increase in relative price. A decrease in price is a decrease in relative price. At the same time, all the prices in the economy are real prices and nominal prices and absolute prices—and most significantly, they are all objective prices by Ayn Rand's definition of objective.

There is more to the doctrine of relative prices than the idea that an increase in price is real only if it is greater than the inflation rate (which is unknowable without a price index). Consider the difference in meaning between these two prices: $200 for a pair of shoes in New York City and 50,000 toskas for a pair of shoes in Quasiland. Citizens of the United States know how much $200 is, but not so 50,000 toskas. Because we are told that 50,000 toskas is a price, we know that a toska is a unit of money in Quasiland, and that one must pay 50,000 of those units to buy a pair of shoes. But we do not know *how much that is*; we do not know whether shoes are cheap or expensive in Quasiland, we do not know the *value* of 50,000 toskas.

What is the value of a sum of money? The meaning of value in this context is: "the attributes or consequences of an item that make it a means to an end" (chapter 2, pp. 34–35). Putting aside the pathology of misers, money is always a means to an end—the end of acquiring goods and services. Rational men save money *because* it is a means to that end. The value of a particular sum, therefore, is its efficacy as that means. That efficacy is measured by its purchasing power. The value of $200 is what you can buy with it. When you know the purchasing power of $200, you know that $200 can buy, for example, 100 bars of soap, 50 pounds of rice, four shirts, three pair of jeans, dinner for two at the neighborhood restaurant, one hundredth of a new car, one thousandth of a small house, and so on.

The knowledge that underlies one's grasp of the meaning of $200 is the approximate prices of literally hundreds of goods and services that one sees, hears, considers, compares, pays, or decides not to pay, in an economy where dollars are the medium of exchange. (Money is defined as the medium of exchange.) With no conscious effort, one's subconscious mind registers an approximation of all the prices that one observes and puts those prices together to yield the automatic awareness of the meaning of $200. If anyone doubts he has this knowledge, imagine you were offered $10,000 for the price of every product you could estimate within ten percent of its actual price.

In most economies, prices change slowly over time. Consequently, as people continuously pay prices of various items in an inflationary economy, they notice a higher price for first one item and then another. The result is that the meaning of a sum of money in their minds changes slowly over time to reflect the changing value of money, the change that later may be measured by economic statistics.[12] The meaning of $200 to the average person in the United States today is certainly less than it was ten years ago, and very much less than it was fifty years ago.

The real price of anything is the money stated in the price, as grasped by people who use that money. More widely, people know the meaning, not just of prices, but of all the sums of money expressed in their monetary medium. For each sum, the meaning is its purchasing power, which people grasp through the prices of hundreds of goods and services, automatically stored and put together by the subconscious mind of a rational being.[13]

Prices are objective in the exact sense defined by Ayn Rand. To be objective is to be a joint product of consciousness and existence—it is to be a fact of reality as grasped by a conceptual consciousness. The meaning of a price, the meaning of its purchasing power, is the sum of money named by the price as grasped by the minds of people for whom that money is the medium of exchange.

Every price is an *objective* price. Every price is a *real* price. Every price is a *relative* price, that is, one's grasp of its meaning depends on grasping its relation to countless other prices. And, every price is an *absolute* price—its absolutism consisting of the sum of money it names and its objective relation to other prices.

C. The Opportunity Cost Doctrine

In contrast, modern economists hold explicitly and adamantly that the real price is *not* the money. The basis for their position is the opportunity cost doctrine. This doctrine says that the *real* cost of anything is the value of the best foregone alternative. The value of the best foregone alternative is the ranking of the item next in line after the item one chooses.

The idea of opportunity cost typically is presented by means of an example. Suppose both apples and oranges are selling for a dollar apiece and a consumer has a dollar to spend. If he buys the apple, the real cost, it is said, is not the dollar he spends on the apple, but the orange he does not buy (forgoes) in order to buy the apple.

The plausibility of this argument depends on the artificial context created by the example. The value of money is what it can buy, and the example gives only one alternative purchase for the dollar. If such a case were possible, then the value of the orange would be the full meaning of the purchasing power surrendered in buying the apple. In this context, there is no difference between the cost measured by the value of the money and the cost measured by the value of the orange.

In reality, there are always many alternatives. The buyer's estimate of the purchasing power of a sum of money reflects the whole galaxy of alternatives with whose prices he is familiar, not just the best foregone alternative. Indeed, for most purchases, the buyer could not identify his best foregone alternative and it does not enter into his decision[14].

As described, opportunity cost is not intrinsic, subjective, or objective. It is just wrong. But as it is most widely understood, the value of the best foregone alternative is identified with the good feeling (utility) one would have received from that alternative, a phenomenon inhering entirely in the mind of the individual (Buchanan 1969). On this interpretation, the real cost is not just subjective, but something even more tenuous: the satisfaction one does not receive from the good one does not buy because one buys something else.

The widest meaning of cost is *the value one gives up in order to obtain a higher value*. To give up a value, one must first possess the value. The opportunity cost doctrine identifies cost with something one does not possess and chooses never to possess—the value one foregoes.

The truth is that the economic cost of a good or service is a sum of money—the sum of money the buyer exchanges for an economic value—the sum of money whose value is grasped by each man who buys and sells with that money.

D. The Intrinsic Conception of the Real Price

The intrinsicist thinks of prices as reflecting some external aspect of reality, prior to and independent of the values of men. Consider the following quotations: "Value theory . . . is the name we attach to the search for processes or structures that impart orderly configurations to the empirical world . . ." and "The purpose of value . . . is to provide a means of linking the phenomena of the empirical world, mainly prices, with some principle or structure" (Heilbroner 1988, 107 and 119). Heilbroner believed that value exists as some underlying structure in the world that fixes or determines prices and it is the job of economists to discover what that structure is. Such a structure would be intrinsic value in the exact sense I have defined.

In this same chapter, Heilbroner also makes frequent reference to a "value substance" that prices supposedly reflect. This is an alternative way of referring to something intrinsic in reality. We saw in chapter 2 that the naïve conception of intrinsic value holds that value is a kind of substance or stuffing residing in goods and that prices reflect that substance (p.29).

Intrinsic price in Adam Smith

Let us consider the intrinsicist conception of price expounded by Adam Smith in *The Wealth of Nations*. We have already seen (p.49) the passage in which Smith says he is searching for "the real price of all commodities." He specifies further that he is looking for "the value of any commodity...to the person who possesses it, and who means not to use or consume it himself, but to exchange it for other commodities" (1776, 47).

The concept of value in this passage is a value to someone, that is, to the owner who means to sell it. But it is not personal value; it is not the value to the owner for his consumption, because he is going to sell it. The value Smith is trying to identify is market value, that is, the price. He wants to know the real value of a price to the seller (and unavoidably, to the buyer as well).

Smith's answer is that the real measure of a good's exchange value is the labor commanded by the good in the market, that is, the labor required to produce the goods for which this good will exchange.[15] Good A has a price. When good A is sold, the sale will place in the hands of the seller the amount of money represented by A's price. That money can then be used to purchase goods B, C, and D. The real value of good A's price to the seller, Smith says, is the amount of labor required to produce goods B, C, and D.

There are several arguments in the paragraphs in which Smith presents his position, but the most important for our purpose is his objection to money as the real price. Money (gold and silver), he says, "can never be an accurate measure of the value of other commodities" because it "is itself continually varying in its own value" (1776, 50). In contrast, a given amount of labor always has the same value to the laborer "at all times and places" (1776, 50).

It is true that the value of money varies, even when the money is gold and silver. But it is also true that the significance of an hour of labor to the laborer will vary with the political-economic conditions (slave labor versus wage labor) and the physical and mental requirements of the work. Everyone has had jobs that they liked more than others. Nevertheless, Smith is correct that the labor required to acquire a good or service is the best measure by which its price or value "can at all times be estimated and compared" (1776, 51). The difference between the real price of shoes in the United States and Quasiland is best conveyed by the fact that it takes the average U. S. worker one day to earn a pair of shoes and the average Quasilander one month. Similar calculations for a small range of goods will give one a good idea of the difference in the standards of living in the United States and Quasiland (or in any two countries or in the same country in two different eras).

This is the element of truth in Smith's position, but it is not really Smith's position. In the key paragraph (1776, 50-1), Smith changes the subject from *the labor commanded by a good to the labor required to produce a good*. They are not the same. The labor an individual must put forth in order to buy good A is important to him. The labor someone else had to put forth in order to produce good A is not. That is Smith's error. He holds that the real price of a good is something which in reality men do not care about or think about in connection with the purchases and sales they make.

The root of Smith's error is the concept of intrinsic value. Smith is looking for a measure or meaning of price that is independent of the changing values and evaluations of men—in other words, a value for which there is no "to whom?" Only intrinsic value could fulfill that condition. In reality, there are no economic values independent of human values, and no escape from the fact that men's economic values change. The premise of intrinsic value explains Smith's search for the meaning of exchange value in an unchanging value. This is the premise that led him to find it in labor. The same premise led subsequent authors to the labor theory of value—the intrinsic theory of price.

VI. Competition

Competition is the concept on whose meaning modern economics has gone most totally wrong.

Competition is not unique to economic activity. It is a broad concept, embracing a wide and disparate range of human activities. There is competition in games, in politics, in romance. A valid concept of competition must subsume all of these cases, as well as economic competition. All forms of competition have to be integrated—that is, put together into one coherent conception. What then do all forms of competition have in common?

Outside the realm of economics, the concept of competition probably is most widely used in connection with games. In competitive games, the goal is *winning*; the procedures that must be followed in order to win are defined by the rules of the game. There can be only one winner.

Competition also is used to name the activity of political campaigns. Political competition takes the form of platforms, position papers, advertisements, speeches and rallies, all directed at the election of a particular candidate. Only one candidate can be elected and take office.

In the field of romance, two men may compete for the love of the same woman. It is a competition because, in 21st century America, she has to make a choice; she can marry only one of them at a time.

The common element in all forms of competition is two or more parties pursuing a goal that only one can reach, such as winning the game, the election, or the girl. In the business world, the common value pursued by two or more businessmen is the customer's dollar. Two businessmen are competing when the same customer could potentially spend his money with either of them. Their relationship is competitive because what is potential for both businessmen can be actualized for only one of them— the potential customer can spend a given dollar only once.

Thus, in its widest, all embracing sense, competition is defined as *the activity of two or more parties trying to acquire a value that only one of them can have.* Two features of this definition, as it relates to business competition, need to be emphasized. First, competition is not a state, a situation, or a structure; it is an *activity* or *action.* Second, competition arises when the value pursued can only be had by one—when acquisition of the value by one of the competitors necessarily excludes everyone else from its possession.

Pursuit of the same customers' dollars is what gives rise to all the business activity that people regard as competitive: cutting prices, improving quality, offering better service, giving guarantees, running sales, advertising, providing comfortable surroundings and agreeable sales people, and so on. Specific concrete actions of this kind are what are subsumed under the concept of business competition.

Such actions can be characterized in general as the creation and offering of values. A lower price is a value to a customer, and so is a better product. Pleasant surroundings, good service, and guarantees are all values which businesses offer as the *means of competing.* (Advertising makes potential customers aware that the values offered by the business are available.) These value-centered activities are the content of business competition.[16] Economic competition is defined as *the activity of two or more businessmen pursuing the same customers' dollars by offering the highest values in exchange.*

Based on this definition, there is no connection between the number of firms in an industry and the intensity of competition among those firms. Two firms can, and often do, compete furiously while a hundred firms may barely compete at all. The intensity of competition is the issue of how hard businessmen are working and succeeding at offering higher economic values. This is fundamentally an issue of human volition, of the ambition, purpose, and ability of the competitors, not of any external conditions.

This definition also does not include war as a form of competition. Physical force is not a *means* of competition. Only one party can win a war, but the combatants in a war pursue the destruction of each others' values. Economic competitors create values and offer them in exchange. In their impact on human life, competition and force are opposites.

For the most part, modern economists do not treat competition, as defined here, as a determinant of price. In fact, however, competition is almost always a critical factor affecting price and consequently, it is central to a theory of objective prices. As I develop that theory, I will count on the definition given above. When I use the word competition, that is what I will mean.

CHAPTER FOUR

FOUNDATIONAL THEORIES

This chapter begins the process of applying Objectivism and the concept of objective value to the theories that underlie economics. It is impossible to proceed in economics without these theories. Part I presents the theory of economic choice, which subsumes the theory of consumer choice. Part I also answers some errors caused by the idea that the value of added income declines. Part II uses the theory of consumer choice to prove the law of demand. Part III proves the most important principle of economics, the principle of gains from trade. Part IV presents the theory of objective business costs. Each of the four parts is preceded by a brief overview (in italics).

I. The Theory of Consumer Choice

Men choose what to do based on their values. They act to gain and keep the things they value more. They pass by the things they value less. In the economic realm, values have prices. Consequently, in choosing what to buy, men rank good-and-price combinations, such as a $600 Apple computer versus a $500 PC. They buy the highest ranked good/price combination.

A. Hierarchies of Values

The second of the three concepts of objective value identified in chapter 2 was the ranking in one's mind of something one acts to gain and/or keep—the ranking of some goal, end, or purpose. If something is ranked high, such as one's wife, it has a high value. If it is ranked low, such as a new acquaintance, its value is low. If it is something like garbage or trash, it is ranked below zero; its value is negative; it is a disvalue—and its removal is a value. Preferring some things to others is a universal feature of human valuation. Ranking is the form value takes in our minds; we prefer values with higher rankings to values with lower rankings.

Hierarchy of values is a concept critical to everything that follows in this section. A hierarchy is defined as a graded or ranked series, one thing above another, such as the ranks of authority in a church or an army. A hierarchy of *values* is a series ranking the things (values) that a man acts to gain and/or keep in the order of their importance to him. A hierarchy of values is a phenomenon of one's mind, but its content consists of the things in existence that one ranks or values.

Something becomes a value through its relationship to a human being. That relationship is a means to an end, grasped and ranked by reference to some standard(s) by an individual human consciousness. For example, a man looking for a car to get to work may rank alternative cars according to their reliability and comfort. His ranking of the cars measures their relative importance to him. A man's complete hierarchy of values consists of all the values that he has ranked in this manner. He may use different standards in different contexts for different hierarchies. However, every standard ultimately is reducible to his life—if his values are objective.

Ayn Rand identified that men's hierarchies of values can be divided into two broad categories: economic values (what she called material values) and moral or spiritual values (values pertaining to consciousness) (Rand 1990, 33–34). In this section, I am primarily concerned with spiritual values. I take up economic values in part B.

Spiritual values are values that are *not* bought and sold; they include such things as other human beings, virtues (honesty, integrity, justice), values of character (self-esteem, reason, honor), political conditions (freedom, rights, democracy), social conditions (poverty, wealth, security), career goals (getting a promotion, writing a book, learning a skill), and so on. The currency or medium of exchange for spiritual values is time, that is, one's life (Rand 1990, 34).

Spiritual values are fundamental. The things a man values in this realm determine his tastes, preferences, and values in the economic realm. If he values thought, discrimination, effort, creativity, drama, excitement, he will buy goods that reflect those values. If he values thoughtlessness, safety, mental passivity, lethargy, the opinions of others, he will buy goods that reflect those values.

A hierarchy of values does not consist of a single ranking from bottom to top of all the values one holds. Such a hierarchy would be impossible to form (a normal adult has hundreds, if not thousands, of values), and useless if it were done. A hierarchy of values is more like the profile of a city with buildings of all different heights across the landscape, each building representing a different field or subject area or activity in which one has formed values. The distinction between economic values and spiritual values divides the value landscape into two parts with many connecting links, like skywalks, bridges, and roads, all running in one direction, from the spiritual part to the economic.

The height of each building relative to the other buildings represents the relative importance to the individual of the highest value in that hierarchy, that is, the highest value in a high building is higher than the highest value in a lower building.[1] Thus we are able to rank very different values in a single hierarchy when we need to. For example, the hierarchy for my time today might be: (1) preparing a class lecture—from my work hierarchy, (2) playing with my son—from my people hierarchy, (3) watching a program on television—from my entertainment hierarchy, and (4) paying bills—from my hierarchy of necessary disvalues.

There are also values that one holds that are not part of a hierarchy of similar values—for example, a promotion at work, building an addition on one's house, celebrating a holiday. In a hierarchy profile, such values can be thought of as high spires, though not necessarily higher than many other buildings. Such spires are integrated into one's hierarchy of values when they are compared to other values. For example, one may skip a party in order to finish a job at work—or one may stop purchasing many lower ranked economic values in order to save the money to add a room onto one's house.

An ordinary human being will have many, many hierarchies. A skier, for example, has a hierarchy of ski areas, a hierarchy of ski slopes, a hierarchy of skis, a hierarchy of ski clothing. Between and among hierarchies, there are also many cross references and connecting lines. For example, a type of ski may be good for one ski area, but not for another. In his hierarchy of forms of entertainment, the skier may rank skiing fifth.

His most preferred entertainment may be reading. Within the category of reading, he has a hierarchy of the kind of books he prefers to read and perhaps additional hierarchies of his favorite books and authors in each literary genre. Another hierarchy may consist of his all-time favorite books independent of genre.

A hierarchy of values does not have to have a rigorous order of first, second, third, and so forth. A man may have two books which he likes equally and which jointly occupy top place in his hierarchy of books. Alternatively, and perhaps unavoidably, he may be unable to give an order to the many books he might put in tenth or twentieth place—books he liked, but without enthusiasm.

Each man erects his own hierarchy of values over time in response to all the experiences and events of his life and how he chooses to deal with them. Technically, the origin of hierarchies of values is a topic in developmental psychology. Nevertheless, a few introductory observa-tions may be helpful.

Objectivism holds that thinking is man's basic act of choice. By consistently choosing to think, one builds up over a lifetime a body of knowledge and a hierarchy of values, both of a particular kind—that is, integrated, consistent, non-contradictory, realistic. If one chooses to think half the time, occasionally, or not at all, one builds up a body of knowledge and a hierarchy of values of a different kind—partially or completely unintegrated, chaotic, inconsistent, contradictory, unrealistic. These are the two extremes; most men are somewhere in the middle.

Every choice a man makes reflects these three fundamentals: his hierarchy of values, his knowledge, and his thinking—his current thinking and the thinking he has done up to this point. The more thinking he has done, the more knowledge he will have and the better defined his hierarchies of values will be. Developmentally, thinking comes first.

Men's hierarchies of values are the primary motivation of all the actions of their lives. Hierarchies change over time as the facts of one's life change, as one acquires new knowledge, and as one changes one's mind about ideas, people, and things. (In this context, the analogy between hierarchies and buildings breaks down. Buildings are relatively immutable; many hierarchies are not.) However, in every area of one's life, one's current choices and actions are governed by one's current hierarchy of values—*in so far as one chooses to engage it.* Men have to choose to focus on their values, to be loyal to them, to act on them—if they are to reach their values.

The primary evidence for the existence and nature of hierarchies of values is introspection. If we turn our mental attention inward, it is clear that we prefer some things to others, some people to others, some values to others. These preferences are the product of evaluation, of ranking things as means to an end. The number and variety of our hierarchies reflects the fact that in reality we are confronted with endless alternatives.

Depending on the individual, many or most of his hierarchies may be below the level of conscious awareness. However, no matter how repressed he may be, he cannot avoid knowing that in field after field, he values some things more than others. Most men form values in most aspects of their lives—and for every aspect, there is a hierarchy. In all the different fields and subjects to which we have given thought, we find a hierarchy of values.

Secondary to introspection, we have a continuous flow of indirect evidence for hierarchies from what people say about their values and from what we observe about their choices and actions. Finally, there are all the great works of literature that identify the motives of their protagonists by revealing their hierarchies of values.

The subject of hierarchies is necessary to understand economic choice and the role played by price in that choice. Now we can take up the question of how people choose what to buy.

B. Consumer Choice

The subject matter of economics is human beings acting to gain economic values. Man has to act in order to live. In order to act, he must know what he wants. He has to figure out what to do, what action to take to get what he wants, in every area and interest of his life. Among all his other actions, he has to choose what to buy with his money.

There are also many other economic choices. He has to choose what job to take; what career to pursue; whether or not to ask for a raise; whether to look for a new job; whether to buy a house or rent one instead; whether to borrow money to buy a car; and so on. In any economic issue, any issue that involves buying or selling, the individual has to rank his alternatives. This usually involves at least two alternatives, and often more than two.

Part A noted that the clarity of one's hierarchy of values varies with the thinking one has done. The following discussion presupposes an ordinary man trying to do the best he can for his life and his loved ones with the money he has available. I am assuming ordinary clarity in his hierarchies of economic values, but I am assuming clarity. Undoubtedly, the hierarchies of many people are not as clear and therefore they act with less success in their economic purchases. In addition, there is impulse buying, careless shopping, and mindless shopping. The process I am describing is certainly not universal, but it is also certainly the norm—that people figure out what is the best course of action, given the prices they face, their income, and their hierarchies of values.

Some of a man's hierarchies of economic values consist of rankings of all the goods and services he regularly purchases. Unlike non-economic hierarchies, economic hierarchies are dual in nature. First, men rank goods of a specific kind relative to other goods of the same kind, and second, they rank the same goods relative to their prices. For any specific good or service, the basic principle of consumer choice is: *buy the highest ranked item/price combination.*

For example: a man has a hierarchy of beverages or liquid refreshment. Let us say that he prefers beer. Consequently, he has a hierarchy of beers, for example, (1) Guinness, (2) Bach, (3) Boddingtons, and so on—all of which are relatively expensive and which normally he does not buy, even though he prefers them. Therefore, he needs and has a parallel or co-hierarchy of beers that takes account of price. In his price-driven hierarchy, he links each beer to its price, and ranks it above its price, considered independently of the other beers and their prices. In other words, considered alone, he values each beer more than the money he would have to pay for it.

His hierarchy of beer/price combinations might be: (1) Budweiser @ $2.49/six pack, (2) Coors Long Necks @ $2.99/six pack, (3) Millers @ $2.39/six pack, and so on. Budweiser is neither the most expensive nor the cheapest beer in this hierarchy. He ranks it number one because he likes Budweiser, and at these prices, Budweiser is the beer he prefers. At the same time, considered in the context of Budweiser @ $2.49/six pack, the other beers are ranked below their prices. And that is the limit of what one can say about a good/price hierarchy.

Specifically, we cannot say that the difference between the ranking of Budweiser and the ranking of $2.49 is greater than the difference between the ranking of Coors Long Necks and the ranking of $2.99. The typical beer drinker probably could not tell you about those differences, but let us suppose he can. He says, "Yes, I like Coors Long Necks a lot more than Budweiser. The personal value to me of Coors Long Necks is about $4.00 a six-pack while for Budweiser it is about $3.00. However, most of the time, I cannot afford[2] to pay $2.99 for Coors. That is why I buy Budweiser." There is no objection to that reasoning. He ranks Budweiser higher than $2.49 and he buys Budweiser.

What if Coors Long Necks also cost $2.49? Given that he prefers Coors Long Necks to Budweiser, he would buy Coors Long Necks. Unless his tastes change, he would never buy Budweiser. The correct interpretation of his hierarchy is that when Coors Long Necks cost $2.49 or less, he ranks Budweiser below $2.49.

For many goods and services that are repeatedly consumed, a consumer's hierarchy comes down to one item that is his settled choice at the price—against the background of the other alternatives that are available and their prices. In these cases, the hierarchy consists of the good ranked above the price. For other products (like fresh fruits, vegetables, meats), the price changes frequently and the consumer's ranking of the product varies with the price. For still other items, and particularly foods, his hierarchy will shift with consumption of the item. For example, one's favorite food may be steak, but if one has had steak three times in the last week, today's hierarchy may not include steak at all.

For items a consumer purchases on a weekly or even a monthly basis, he is familiar with the prices and in his price-driven hierarchies, he ranks each item he buys above its price. In determining his choice, the hierarchies that are independent of price exist in his mind as a background context until he calls them up—because his income increases or he wants to do something special. In such cases, the hierarchies independent of price become price-driven and the ranking of an item may shift up relative to its price so that now it is ranked above its price. For example, a young man normally ranks $30 above a dozen roses, but when he meets a girl he wants to impress, his ranking changes; he ranks a dozen roses above $30.

For things the consumer seldom purchases (such as a computer, a TV set, a house), his hierarchies are necessarily unclear. For example, an individual who does not own a computer may have only a vague idea of what a reasonable price would be for a new computer; he may have some ideas about alternative features available on computers; he may have a notion of which brand has the best reputation; or his ideas may be all wrong. This lack of clarity has no effect on his choices or well-being until he decides to buy a computer.

If a man's hierarchy of values is unclear for a product he wants to buy, he may clarify it by acquiring knowledge. He can examine alternative products, read brochures and magazines devoted to the product and talk to sales people. As part of this process, he may discover that the current price is much higher than expected. Often this causes a shift in one's hierarchy of values, and a price one would have considered untenable prior to the search now looks reasonable. Alternatively, one's hierarchy of values may not shift, or may not shift sufficiently, and one ends by ranking the item below its price and forgoing its purchase.

This process is a type of *shopping*—one spends time looking for a product to buy when one is unfamiliar with its features. Shopping is how we acquire the relevant knowledge. That knowledge may be used to create two simultaneous hierarchies of values, hierarchies that are already established for goods and services we buy regularly: First, a hierarchy of the different versions of the good ranked by the standard "best for my life" or "best for my family" or the equivalent. This hierarchy does not reflect prices, but it is restricted by price. One does not spend time ranking items that are financially out of the question. The point is to survey the alternatives and get a general idea of what is available and what one wants.

Second, a hierarchy of the versions ranked according to the standard "best buy" or "best deal" or "best we can afford." In the second hierarchy, each variation is linked to the price (as the beers were in the preceding example). The minimum requirement for entering this hierarchy is that each variation, considered separately, is ranked above its price. This second hierarchy then is a ranking of item/price combinations.

When people have identified the highest ranked item/price combination, often they proceed to inspect other sellers, looking for a better price. Other things equal, a particular product at a lower price is always ranked above the same product at a higher price. Eventually the buyer becomes satisfied that he has found the best price or near-best price and buys the item.

All three of these steps usually go on simultaneously. For example, suppose a man is looking for a new TV set with a particular screen size. (1) The first step is to get an idea of what is available by shopping in the familiar way. This process will result in a rough ranking of "good, better, and best" according to the evident quality and features of the different sets. At the same time, as he is shopping, he notices the prices and (2) estimates whether each set is worth more to him than its price. At the same time he is ranking each set relative to its price, he is (3) looking for the best price.[3]

Exactly how an individual proceeds in any particular case will depend on what the product is, what he knows about it in advance, how much money is at stake, and so forth. A wealthy man may buy the highest priced product on the principle that quality tends to rise with price. For most people, however, if the product is not known, some knowledge of the features of alternative versions has to be acquired before one can start ranking versions in conjunction with their prices. Then, one may start shopping for the lowest price. Or, one may begin and end the whole process in one place by shopping in a discount store. Or, in the process of shopping for a lower price, the buyer may find a product at a price he can afford which he had previously dismissed as "too expensive." This then becomes the highest ranked item/price combination. The alternatives are virtually endless.

There is one constant. The overarching principle of economic choice is that one chooses the highest value in one's price-driven hierarchy—the highest item/price combination.

C. The Diminishing Marginal Value of Money

Closely related to the analysis of the preceding two sections is the subject that economists call "the diminishing marginal utility of income." Chapter 2 noted that I have abandoned the term utility. In addition, one can get money in forms other than income. Consequently, let us call this principle *the diminishing marginal value of money.*

The marginal value is the additional value. Thus, this principle means that as one acquires more and more money, any given sum is ranked lower and lower relative to the other economic values in one's hierarchy. Because the doctrine is in terms of "marginal" value, economists typically take the sum of money at stake as one dollar. (By convention, the marginal sum is usually a dollar.[4]) Thus, one ranks each additional dollar lower and lower relative to the goods and services in one's economic hierarchy. Why? Economists say it is because as we acquire additional dollars, we use them to buy lower and lower ranked values.

The standard argument for the diminishing marginal value of money is this: whatever the amount of money you have at your disposal, you spend it on the goods and services that you rank highest.[5] If you win a hundred dollars playing bingo, then you use it to buy something that you could not buy before, something that has less value to you than any of the things you were previously buying. As we get more and more money, we work our way down our hierarchy of economic values, buying things of less and less value, of lower and lower ranking, until, if we have enough money, we buy things which have no value to us at all and without which we would be no worse off.

The preceding paragraph pushes the argument a little further than it is usually pushed to make a point—that this is a total misunderstanding of the significance to people of additional sums of money. We do not spend our economic lives working our way down our hierarchy of economic values—working for a raise so we can buy something of less value than what we bought with the last raise. This idea represents an attack on economic progress as such. It says that, for the individual, a rising standard of living is nothing more than acquiring items of continually diminishing importance—and ultimately, of no importance at all.

The truth is that we spend our lives working our way *up* our hierarchy of values. More and more money is not used to acquire values ranked lower and lower. More and more money is used to acquire values ranked higher and higher.

The flaw in the standard argument is that it focuses on adding first one dollar to a man's income and then another dollar. In today's economy, a dollar might as well be a penny; neither can raise one's standard of living. If you received first one dollar and then another, each successive item you bought with each additional dollar would be ranked lower and lower and nothing you bought would be of consequence.

To grasp the truth, we need to think in terms of larger amounts of money. Suppose a man is making $100 a week, living with his parents, taking the subway or walking to his job. If his income increased to $1000 a week, he could buy a used car, stop taking the subway, and maybe move into a little place of his own. For $10,000 a week, he could buy a house in the suburbs with a swimming pool; he could eat at fine restaurants, take tennis lessons, and go to the theater. This is how increases in income work. With every increase, you are able to buy higher ranked values, and in the modern world, there is no effective limit to how high you can go.

The marginal value of money diminishes, not because we buy lower and lower ranked values with additional money, but because as we acquire more money, any given sum represents a smaller proportion of the total.[6] Thus, $1000 is 10% of $10,000, 1% of $100,000, and 0.1% of $1,000,000. This is why $1000 is much more important to a man with $10,000 than to a man with $1,000,000. As one acquires additional money, all individual sums, such as $1000, shift down relative to one's hierarchy of economic values. This is why we buy higher ranked values when we get more money.

In effect, in our economic hierarchies of values, the ranking of sums of money and of economic goods are in the same hierarchy. When our income increases, the sums of money shift down relative to the economic goods. At a man's current income level, he may rank $5000 far above an entertainment center costing $5000 that he admires. Then he wins the lottery and his ranking of all sums of money, including $5000, falls relative to all his economic values, including the entertainment center. Now he ranks $5000 below the entertainment center and it is the first thing he buys.

As our income rises, a significant portion of our additional expenditures go for better versions of things we were already consuming. Economists call the things we give up inferior goods; they call the better versions we buy with more money normal goods. We have seen why the demand for normal goods increases. One gives up inferior goods at higher income levels for a related reason.

Suppose a man ranks red beans and rice above $50 and he has been spending $50 a month on red beans and rice. Now an increase in income reduces the marginal value of money to him. Considered alone, this suggests the ranking of $50 falls further below the ranking of red beans and rice. However, the increase in income that reduces the ranking of $50 also reduces the ranking of $100, which, let us say, is the cost of a month's worth of hamburger. The fact that he can now afford hamburger reduces the ranking of red beans and rice below $50 and he eats hamburger instead.

The last paragraph reflects an important principle. The ranking of goods does not exist in isolation. For example, a man may be about to buy one TV set when he finds a better TV set for the same price. The immediate effect is to reduce the ranking of the first TV set below the price he was about to pay. Thus, the ranking of any economic good relative to its price by any individual depends on the context of the whole network of alternatives in which that good exists and of which he is aware.

II. The Law of Demand

The law of demand says that customers want to buy more of a good when the price falls. The cause is men's differing hierarchies of economic values. As the price of a good falls, the ranking of the sum of money represented by the price falls below the ranking of the good for more and more people.

What is the basis for the law of demand? Why is it true? The standard answer in modern economics is that decreases in price cause individuals to buy more units of the same good. In fact, this usually is not the case.

There are relatively few goods of which people buy more than one unit at a time, where all the units are identical, and where a decrease in price might induce them to buy a larger total amount. These are products like heating oil, water, gasoline, electricity, and perhaps some food items such as butter and eggs. For almost everything else we buy, including most food items, the units are not identical and we do not want more than one at a time: a steak, a bunch of bananas, a pair of shoes, a shirt, a skirt, a lamp, a rug, a TV set, a VCR, a CD player, a movie ticket, a restaurant meal, a car, a house, and so on. In this context, if the additional units are not identical, the second unit is not a unit. It is something else.

Suppose, for example, you were about to buy a thirty-six inch television set for $800 and the store reduced the price to $600. The modern proof of the law of demand implies that you (or somebody) would then buy two thirty-six inch television sets instead of one. If instead, you buy the thirty-six inch set for $600, and then, with the $200 you saved, you buy an eighteen-inch set, that is not an increase in sales of thirty-six inch sets. Of course, *sometimes* an individual may buy more units of the same good when the price falls, but the law of demand is not a sometime thing.

The cause of the law of demand, and particularly its universality, is that people have different hierarchies of economic values. They value some things more than others and everybody is different in what they value and how much they value it. If in his hierarchy of economic values, a man ranks the amount of money that an item costs higher than he ranks the item, he does not buy it. As the price rises, it reaches this level for more and more people. This is why the quantity sold decreases as the price goes up.

The reverse is true for a fall in price. As a good's price falls, it falls below its ranking for more and more people. If an individual ranks a good higher than he ranks the money he must give up to get it, he buys the good. As the price falls, it reaches this level for more and more people. This is why the quantity sold increases as the price falls.

All the preceding depends on the assumption of "other things equal" (p. 15). Specifically, we have to assume that men's hierarchies of values do not change when the price changes. That need not be true. As I noted in chapter 1 (p. 15), at the same time the price of chicken rises, the housewife may decide that chicken is better for one's health or the price of beef or pork may also rise. These changes raise the ranking of chicken in the housewife's hierarchy, so that instead of buying less chicken at the higher price, she may buy more. The law of demand is still valid in the face of all such changes because, even though she buys more chicken at the higher price, she buys *less* chicken *than she would have bought if the price had not risen.*

To make this clear, let us suppose that normally a housewife buys ten pounds of chicken a week when the price is $3.00/lb. and eight pounds a week when the price is $4.00/lb. Now she becomes convinced that chicken is good for one's heart and at the same time the price rises from $3.00/lb. to $4.00/lb. Her new conviction means that she ranks chicken higher, so let us say that now she buys eleven pounds a week at $4.00/lb. instead of eight. But if the price had remained at $3.00/lb., she would have bought, let us say, twelve pounds instead of ten. Thus, at the higher price of $4.00/lb., she buys less than she would have bought if the price had not risen.

This result is not guaranteed. Possibly the housewife would have bought eleven pounds at both $3.00 and $4.00. However, she certainly would not buy more at $4.00 than at $3.00, and if some people buy less at $4.00, the law of demand is confirmed: even when the quantity demanded is higher at a higher price, it is less than it would have been if the price had not risen.

The law of demand is a law of markets. It is a law that depends on large numbers of people. Individuals can violate the law. For example, a very rich man may buy less of a superior champagne when its price falls because it is no longer expensive enough to serve to his guests. But that individual's choice is swamped by all the people who are eager to buy superior champagne at a lower price—that is, all the people for whom the ranking of the price has fallen below the ranking of the champagne.

The law of demand is reached by looking at the facts of a market economy and the nature of the human beings that compose it. That people have widely varying hierarchies of economic values is an elemental fact. That they compare the ranking of goods with the ranking of sums of money is the essence of economic choice.

III. The Principle of Gains from Trade

Exchange by its nature is self-interested. Both parties to a trade intend to gain by it and both do gain if they are rational and neither makes a mistake.

The principle of gains from trade is the most fundamental principle of economics. Those who have not grasped it know essentially nothing about how an economy works while those who have grasped it know the essence of a free market. A preliminary statement of this principle is that both parties usually gain from an exchange. If that sounds innocuous, it has to be contrasted with the view of the entire pre-capitalist era (pre-1800) and of most of the world's population today.

Let us call the alternative view the principle of losses from trade. It holds that the nature of exchange is that one party wins and the other party loses—that one party's gain is the other party's loss—that the greater the gain of the first, the greater the loss of the second—that if neither party gains, then neither party loses—and that this last result, infrequent as it is, is the best that can be expected from trade or exchange, which this principle regards as immoral.

Exchange by its nature is self-interested. If one of the parties is *not* acting in his own interest, then he is engaged in charity, not exchange. The medieval morality of altruism held that self-interest is evil and so is anything that proceeds from it. Altruism made the principle of losses from trade seem self-evident. This was *the* mortal blow against trade in the medieval era, and there was essentially none. Trade was damned, exchange was damned, and so were the men who engaged in it. This condemned most of Europe's population to an existence of bare subsistence and of premature death from malnutrition and famine. The Dark Ages was the era in the West when the principle of losses from trade was uncontested.

Let us consider the specific conditions that define the context of any trade or exchange—the conditions under which the principle of gains from trade is true. In addition to the condition that both parties are acting in their own interest, exchange also requires that neither of them is physically threatened or lied to. If one of them is physically forced or deceived, then it is robbery or fraud, not exchange. The concept of exchange applies only to mutually voluntary, self-interested trades.

For an exchange to take place, each party must own one or more economic values which he is willing to exchange. Further, if both parties are to gain from the exchange, both party's offerings have to be *objective* economic values. One does not gain from an exchange if the value one secures harms one's life. Such values are nonobjective values or disvalues (chapter 2). Their acquisition is not a gain but a loss.

Since both parties are motivated by self-interest, each party will enter into an exchange only if he expects to gain. For each party, the condition for gaining from an exchange is that he values the good he receives more that the good he gives up—that in his hierarchy of economic values, the good he receives is ranked higher than the good he surrenders. If, as is the norm, the exchange is the result of buying and selling a product, then the buyer values the product higher than the money he has to pay for it and the seller values the money higher than the product.

Gains from trade require not only that both men intend to gain; but also that both men's hierarchies of values are sufficiently clear that they know what to do in order to gain. With respect to economic goods and services, this is the normal case. But it is not guaranteed. When men's hierarchies contain internal contradictions, they may choose to take actions that make themselves worse off—including buying something they cannot use or cannot afford or both.

The primary requirement for gains from trade is reflected in the immediately preceding paragraph. That requirement is rationality. The exercise of reason clarifies one's hierarchies and the failure to exercise it generates contradictions. In the context of exchange, to be rational means to be focused on the facts that are relevant to the exchange. This focus requires an act of will: refusing to be driven by an emotion of the moment, refusing to evade some unpleasant fact, keeping reason in charge of one's choice—all with the purpose of achieving one's long-run self-interest. If reason is not in charge, one may have the necessary knowledge while evading it or refusing to activate it. For example, one may have a succession of feelings which, if translated into words, would be: "We can't afford to buy that. Ignore that thought." Many people proceed in this manner and insure that sometimes they lose from exchange.

Finally, buyers and sellers are not omniscient; they can make mistakes. One may be uncoerced, acting in one's self-interest, with a clear hierarchy of economic values and with reason as one's guide, and still make a mistake—by misapprehending what one is buying, by following bad advice from a friend, by buying something that sounds good in an advertisement, and so forth. But if both parties follow reason, and neither of them makes a mistake, then each party gets what he wants, each party goes away happy, and neither has any reason to regret the transaction— which is the usual case.

The preceding points are necessary to prove the principle of gains from trade. It may seem that much is required if both parties to an exchange are to gain, but in fact, all those points come down to one thing: both parties have to focus on the relevant facts. In reality, most people are rational when they buy or sell, mistakes are infrequent, and consequently, most people, most of the time, do gain from trade—something almost everyone can confirm from personal experience. The principle of gains from trade is that *in any trade or exchange in which both parties are rational and neither makes a mistake, both parties gain.*

Having established the principle of gains from trade, one can then apply it to concrete cases of exchange and predict that both parties will gain. But to apply it, one must know the context—that the case is one of exchange and not of charity or robbery or fraud, that both parties are acting rationally and that neither is mistaken. One can know these things only by examining the facts, which in this context means by talking to the parties to the exchange.

The more important application of the principle of gains from trade is to the totality of a capitalist system. A market economy is characterized by trade for mutual gain—at the top, at the bottom, and at every level in between; in each of the millions upon millions of exchanges that take place every day; in every loan, job, salary, contract, sale, mortgage, rental, lease, and purchase; from contracts between major corporations to exchanges between two individuals at a yard sale. If the parties participating in those exchanges are rational and not mistaken, they gain. This is a fundamental attribute of a capitalist economy—no one is sacrificed; everyone moves forward together.[7]

IV. The Theory of Objective Business Costs

Businessmen follow widely varied, inconsistent, and unsystematic procedures in allocating their costs to the products they sell. There are many problems with no obvious solution. Nevertheless, business costs are objective because they reflect businessmen's best rational grasp of the relevant economic facts.

A. Alternative Concepts of Business Costs

The standard practice in economics is to divide business costs into variable costs and fixed costs. The standard definition of *variable costs* is costs that change with the quantity of output—primarily the cost of employees and materials. Usually, a businessman must hire more workers and buy more materials if he wants to produce more. If he wants to produce less, he may lay off workers and he will definitely buy a smaller quantity of materials. Consequently, total variable costs increase with increases in output and decrease with decreases in output.

The standard definition of *fixed costs* is costs that do not vary with the quantity sold. A businessman's total fixed costs are the same if he produces nothing or if he produces up to the limits of his capacity. Fixed costs usually include the cost of administration, depreciation on plant and equipment, interest on debt, rent, insurance, and other costs that have to be paid regardless of the quantity sold. Fixed cost often are called *overhead*, particularly in retail businesses.[8]

There are two concepts of cost that businessmen use in setting their prices: (1) average cost and (2) average variable cost. Both of these are measures of unit costs or cost per unit of output. As a first approximation, average cost is calculated by dividing the total costs of the business (both fixed and variable) by the number of units produced. Suppose a businessman is producing 1000 units, his total fixed cost is $4,000 and his total variable cost is $6,000. Then his total cost is $10,000 and his average cost of production is $10 a unit.

Average variable cost is the total variable costs of the business divided by the number of units produced. In the preceding example, the average variable cost is $6 a unit ($6,000/1000).

When the businessman refers to average cost as a guide in setting his price, economists call it average cost pricing or full cost pricing or cost plus pricing. If he refers to average variable cost as the guide, economists call it variable cost pricing or marginal cost pricing. Average cost pricing is by far the most widespread alternative chosen by businessmen. (See appendix C for a critique of marginal cost pricing.)

The cost-of-production theory of value is consistent with either of these two approaches. It says that the prices of products are determined by the costs businessmen incur in producing their products. This theory goes back to Adam Smith and is still widespread. Part B following presents many facts that contradict the cost-of-production theory of value.

B. Problems in the Calculation of Business Costs

The above formula for calculating average cost is valid if the business is selling only one product. However, one product is far from typical among businesses in the economy. It is much more common for a businessman to offer for sale many different products and many variations of each product. In businesses producing and/or selling many products, the average cost of each unit has to be determined by allocation, that is, by dividing up each of the business's costs and allocating a portion to every unit of output.

For example, if the firm's administrative costs are 100 dollars, and the firm produces 10 widgets and 10 smidgets, one way of allocating the administrative costs would be to assign 5 dollars to each of the 20 units. If the smidgets require much more administrative oversight, then 3 dollars might be allocated to each widget and 7 dollars to each smidget. Cost allocation is a universal problem of businessmen in calculating average cost.

For the purposes of economic theory, this problem could be solved by holding that all unit costs are objective and provide an objective basis for price. The obvious objection to this solution is the highly varied and unsystematic ways that businessmen allocate their costs. An economic theory based on objective value must deal with the obstacles to accurate cost allocation. I have to make clear what the difficulties are and show that business costs are objective in spite of them. The difficulties are more widespread than is commonly understood. Most economists know that allocating fixed costs to individual items of output is a hard problem. They do *not* know that there are equally hard problems involved in allocating variable costs.

The only economist I have found who has documented the problems of cost allocation is Bjarke Fog (1960). Over a four-year period, from 1951 to 1955, Fog interviewed 185 firms in Denmark. He asked them about the economic details of their operations. He was not the first economist or the last to ask businessmen what they do and why, but he was by far the most skilled in eliciting information. His book is filled with anecdotes about the problems and practices of businessmen that would astound most economists (and astounded me).

Fog's information originates in interviews conducted over fifty years ago and, undoubtedly, some of the conditions he describes have changed. But most of the problems and the solutions Fog describes are inherent in operating a business. It represents a huge loss of basic factual knowledge that Fog has been largely ignored, including by economists who have done empirical studies. Blinder and others dismiss his information as not "suitable for statistical analysis" (1998, 41)—which it is not, but the value of empirical work is not limited to statistics. What follows depends completely on Fog's work and for the remainder of this section, unless otherwise indicated, all page references are to his book.

One of the results Fog did not expect is that he found it impossible to adhere to the distinction between fixed and variable costs. Costs which appear fixed, he says, on closer examination turn out to be variable (pp. 70 & 80). As an indication of the problem, labor is always regarded as a variable cost and depreciation is always regarded as a fixed cost. But if firms are reluctant to fire workers when demand falls, they turn their labor force into a fixed cost, and if a machine is worn by use, its depreciation is in part a variable cost (p. 50). Blinder and others also found that many businessmen could not distinguish fixed costs from variable costs (1998, 101). Blinder mentions this without comment.

Fog's solution is to substitute the concepts of direct and indirect costs.[9] Fog defines direct costs as "those which can be assigned to the individual product by direct observation." If you see a man working on the assembly line of an automobile, you know that his salary should be included in the cost of producing the automobile. Indirect costs are costs that cannot be assigned to the product by direct observation "because they are considered too difficult to divide or because it is not feasible to do so" (p. 62, note 1).

Direct costs are variable costs; they are easy to allocate. But it would surprise most economists that variable costs may also be indirect. When they are, they are as difficult to allocate as fixed costs, which are usually indirect costs (p. 63, note 2).

1. Anomalies in cost allocation

Fog found that the calculation of costs by businessmen differs greatly from the calculation pictured by economists. The same firm may use one method of measuring costs for some of its products and a different method for others. A definite system may be used in principle, but not used consistently. The costs of some products may not be calculated at all (p. 69).

Fog identified many difficulties that businessmen have in allocating costs to products. The next few pages present some of them. Most of these anomalies are the consequence of indirect costs in conjunction with the fact that most businesses produce and/or sell more than one product. The standard assumption of economic theory is that each firm produces a single product—an assumption economists know is untrue, but which they believe does not affect their conclusions. In that, they are mistaken—it has made all the problems of cost allocation invisible to them and consequently, they have no theory regarding it.

Labor costs

How would one allocate the wages of these workers to the cost of the final product? (1) There are workers (foremen, shop bosses, overseers) whose job is to help and/or direct the laborers who work directly on the product. The cost of these "auxiliary workers" is indirect; they may over-see many workers working on many different products. (2) The same worker may take part in the production of several different products. (3) A worker may "handle several different manufacturing processes at the same time." In the "paint, dyestuffs, and varnish" industry, Fog found that a worker normally handles three manufacturing processes. If man-agement tries to solve one of these ambiguities by asking the workers to keep work records, the workers may resent it and keep inaccurate records (p. 63). In addition (my own observation), there are time costs involved both for the workers in filling out work records and for management in creating an environment in which they will do so. How should that cost be allocated?

A firm manufactured one product on the first shift and a different product on the second shift. Labor costs were higher on the second shift due to shift premiums. Originally, the firm calculated the labor cost of the different products by the wages actually paid. Later, it calculated the labor cost "on the basis of the average of both shifts combined" (p. 68). Which practice was right?

The same product may be produced by a journeyman or an appren-tice. Should the product be considered cheaper to produce when it is pro-duced by the apprentice, who is paid less? "Some firms adopt the former point of view, others the latter" (p. 68).

Materials costs

It is frequently impossible to determine the cost of the materials con-sumed in the production of each individual product. For example, "In the tobacco industry . . . the tobacco leaf is regarded as an indirect cost be-cause the different parts of the tobacco leaves are used for different qualities and products. . . . In a shoe factory, the same kind of leather is used for men's and children's shoes. . . . In a hosiery mill . . . the same kind of yarn is used for twenty different designs" (p. 63). There are countless such cases, including the cost of fuel, electricity, and water which normally are indirect variable costs.

Another anomaly is the basis firms use to record the cost of their ma-terials. There are four possibilities: (1) original cost, (2) expected re-placement cost, (3) current price, and (4) standard cost (average over time). Fog found it was impossible to classify firms according to which basis they used. "…only a few firms adhere consistently to a single prin-ciple." It is more common that the same business uses "different costing methods in different situations and . . . all possible intermediate forms occur." Thus, many businessmen use an average cost for their materials: either (a) an average of the prices of materials acquired in different purchases, or (b) an average of the prices paid for materials in inventory with current prices, or (c) an average of inventory prices and anticipated future prices (p. 64). Each of these averages yields a different cost.

Machine costs

Using the costing procedures allowed by the government, some firms had written off machines three of four times. Other firms reduced their prices after a machine's cost had been written off the balance sheet (p. 82).

A hosiery mill allocated the machine cost to its products based on the machine cost per hour for each of the different machines used to produce each product. The machine costs per hour varied, so the cost of each product depended on which machine was used. This resulted in variations in final prices which the businessman found impossible to explain to his customers. Consequently, the practice was abandoned and a general machine cost per hour, the same for all machines, was substituted (p. 84).

Handling and carrying costs

Handling and carrying costs are another indirect variable cost. In the process of deciding how to allocate these costs, a businessman considered the following alternatives and the objections to each: (1) Value—but a $1 product and a $100 product could require the same amount of handling. (2) Weight—but twenty bottles weighing the same as a box would require more handling. (3) Number of units—but fifty identical units would require less handling than five different units. (4) Number of handlings—but handling and carrying did not increase proportionately with the size of orders.

Clearly, there was no "right" answer to this problem. The businessman chose value as the basis for allocation. He decided some method was better than none (pp. 72–73).

Administrative costs

Fog notes that administrative costs typically have both a fixed component and a variable component. Salaries at upper levels of management are fixed, while lower level administrators may be hired and fired with changes in demand and output. However, even those administrative costs that can be regarded as variable are not closely tied to changes in output. This makes it very difficult for firms to determine a basis for allocating administrative costs. Fog says that a majority of firms do not adopt any basis, and others adopt an entirely different basis from that which they use for other costs. The firms that Fog interviewed used the following bases for allocating administrative costs among departments:

(1) Equal amounts to each department.

(2) Allocation according to the number of employees, or according to the amount of wages paid, or according to turnover.

(3) Allocation according to the number of invoices, or according to the number of lines on the invoices.

(4) Arbitrary or estimated allocation, or partial allocation, or no allocation (p. 73).

Some firms had a tripartite division of costs: "(1) variable costs, (2) allocated fixed costs, and (3) costs which cannot be allocated" (p. 88).

Advertising and promotion costs

Advertising and promotion costs can be considered as either fixed or variable costs. Normally the relation between the volume of goods sold and what is spent on marketing is not close, so there is no good basis for allocating marketing costs. Most of Fog's businesses just added a fixed percentage for marketing to the manufacturing cost of each product. Frequently there were products that required more or less sales effort than others, but businessmen considered it impossible and unprofitable to try to adjust for the differences (pp. 73–74).

2. Erroneous cost calculations

Fog also found numerous instances where the cost calculation by the business was wrong.

A factory added "the same percentage of additional charges…for all departments and all products in spite of the fact that [different kinds of] goods of varying sizes and of different materials were being manufactured." In a cannery, the charge for steam was the same in the slaughterhouse as in the canning department even though the consumption of steam was ten times greater in the cannery (p. 72).

Machine costs are usually allocated by adding a fixed percentage to labor costs. This gives inaccurate results for products that require much machine time but little labor time. A chocolate factory added the same additional charge for assorted chocolates as for chocolate bars, even though assorted chocolates required primarily manpower and chocolate bars required primarily machine power (pp. 82–83).

A business calculated that its selling costs constituted eleven percent of its selling price. Consequently, they added eleven percent, not to the selling price, but to their variable costs. When Fog objected that this could not be right, they agreed it was an error, but "we have to do it because, otherwise, there would be no profit to ourselves" (p. 99). Another business added the same percentage for selling costs to all deliveries whether or not the sale involved any selling costs (p. 114).

A business purchased a machine that could not be used satisfactorily. The business therefore wrote off the fixed cost and only counted the variable costs associated with the machine's use. On this accounting basis, the machine was highly profitable, so the business purchased another one (p. 81).

3. Costs calculated by reference to the selling price

Fog shows that the traditional interpretation of the cause and effect relation between price and cost is frequently reversed. The "desired selling price . . . determines the calculated costs instead of vice versa." (p. 98). Fog says that if a firm finds it impossible to charge the price that is indicated by one costing method, the general rule is to adopt a different costing method (p. 65).

Some examples of using the selling price to determine costs are: (1) Depreciation on plant and equipment can be calculated "on the basis of either initial cost or of replacement prices." Most firms used original cost prices. One reason given was that if replacement costs were used, the price required to cover costs would be too high. "If we were to write off on the basis of replacement costs, we might as well shut down" (p. 82). (2) Another firm determined its price by allocating its fixed costs "according to current sales prices" and then adding a traditional profit margin. When sales dropped, it became impossible to charge the prices calculated by this method, so the firm changed to a different method (pp. 86–87). (3) A weaving mill calculated the cost of a big order on the premise that it would be produced on its most efficient looms, even though these looms were not available to produce the order (pp. 99–100).

Fog raises the question of whether businessmen actually use their cost calculations to set price. The answer frequently was "no." Although some managers considered the cost calculations binding on their price decisions (p. 90), more commonly, the cost calculation was viewed as advisory, as only an indication of what the price should be. Fog observes that in setting prices, firms "disengage themselves" from the cost calculations and set the prices "on the basis of other considerations" (p. 92).

For example, one corporation, after looking at the cost calculations, "set its price exclusively with a view to competition and to market conditions." Fog asked what the cost calculations were being used for. The answer was: "They are used more or less as a kind of statistics." In a similar case, the manager answered, "It is nice to be able to sit down and look at the figures" (p. 92). In a more obvious instance of the same policy, the selling price was set in advance and the purpose of the calculated cost was to justify the price the manager had already decided upon. If the calculated cost did not justify the price, it was thrown out and a new cost was calculated. This continued until a cost was reached that justified the price (p. 100).

4. Summing up

Variable costs often have an indirect component which makes them as difficult to allocate to units of output as fixed costs. Often there is no clearly "right" way to allocate a cost. In recording their materials costs and allocating their administrative costs, different firms use different methods, and different departments in the same firm use different methods. This means that two firms could be the same in every way—producing identical products, using the same plant and equipment, the same materials, the same labor force, paying the same prices for their factors—and yet calculate different costs for their products. In addition, businessmen's cost calculations frequently are wrong. And, as the final nail in the coffin of the cost-of-production theory of price, businessmen routinely calculate their costs by reference to the price they want to charge.

These are all facts. A valid theory of business costs must encompass them. It must apply to the costs of every business in the economy, including all of the above cases from Fog.

C. The Theory of Objective Costs

The anomalies I have presented from Fog fall into three categories: problems, mistakes, and price determining cost. Let us consider the mistakes first. With the exception of the firm that bought a second unsatisfactory machine, the errors Fog describes are small. One would not expect them to have much impact on a businessman's prices. Further, businessmen that consistently made serious errors in calculating their costs would misprice their products, undermine their profits, and eliminate themselves from the market. Consequently, we can dismiss actual errors in allocating costs as inconsequential.

The second category is problems—there are many cases where there is no clear right method for the allocation of costs. The consequence is that human beings have to figure out what method to use. The theory of objective costs says that whatever the unit cost men figure out, to the best of their conscientious ability, under the existing conditions—that is the *objective* unit cost. An objective cost is a cost grasped (that is, figured out) by a rational mind guided by nothing but the facts. That is what it means to be objective—not a gift from God—but the product of a rational process.

There is no necessary or mandatory method for allocating many indirect variable costs and fixed costs. The same firm may use different methods under different circumstances, and identical firms may calculate different unit costs. This is all irrelevant to the objectivity of the cost calculation. Objectivity is an issue of method. There is no way to determine the objectivity of a result other than by looking at the method by which that result was reached. If the method is based on facts, if it reflects a rational attempt to grasp reality, if nothing relevant is deleted or evaded, and nothing extraneous is introduced, then the resulting unit cost is objective.

Fog describes the allocation of fixed costs as "arbitrary" (p. 80). This is a misnomer in light of the conscientious, painstaking thought businessmen invest in figuring out various allocations (for example, above, handling and carrying costs and administrative costs). There is nothing arbitrary about it. Fog's businessmen do not allocate costs by doing whatever they feel like, following whatever emotion strikes them at the moment. If one has no objective basis for choosing one method of allocation over another, then one may do the equivalent of flipping a coin. That is the method required by the facts. It has nothing in common with being arbitrary.

The premise that makes the above anomalies shocking is intrinsicism—the premise that reality should dictate the cost, that the facts should imprint on our minds the one accurate measure of cost. But, as we have seen, it does not. Average cost and variable unit cost are not intrinsic. There is no voice of God telling businessmen the right unit cost for a particular product, or for that matter, the right price at which to sell it.

Let us pause for a moment on the fact that subjectivism is much less tempting in the context of calculating business costs than in valuing consumer goods. Subjectivism would mean that the businessman made up any unit cost that he felt like making up, without reference to the facts of production, as his feelings saw fit. Obviously, such an approach would be suicidal. If one understands the point, subjectivism is equally suicidal for consumers. While businessmen have to test their choices in the market, consumers have to test their choices in their lives.

What about the fact that sometimes the selling price determines the unit cost, and sometimes businessmen set their prices without reference to their unit cost? The principle explaining both cases is the same. To stay in business, the businessman must be able to sell his product and to do *that*, he must have a competitive price. It is a survival requirement that the businessman subordinates his cost calculations to competitive prices and that sometimes he sets his prices independent of cost. Such costs are still objective in exactly the sense identified above. They reflect the businessman's grasp of the relevant economic facts.[10]

CHAPTER FIVE

INTRODUCTION TO THE THEORY OF OBJECTIVE PRICES

I. The Three Theories of Price

Ayn Rand's trichotomy of the intrinsic, the subjective, and the objective implies three theories of price. Fundamentally, these three are the only possible theories of price. Other theories represent attempts to combine two or more of these basic theories. Such combination theories are internally contradictory. In the pure, consistent, undiluted form, there are only three.

A. The Intrinsic Theory of Price

Historically, the most sophisticated and realistic of the intrinsic theories of price was Ricardo's labor theory of value. The labor theory held that the conditions of production determine prices, particularly the condition of the amount of labor required to produce goods. As we saw in chapter 2, this theory holds that if avocados require twice as much labor to produce as apples, then the price of avocados will be twice the price of apples. The addition of a normal return on investment does not change the relative prices (that is, a normal return of ten percent added to prices of 50 dollars and 100 dollars yields prices of 55 dollars and 110 dollars, with the second still double the first.) However, Ricardo showed that relative prices also reflect differences in the time required for production, which causes relative prices to diverge from their labor-determined values. Marshall argued that the addition of time to the determinants of price makes Ricardo's theory a cost-of-production theory (Marshall 1920, 670-76), the theory of the British classical school.[1]

However, the premise that gave rise to Ricardo's theory is the same premise that gave rise to the pure labor theory of Marx. That is the premise of intrinsic value. If value is something in reality, prior to and independent of the thoughts and desires of men, then it follows that the measure of value (the price) must have the same origin. Only some fundamental fact of economic reality, the intrinsicists thought, could determine prices independently of the constantly shifting, changing wants of human beings. The proper chain of cause and effect is first, some external economic fact fixes the price; and second, men adjust their desires to that independently given price. This is a conception of prices as *intrinsic necessities*.

We saw in chapter 2 that the intrinsicists think reality, somehow, imprints itself on our minds. In this case, they think that reality dictates the price to men, and men have no choice but to accept and implement the price that reality gives them.

B. The Subjective Theory of Price

The subjective theory of price holds that the feelings of some economic actor or actors determine the price. In its pure form, the subjective theory abandons any attempt to devise a theory of price. The subjectivist recognizes that there are no intrinsic factors in the world dictating prices independently of men's desires, and that therefore the intrinsic theory is wrong. He concludes that human desires are primary and that a price can be anything the price-setter wants it to be. In its primitive form, the subjective theory claims that the seller sets any price, the banker sets any interest rate, and the employer sets any wage rate that any of them feels like setting, apart from and independent of the facts. Though this primitive view is very popular with the average man, most modern economists would reject it. Nevertheless, the primacy of subjective preferences in modern economics is manifest and consistent with this basic subjectivist position.

The most prominent early advocate of this viewpoint in the English-speaking world was Jevons. Jevons said, "*value depends entirely upon utility*" (Jevons 1871, 1; his italics). He does not tell us what he means by "value" in this statement, and later (p. 81) he rejects the use of the term altogether as dangerous and confusing. Nevertheless, let us take "value" in that quotation as meaning "price," which is the most plausible interpretation. Then the question is: what does Jevons mean by utility? The answer to this is not entirely clear either. Early in his book, Jevons says utility is "the abstract quality" of an object that makes us desire it (p. 38)—which is meaningless. Later he says that utility is "identical with the addition made to a person's happiness. It is a convenient name for the aggregate of the favourable balance of feeling produced—the sum of pleasure created and the pain prevented" (p. 45). And still later, "Intensity of feeling, however, is only another name for degree of utility" (p. 65). The conception of utility reflected in these last two statements—the feeling produced by an object—is the conception that is consistent with the subjectivist agenda. Thus, in the quotation beginning this paragraph, Jevons says that price depends entirely upon feeling.

However, this was not the position Jevons maintained in the actual content of his theory of price. Jevons stated his central position as follows:

> *Cost of production determines supply;*
> *Supply determines final degree of utility;*
> *Final degree of utility determines value.*
> (Jevons 1871, 165, his form and italics).

This statement seems to say that at the base of things, the cost of production determines price. This is decidedly not the subjectivist position; it does not make feeling the fundamental determining factor. However, the only cost of production that Jevons considers in this context is labor, and on the next page he says the value of labor "*must be determined by the value of the produce, not the value of the produce by that of the labour*" (p. 166, his italics).

This last statement is the subjectivist position, and identical with that expounded by the Austrians. They too reversed the line of causation projected by the labor theorists. First, the foundation of value is the value placed on an item by consumers. That is the starting point. Then that value is reflected back to the factors that produce the item. A factor that is required to produce something that consumers value highly will itself be valued highly for that very reason. The price of a consumer good will tend to equal its cost of production, but that is because producers bid up the prices of labor and materials according to the price for which they can sell their products. (Chapter 12 answers this idea.)

We saw in chapter 2 (p. 37) that a consistently subjective theory of price holds that the immutable first cause on which everything else is based is consumer desires. The rest of the productive network, including all its prices and quantities, adjusts to the fundamental fact of what consumers want and how much they want it. We also saw in chapter 2 (pp. 30–31 above) that subjectivists frequently hold that consumer desires themselves are uncaused, arbitrary, and not subject to rational examination. Thus, the door is closed on reason, and the essential subjectivist theory emerges: prices are arbitrary, the product of *subjective feelings*.

C. Marshall's Theory of Price

The modern version of the law of supply and demand originated in the economics of Alfred Marshall. Marshall was the first to think of combining the two competing theories of price that dominated his time: Ricardo's cost-of-production theory and Jevons' subjective utility theory.

Intrinsic considerations (the cost of production), Marshall held, determine the supply side. As we have just seen, the premise underlying the intrinsic theory is that factors inherent in reality determine price prior to and independently of the desires of human beings. Subjective considerations (the intensity of desire), Marshall held, determine the demand side. The premise underlying the subjective theory is that price is the product of subjective feelings, independent of the facts of reality.

Marshall's theory *is* the modern version of the law of supply and demand. However, the two theories of price which compose it are mutually exclusive. It is not surprising, therefore, that a theory of price that attempts to combine them is in principle unable to explain the origins of price (appendix A).[2]

D. The Objective Theory of Price

The objective theory is that prices are not determined by reality independent of man's mind, or by man's mind independent of reality. Rather, prices are the joint product of the mind and reality. Every market price is the consequence of a human mind grasping the relevant facts and acting accordingly (asking a price, bidding a price, paying a price, refusing to pay a price, and so on). We can sum up the objective view by saying that prices reflect *objective choices*—the objective choice of everyone buying and selling a particular product at a particular time, from two fundamental perspectives: (1) The man who asks a price chooses that price based on his grasp of the facts; (2) The man who pays a price chooses to pay based on his grasp of the facts. Prices are objective.

The intrinsic theory and the subjective theory are wrong. There is nothing in reality that forces men to set one price rather than another. Human beings are not automatons; they have free will. (In this sense, a businessman *can* charge any price he wants.) But neither are businessmen unconstrained by facts in the prices they set. If they wish to succeed, if they want to make profits, they have to consider the whole network of economic facts within which their businesses function when they decide what price to charge. For example, the retail prices set by retail firms reflect the facts grasped by retail merchants; most prominently, the fact of their costs at wholesale.

II. Background Considerations

A cursory overview of the most obvious economic facts suggests that the objective theory of prices is correct, that most prices do reflect the economic facts grasped by the men who set and pay the prices. Nevertheless, "most prices are objective" is not a theory. A theory has to be in the form of a general proposition, that is, a proposition at least implicitly incorporating the word "all." "All prices are objective" would be such a proposition. However, that proposition is false.

In addition, for a theory to be rationally usable, the theoretician has to specify the surrounding context. In this case, that context takes the form of answers to a number of questions. For example:

If most prices are objective, how many is most? Which prices are objective? Why are those the ones?

What is a nonobjective price? How many of those are there? What is the relative importance of objective and nonobjective prices in the economy?

What is the significance of objective prices for how the economy works? How can its working be reconciled with the existence of nonobjective prices?

What is the relation of objective prices to the law of supply and demand? Fundamentally, only individuals make choices; the choices of groups are the product of the choices of their individual members. If objective prices are objective choices in the sense described above, then the choices of individual human beings create objective prices. However, according to modern economics, the impersonal market forces of supply and demand determine prices. The individual has nothing to say and no choice to make; he is at the mercy of the market forces and must adjust to them. What are the implications of a theory of objective prices for that view?

We have to answer these questions before we can establish a general theory of objective prices.

Finally, there is the meaning and application of the concept of objective prices to the prices that exist in the real economy. What does the theory mean in practice? How can we tell when a price is objective and when it is not? Consider the following prices and the means by which they are set.

A. Case 1

For many years, U. S. Steel was the price leader for the steel industry. U. S. Steel initiated all changes in the prices of steel products which were then exactly duplicated by every other steel firm in the country, often down to the thousandth of a cent (Adams 1977, 107). In addition, a basing point system was used to price the products to the customer, the famous "Pittsburgh plus" system. No matter where in the country the steel mill was located, and no matter where in the country the customer resided, the delivered price of steel to him was the cost of the steel plus the cost of freight from Pittsburgh. The basing point system, plus the price leadership of U. S. Steel, meant that every steel firm in the country quoted the same delivered price to every potential customer.

The method by which U. S. Steel determined its prices (and hence the prices of all steel products in the country) was average cost pricing (p. 75 above). To the estimated cost per unit of the product, U. S. Steel added what it considered a "fair return" for its profit. The sum of these two elements was U. S. Steel's price (Kaplan, Dirlam & Lanzillotti 1958, 169-70), and shortly, every other steel firm's price. Was this an objective price?

B. Case 2

When a doctor wants to sell his medical practice, how should he decide what price to ask? In a 1994 article, Goldberg described three common methods and advocated a fourth:

(1) The net worth method: Take an inventory of all "the furniture, equipment, and supplies" and have "it all appraised at fair market value." Then, from that total, subtract the "outstanding debts and other liabilities," and the result is the asking price.

(2) The gross income method is a popular rule of thumb: the doctor's asking price for his practice is last year's gross income.

(3) The distress sale method was used when a doctor had a stroke and his wife could not find a buyer for the practice. Eventually all she could do was "sell off the equipment and other tangible assets."

(4) Goldberg recommended the debt capacity method: Given the net annual earnings of the practice, determine the maximum loan that a bank would make based on that income stream. That figure will allow the buyer to pay the essential practice expenses, take home a living wage, and repay what he borrowed to buy the practice.

(5) Goldberg did not mention the method most economists would endorse: project the net income stream into the future, discount that stream by the current interest rate and the resulting present value is the price of the practice.

In reality, all five of these methods are used to determine the value of doctors' practices. The problem faced by a theory of objective prices is, which of these methods yields an objective price and why?

C. Case 3

Finally, consider this case:

> A major capital equipment manufacturer wanted to significantly increase its share of revenue from non-U.S. sales. A study of its current pricing practices made it evident that not only was there no coherent approach to pricing, but its prices were primarily being set by distributors, who adjusted prices virtually at will. In addition, the company was unable to piece together a coherent account of what was happening because the ordering processes bundled different customer orders into one order, obscuring which sales were being made at what price levels. This meant that control of its price-points had essentially been lost . . . (Sinclair 1993, 18).

Were this company's prices objective?

We could multiply examples of this kind indefinitely. Their point is that the meaning and interpretation of a theory of objective prices is not self-evident. The remaining pages of this chapter and the next three chapters develop that meaning and interpretation. In the end, we will have a general proposition, an exact understanding of what the theory means, and evidence that the theory is both true and important.

III. How Prices Are Created

Fundamentally, every price originates in the mind of an individual human being. But an individual can make up any price he wants, such as a million dollars for a pencil. To be objective, a price must be based on the facts. Consequently, we will restrict our attention to prices at which the price-setter intends or expects or hopes to make a purchase or sale. Such prices are not guaranteed to be objective, but limiting our subject to such prices excludes prices that are a pure individual fantasy.

How do prices at which exchanges are made come into existence? To answer that question, we have to survey the ways that prices are established in the economy. We also want to know, are those prices objective? To answer that question, we need to see the extent to which facts lie at the base of prices, and what those facts are. Both questions require that we examine the methods by which prices actually are set. The next section surveys all the markets in a free economy, classified according to the product or service sold, and identifies the methods by which prices are established in each market.

A. Preliminary Comments on Terminology

First, a word about the concept of "price determination": In modern economics, the term "determination," in the context of price theory, carries the connotation that something *fixes the price in advance* of human calculation or choice. An example is the modern interpretation of the law of supply and demand (appendix A). In this respect, there are intrinsic elements in much of modern price theory. I deny that prices are fixed by any factors prior to human choice. All the facts that are relevant to the choice of a price operate only *through* a human grasp of those facts, and the price is the result of human calculation or processing based on those facts. Consequently, I will avoid the term determination. Instead, I will use the words "price creation" to refer to all the ways in which human beings bring prices into existence.

In modern economics, "firm" is the standard term for a business—a unit of production, organized to produce and/or sell at a profit. Without being obsessive about it, I avoid using the word firm. It has the effect of depersonalizing businesses and unnecessarily raising the level of abstraction. In fact, of course, firms do not do anything; all the actions of businesses are the actions of individual human beings. Consequently, in the rest of the book, I usually will use the term businessman when action by an individual is the subject, and the terms business or firm only when the whole organization is the subject.

My concern is with price creation in a free market. I assume laissez-faire capitalism throughout, as defined in chapter 1—specifically, that the government does not set, control, or charge any prices.

B. The Markets of a Free Economy

1. New consumer goods and services
Consumer goods and services are sold to consumers by businesses. Usually the businessman sets the price, though there are goods, such as new cars, where the buyer may negotiate with the seller over the price.

2. Used consumer goods
This market encompasses houses, cars, art works, collectibles, antiques, and items sold at garage, tag, yard, and barn sales. The prices of used houses and used cars are typically negotiated. When art works, collectibles, and antiques are sold by a business to an individual, the businessman names a price, but that price frequently is open to negotiation. High-end art works, collectibles, and antiques usually are sold at auction. The things sold in garage, tag, yard, and barn sales tend to be very inexpensive and, depending on the predilection of the seller, may or may not be subject to negotiation.

3. New producer goods and services
These are goods and services which businesses sell to each other for production or for resale at a profit. New producer goods include parts, materials, ingredients, finished goods at wholesale, machinery, tools, plants, and structures. New producer services include things like advertising, accounting, banking, insurance, and legal advice, when one business hires another to provide the service. The selling prices of these goods and services are given by the seller, or by the buyer, or the price is negotiated. For construction projects, the price usually is determined by sealed bids.

4. Producer worker services
These are all the employees in the economy. They include essentially everyone who is not self-employed. Usually the business tells potential employees what the wage rate is. In the cases of union workers and executives, the wage usually is negotiated.

5. Used producer goods
Used machinery, tools, plants, structures, and entire businesses are sold by one business to another for productive purposes. The seller may

set the price or the price may be negotiated. Expensive used machinery often is sold at auction.

6. Stocks, bonds, and commodities

These items are sold by both individuals and businesses to both individuals and businesses. Their prices are the ones people most frequently describe as determined by supply and demand. I disagree with this description. Consequently, I will call these prices *brokered prices* and this method of price creation the brokered method.

7. Not-for-profit corporations

It is doubtful that such firms would exist under laissez-faire capitalism. Since there would be no income taxes on either individuals or corporations, not-for-profit corporations would have no advantage over ordinary businesses. In any case, not-for-profit corporations do not have any special method of setting their prices and we will not consider them further.

C. The Five Methods of Price Creation

On the basis of the preceding survey, we now can make an exhaustive list of the methods by which prices come into existence. There are five.

1. Someone sets the price

One party gives or announces or states or prints the price, and the other party pays the price or accepts the price without quibbling. In exchanges between individuals and businesses, the price almost always is set by the business. "Someone sets the price" is virtually the exclusive method of price creation for new consumer goods and services and producer labor services. It is the primary method for used consumer goods when a business (excluding auction houses) sells those goods. Probably it is also common for new producer goods and services. We will call these prices "set prices" when the context allows us to do so without confusion.

2. Negotiation

Prices are created by negotiation when they are the result of discussion between the two parties, usually characterized by a series of offers and counteroffers. Some prices are created by negotiation in each of the six markets listed above, most frequently for producer goods and services, executive salaries, union wage rates, new and used houses, new and used cars, and other used consumer goods.

3. Sealed Bids

In this case, businesses compete for a specific job by submitting sealed bids. The bid is a unique price for a unique piece of work.

4. Auction

There are many kinds of auctions around the world. We will restrict our consideration to the kind dominant in the United States, where individuals bid up the price of a good in fixed supply. The auction method of setting price is used primarily for used consumer goods, especially art works, collectibles, and antiques. Used producer goods and perishable products like fish also are sold at auction. In addition, new goods which were produced for inventory by a bankrupt firm may be sold at a liquidation auction.

5. Brokered Prices

In this method of price creation, buyers and sellers function independently of one another. Buyers create the "bid price," sellers create the "asked price," and a price is set when those two prices coincide. Economic items priced by this method include stocks, bonds, commodities, futures contracts, foreign exchange, and interest rates.

Barter is not a method of setting prices. Barter characterizes the terms which define the price, not the method by which those terms are reached. The usual method of creating barter prices is negotiation.

A general theory of price must embrace these five methods of price creation. In order to reach that general theory and the evidence that confirms it, we have to identify the facts men grasp when they establish a price by each method. Consequently, in the next two chapters, that is what we will do. In identifying these facts, we will establish a basis for estimating how widespread objective prices are and the extent of nonobjective prices. This network of facts also will be the basis on which we will apply the theory to an analysis of how wages change when the facts change (chapter 9), how other prices change when the facts change (chapters 10 and 11), and the role of prices in distributing the economy's productive resources to its businessmen (chapter 12).

The following pages do not identify every fact that might enter into the creation of a price—which would be an endless list. Many readers will be able to add relevant facts based on their specialized knowledge. My purpose, however, is only to indicate the extent to which facts are relevant in the creation of prices in each of the five settings I have identified. The point is to show that in a free market, men create prices based on the facts. Chapter 6 identifies those facts when someone sets the price.

CHAPTER SIX

SOMEONE SETS THE PRICE

I. Introduction

When someone sets the price, there are three facts the price-setter is likely to consider. The following discussion is not in order of importance. I do not think that any one of these facts can be demonstrated to be more fundamental than any of the others.

The first is demand, that is, what people want and how much they want it, as reflected in the quantity of a good they will buy over a range of prices. In setting a price, a crucial consideration for the businessman is the total quantity he can sell over, let us say, a month. The relevant concept of demand is represented in the difference between the demand for chocolate covered cherries and the demand for chocolate covered ants. Demand means the broad range of output the firm can sell, given normal variations in price.

The second fact is the business's cost per unit of production, that is, its average cost or its variable unit cost. There is a long history of controversy in economics over the relevance of these two concepts. Part IV of chapter 4 dealt with some of these issues and appendix C gives my position on variable unit cost (that is, marginal cost). There is no question that average cost is by far the most widespread concept of cost used by businessmen. That is sufficient justification for this chapter's focus on average cost.

Average cost may rise or fall or remain unchanged as a business increases its output within its normal range. If average cost rises with increasing output, an increase in demand will be associated with a rise in average cost as the businessman increases his output to satisfy the increasing demand. If average cost falls with increasing output, an increase in demand will be associated with a fall in average cost.

The third fact is competition. Two attributes of competition affect the price a businessman charges: (1) the prices charged by competing businesses, and (2) the quality of competing products relative to one's own product. Both of these have a direct effect on the demand for the businessman's product and, through that, an indirect effect on the businessman's average cost—if average cost changes with changes in the quantity of output produced.

This chapter considers the effect on price of each of these factors for a consumer good or service. The purpose is to show in principle how demand, cost, and competition affect the price the businessman decides to set. Chapter 10 explains how the price changes in response to changes in each of these factors.

As background for everything that follows here, we need a clear conception of profit.

The Calculation of Profit

A businessman's profits are defined as total revenue minus total cost. If the businessman charges everyone the same price for a particular product, his total revenue is equal to the price charged (P) times the quantity sold (Q). If he sells 1000 units at $10 each, then his total revenue is $10,000.

A business calculates the average cost (AC) of producing each of its products by allocating its various costs to the individual units of each product, as we observed in chapter 4 (part IV). The total cost of producing each product is its average cost times the quantity sold. If a businessman's average cost is $9 a unit and he sells 10,000 units, then his total cost is $9000.

Thus, the equation for profits is:
$$\text{Profits} = PQ - (AC)Q$$
If $PQ = \$10,000$ and $(AC)Q = \$9,000$, then profits = $1,000.

II. Demand

Production is the first cause in economics. There is no demand if there is no production. This would be literally true in a barter economy where one man could demand another's product only by offering in exchange something he had produced. When money is the medium of exchange, almost every exchange is for money, and demand takes the form of offering money. Production still has priority—without production, there would be nothing to offer the money *for*.

Nevertheless, demand is crucial to the producer—that is, there is no production, there are no products, there are no businesses, there are no businessmen, absent the expectation of sales. Consequently, the businessman must have some idea of the quantity he can sell at the price he chooses to set. Under some circumstances, this estimate can be very casual. In other cases, an established history of demand may mean that he can take demand for granted. But in principle, expectation of demand is a prerequisite for establishing a business of any kind.

Usually, the businessman's estimate of demand is not and does not have to be precise. Businessmen build, buy, or rent their plant or facilities to produce a certain level of output. Usually that level is not a precise number, but a range within which the business's unit costs are acceptable. The businessman chooses a price that he believes is consistent with a quantity demanded that falls within the required range.

When the relevant concept of demand for a business is a range of quantities, the businessman may be able to consider his demand independently of what the competition is doing or will do. What the businessman needs to know is not the exact amount, but the approximate quantity that he can expect to sell over a normal range of prices—both his own price and the prices of his competitors.

Socially Objective Value

Ayn Rand's distinction between socially objective value and philosophically objective value adds an important dimension to the meaning of price vis-à-vis demand. She defined *philosophically* objective value as

> a value estimated from the standpoint of the best possible to man, i.e., by the criterion of the most rational mind possessing the greatest knowledge, in a given category, in a given period, and in a defined context (nothing can be estimated in an undefined context). For instance, it can be rationally proved that the airplane is *objectively* of immeasurably

greater value to man (to *man at his best*) than the bicycle—and that the
works of Victor Hugo are *objectively* of immeasurably greater value
than true-confession magazines (1966, 16-17, her italics).

She defined *socially* objective value as "the sum of the individual
judgments of all the men involved in trade at a given time, the sum of
what *they* valued, each in the context of his own life" (1966, 17). She argued that the free market prices of goods and services "reflect" or
"represent" their socially objective value, "not necessarily…their philosophically objective value" (1966, 17).

In her definition of socially objective value, I take the word "sum" to
mean not a literal addition, but an array of the rankings of the values of
all "the men involved in trade at a given time." Thus, a product's socially
objective value is the value of the product to the buyers. Prices reflect
that value in the sense that businessmen choose prices that buyers are
willing to pay, and to pay in sufficient numbers to keep the firm in business, given the facts of cost and competition. When men know a product's philosophically objective value and value the product on that basis,
then the price reflects that value.

It is also true that the businessman wants to charge whatever the
market will bear, that is, the highest price people are willing to pay. If a
businessman can identify customers who value the product more, and
charge them a higher price, he will do so. This is called price discrimination, a term with negative connotations, but denoting an entirely ordinary
and moral business practice. For example, much of the advertising by
businesses is directed at attracting customers who will pay higher prices.
Price discrimination is an instance of the principle that the prices of
products reflect their socially objective value.

However, the value of a product to an individual buyer depends on
the entire economic context, on the whole constellation of facts within
which the product is sold. The value to the buyer is not a result of just the
buyer's values and income, but also of the competitive context, that is,
the availability of substitute products, their relative quality, and their
prices (p. 69 above). Consequently, when a businessman considers alternative prices, he often needs to consider how his competitors will respond to those prices. This means that in selecting a price, the businessman needs a standard that integrates the facts of demand, cost (p. 98
above), and competition. We will return to this issue at the end of this
chapter.

III. Unit Costs

A price set to exceed average cost covers the business's total cost per unit. If price exceeds average cost for all the units the firm sells, the business's total revenue exceeds its total cost and the business makes a profit. Less frequently, a businessman may set his price by reference to his variable cost per unit. Sometimes a combination of both may be used.

First, let us consider why average cost is the cost that most businessmen choose to measure and base their prices on—*if* they choose to base their prices on their costs. Then we will review the alternative of variable cost pricing.

A. Average Cost Pricing

From a businessman's perspective, the primary advantage of basing price on average cost is that the price includes an allocation for the firm's fixed costs. The price has to cover fixed costs over the long run or the business will fail—that is, the businessman will be unable to replace his plant and equipment as they wear out, pay the interest on his debt when it comes due, or pay salaries to himself and his upper management. A price that exceeds average cost is covering that individual unit's share of the business's fixed cost—a contribution that the businessman naturally considers a necessity if his firm is to continue in business.

Another reason that businessmen prefer to base price on average cost is that costs the businessman regards as fixed may turn out to be variable over time. The businessman may fail to notice that these costs are slowly rising relative to output—a phenomenon sometimes called "creeping overheads." By including all costs in average cost, the businessman does not have to worry that costs like this are overlooked (Fog 1960, 80).

Finally, there is the terrific pressure businessmen are under to cut price in order to compete. Average cost sets a lower boundary for pricing by the marketing department, preventing that department from reducing prices to the point that the business makes a loss. This is not an idle concern. Fog (1960, 79) tells of a business that switched from average cost pricing to variable cost pricing. Subsequently, the marketing department steadily lowered prices across the board until management put a stop to it, modifying the system and raising prices.

B. Variable Cost Pricing

In variable cost pricing, the businessman bases his prices on variable costs. Variable cost pricing has a limited appeal because it ignores fixed costs. At the same time, this is the basis of its attraction. Allocating fixed costs is a very difficult problem, as we saw in chapter 4. If the business does not allocate its fixed costs, cost allocation is much easier and time does not have to be spent figuring out how to do it (Fog 1960, 85). In addition, for particular businesses within their particular market contexts, this may be the profit-maximizing way to set their prices.

There are also businessmen who set their prices by reference to both average cost and variable cost. For example, suppose a manager normally uses average cost pricing. Then a new customer offers to pay a low price for a big order. To decide whether or not to accept the offer, the manager subtracts the average fixed cost from the average cost of the product. The remainder is the variable cost per unit of producing the item. Since producing the additional output will not add to the firm's fixed costs, if the low bid exceeds the variable cost per unit, the manager will accept the bid and add to his firm's profits (Fog 1960, 91). This kind of calculation is not rare.

C. Marginalism

The reasoning reflected in this last example is called *marginalism*. It is the touchstone of modern economics. Used rationally, marginalism is the basis on which businessmen evaluate changes in action and policy; for example, whether or not to run an advertising campaign, whether to build an addition onto the existing plant, whether to build a new plant, whether to buy a new piece of equipment, whether to acquire a competitor, whether to add another airline flight to the schedule, whether to start a new business, whether to add a new product line, and whether to accept a low price for a big order. The marginalist rule is that any action of this kind should add more to the firm's revenues than to its costs. This is a true and valid and useful principle. It is certainly understood by most businessmen, who did not learn it from economists. (See appendix C for my objections to the role of marginalism in modern economics.)

D. The Required Relation of Cost to Price

The first objective absolute of business costs is this: no matter how those costs are calculated, over the long run a business's total sales revenue must exceed its total cost. Usually, there is relatively little difficulty in determining a business's *total* costs.[1] The major problems occur in the attempt to allocate the totals to individual units of output (chapter 4, part IV). The firm's survival does not depend directly on the accuracy of this allocation. The critical requirement is that on average, over the long run, total revenue exceeds total cost; that is, the business must make a profit.

Thus, Fog (1960) notes that some firms do not know what their unit costs are. Four shoe manufacturers made no cost calculations whatever. In answer to the question of how they set their prices, the first firm said, "It's more or less a random guess." The other three firms "admitted that they did not have the faintest idea of the cost of manufacture of the shoes," but set their prices on the principle that if firm A can make this model for X dollars, then we must be able to make it for a little less (p. 170). Evidently this was the case, because these firms continued in business, which means they set competitive prices and earned a total revenue that exceeded their total costs.

Now let us consider the relation between price and average cost. The average cost per unit does not determine price, it does not fix the price in advance—which is why the intrinsic theory of price is wrong—but the average cost *of newly produced products* (as opposed to used products) does set the basic context for the price. Average cost determines the general range within which a price will fall. No matter what the difficulties in measuring average cost, this remains true.

For example, in the first decade of the twenty-first century, in the United States, the price of a pack of gum was in cents, not dollars. The price of a newspaper was in dollars; the price of a restaurant meal was in tens of dollars; the price of a blu-ray disc player was in hundreds of dollars; the price of refinancing a mortgage was in thousands of dollars; the price of a new car was in tens of thousands of dollars; and the price of a new middle-class house was in hundreds of thousands of dollars. (But note that the original cost of a *used* middle-class house had very little to do with its price.) Costs explain differences on this order of magnitude. A difficulty or even an outright error in calculating average cost cannot alter differences of this kind.

There is no particular relation that the price should have to average cost in order for the businessman to maximize his profits. One might think that a minimum requirement would be that the price of each product sold should exceed its average cost, but that is not true. There is such a thing as a "loss leader," a product priced below cost in order to attract customers. Many businessmen find this practice profitable, and the fact that they do refutes the idea that profit maximization requires that a product's price always exceeds its unit cost. Indeed, we saw in Fog (1960) that a businessman may set his price based solely on demand and competition, without any reference to his unit costs (chapter 4, part IV). The most we can say is that *on average*, over the long run, a business's price per unit must exceed its average cost, because only then will the business's total revenue exceed its total cost.

Retail businesses are different. The typical retail store sells many different items and does not price any of them by reference to average cost. Let us see why.

The total cost of a retailer is the sum of whatever he pays his wholesalers for the goods he sells, plus his overhead (insurance, electricity, rent), plus the wages of his employees and his own salary. Average cost would be that total divided by the total number of items he has for sale. A drugstore, for example, might have a stock of 100,000 items, including five electric hair dryers and fifty rolls of toilet paper. The average cost thus calculated would be almost completely without meaning and useless for setting prices.

A retailer sets his price by marking up the price the wholesaler charges him, adding ten percent, fifty percent, one hundred percent or more, depending on the other costs of his business. That markup has to cover all his costs and yield a profit. Price has no relation to average cost in his business. There is no average cost. The only requirement for the survival of a retail store is the requirement of every business: over the long run, the store must make a profit; total revenue must exceed total cost.

E. The Structure of Unit Costs

How does the businessman's average cost change as he increases output? The answer is important in understanding the effect on an industry of a change in demand or competition or the cost of an input—the subject of chapters 10 and 11. What can we say that in principle will be true of all, or almost all, businesses?

First, let us consider the range of output from zero up to the smallest quantity the business might produce. There are two reasons to expect falling average costs as output increases over this range. First, on average, fixed costs are a high proportion of total costs. Blinder and others

(1998, 101) found that an average of 44 percent of costs are fixed (for example, 53 percent are fixed in "transportation, communications, and utilities," 56 percent in "services"). Since fixed costs do not change with increases in output, average fixed costs fall very rapidly when output is low. For example, if fixed costs are $100, fixed cost per unit declines to $50, then $33, then $25 and then $20, as quantity increases from one to five. In contrast, at high levels of output, average fixed cost declines very slowly as each increase in output is a very small change in a large total (for example, from 1,000,010 to 1,000,015).

In retail businesses, "spreading the overhead" is the equivalent of reducing average fixed cost by increasing output. It is clear to every retail businessman that there is some minimum level of sales revenue that is necessary to cover his overhead costs before there is anything available to pay his other costs or contribute to a profit.

Second, the main component of average variable cost is the wages of employees. As output increases, more and more workers can be assigned to jobs that are more and more specialized. Increasing specialization of labor increases the output per worker and reduces the labor cost per unit.

If both average fixed cost and average variable cost decline, then average total cost, as the sum of both, declines. Looked at from the perspective of reducing output, there is always some decrease in output that will sharply raise a business's average cost. It seems likely that businessmen are aware of this and that they consider it important to keep the quantity they sell above the level where this happens. Often a recession is bad for a business, not just because its sales fall, but also because its average cost goes up.

Now let us consider how average cost varies over the range of output that businesses normally produce. Blinder and others (1998) present direct empirical evidence on this point. Blinder wanted to ask business executives about how their *marginal* costs change with increases in output (see appendix C). He called them "variable costs of producing additional units" (pp. 102 & 216). He found that 41 percent of his firms reported falling unit costs, 11 percent reported rising unit costs, and 48 percent reported unchanged unit costs as quantity increased (pp. 102 & 217). I take these figures as measuring changes in average cost rather than marginal cost for the following reasons:

First, Blinder reports that "in a fair number of cases" his interviewees had a hard time distinguishing fixed costs from variable costs (p. 101; see part IV of chapter 4 above) If businessmen cannot distinguish between fixed and variable costs, it is because in their businesses, fixed and variable costs cannot be distinguished. If this is true, then they cannot understand the meaning of "the variable costs of producing additional units."

Second, Blinder says the question "often had to be repeated, rephrased, or explained," that ten of two hundred firms were unable to answer the question at all, and the others "answered in [their] own words, sometimes at great length" (pp. 216–17). This last, I submit, is the response of men of good will, who are trying to be helpful, but who do not know what you are talking about. Finally, Blinder says it is possible "that some (or even many) of these firms were confusing average cost with marginal cost" (p. 102). In the total context of this question, I think that is a virtual certainty.

If we are justified in taking Blinder's figures as representing average cost, then these numbers represent how average cost changes for firms *over the range of output they customarily produce*. These numbers do not tell us how firms' average costs change over much smaller or much greater quantities of output.

We have already considered smaller quantities. With regard to greater quantities, orthodox economic theory holds that unit costs start to increase rapidly as output approaches capacity. That seems to be correct. For manufacturing firms, this is because of factors like overtime pay, shift premiums, and more spoilage as a result of speeded-up processes. In addition, all of a firm's machines do not reach capacity at the same time and it is expensive to buy (probably from a competitor) semi-finished items which normally are produced by a machine that has reached the limits of its capacity. Also, the maintenance of equipment becomes harder and more expensive when there is no down time.[2] If new workers are hired, they have to be trained by existing personnel, who therefore cannot do their regular jobs, or who cannot do them as well.

Most of the foregoing factors are relevant in explaining why service producers also are likely to encounter rising average cost as they approach capacity. In addition, service producers will face factors like overcrowded office space, overused machines (for example, copiers) with resulting down time, and delayed processing of documents as existing staff fall behind. In the summer of 2009, the demand for refinancing mortgages was so great that the required paperwork routinely arrived a month or more after expiration of the lock-in date for the interest rate (which the mortgage companies honored nevertheless). These same factors may be operative in the offices of manufacturing firms as they approach capacity.

What can we say about retail businesses in this connection, especially since they do not calculate average cost? Most local retail stores are small, but there are some very large chains with very large stores. These chains have been able to achieve significant cost reductions through the enormous quantities they buy from suppliers and the low prices they are able to negotiate. "Economies of scale" is the economic term for these reductions in average cost. Usually economists think of economies of scale as applying only to very large businesses, but they are also relevant to small businesses.

The size of the small local retailer is the product of the economies of scale at his level. For most retail stores, a wide variety of merchandise is a competitive requirement, and a still wider variety is a competitive advantage. (Retailers for whom this is not true, like barbers, can be profitable with less space, which in fact we observe.) Suppose a profitable retailer had a store one tenth the size. With less space, he could carry a smaller variety of goods, which would put him at a competitive disadvantage. His sales would fall, he could not cover his overhead, and his profits would disappear. Retail stores are the size they are because that is the size necessary to achieve the economies of scale available to them.

A retail store reaches capacity when people line up outside waiting to get in. A popular movie can cause people to line up outside a theater and keep it operating at capacity for weeks. There are restaurants so popular that people line up to get inside and every seat is occupied continuously. Is cost higher as a result? Undoubtedly, there is some increase in *total* costs: for the theater, more ushers to keep the theater clean; for the restaurant, more waiters and cooks. But if we think of *average* cost on a per customer basis, it seems unlikely that there is any increase in average cost in such cases. If average cost rose, the owners would have to raise their prices, and we do not observe that. (Of course, we also do not observe retail stores at capacity very often.) In general, it seems safe to conclude that once the retailer has adjusted to a capacity level of business, any higher costs are more than compensated by higher revenue.

In summation, I hypothesize that there is always some decrease in output that will raise a business's average cost, that average cost is constant or increases slowly or decreases slowly over the range of output the business unit is designed to produce, and that, with the exception of retailers, unit cost increases rapidly as the business approaches capacity. The remainder of this book counts on this pattern of average cost.

IV. Competition

Competition includes two central issues that bear directly on the price set by a businessman.

A. The Prices Currently Charged by One's Competitors.

The range of prices charged by other businesses is probably *the* essential competitive condition faced by a business. The general rule is that whatever price the business decides to charge must fall within that range. A price can fall outside that range only if it represents some unusual variation in quality.

B. The Quality of One's Product Relative to Competing Products.

The general rule under this heading is that the price must be consistent with relative product quality. Usually it is economic suicide to try to charge more for an inferior product. It is this fact that accounts for the widespread usefulness of price as an indication of quality.

When a businessman changes his price, sometimes he does not give the competition any direct attention. He does not consider how his competitors might respond. This is particularly common for retail businesses. In retail markets, often the price differentials among stores have existed for a long time, and when, for example, costs increase, the owners do not worry whether their competitors also will raise their prices. Nevertheless, these prices too reflect the state of the competition.

Whether or not the retail-business owner is aware of it, his firm's market position would be radically different if he had many more competitors or none. His stable relations with his competitors are what allow him to ignore them. In such cases, the businessman may have the importance of his competitors forced on his awareness only if something dramatic happens to the market, like a sharp fall in demand or a major new entrant. The fact that competition is always relevant, that it is always there in the background, is confirmed by the fact that the owner of a new, retail-store learns his competitors' prices before he sets his own.

C. Price Leadership

There are two additional facts of the competitive context that a price leader may consider: One is the costs of competing firms. If the price leader is also the dominant firm, normally he will not want to set the price too high above the costs of his competitors. To do so would give those firms the opportunity to accumulate capital, expand, and eventually challenge his dominance (Reisman 1998, 200; Fog 1960, 141, 150-51).

The second fact is the threat of potential competition. A price leader will not want to set the price too high above the costs of potential competitors, making it profitable for them to enter the market. This may also be a consideration for businessmen who are not price leaders.

V. Additional Issues

In setting his price, the businessman needs to consider the facts of demand, cost, and competition. His price needs to be consistent with these facts. One cannot hold as an additional condition that the price should yield a profit. The price *must* yield a profit eventually. However, a businessman may have no choice in the short run but to set a price at which he takes a loss, particularly if the cause of the price change is something bad for profits, like falling demand or rising costs or more competitors selling more output.

A. Expectations

The price-setter also is likely to consider the prospects for change in each of the three factors. The primary reason for this is that it takes time to raise the price. This is true even of consumer goods and services, but it is much more important for producer goods and services, when businesses are selling to other businesses. In such cases, advance warning (three months is not unusual) of an increase in price is normal. The price the business is raising is a cost to his customers and will affect their profits. The advance warning gives them time to figure out how they will deal with the increase in costs—maybe by altering their mix of inputs, maybe by increasing efficiency, maybe by increasing their prices. Giving one's customers advance warning of a price increase is both a competitive action and an act of good will—a helping hand extended to those upon whom one's business depends. It is the same motive that makes it against a businessman's self-interest to raise his prices up and down with every change in demand or cost (see appendix A).

B. Complications

We have not dealt with many considerations that enter into the creation of prices, considerations like using different models and prices for the purpose of price discrimination and market segmentation, and cases of strategic pricing. These topics are treated primarily by the marketing profession.[3] However, they are real considerations. They affect the prices businessmen set. A general theory of price has to include them.

We will not pursue this topic further. When we reach the theory of objective prices, it will be clear that, whatever the impact on prices of these complications, that effect is consistent with the theory.

We have three fundamental facts, but only one price for each individual unit. The beginning of this chapter pointed out that competition affects the firm's demand, which in turn affects the firm's average cost, if it is not constant with increases in output. The three fundamental facts are interconnected, while each of them is independently relevant to the choice of the price. In addition, there may be many other facts that are important to the price in a specific industry or market. Somehow, all these facts have to be tied together so that the businessman's price reflects the entire constellation of facts that are relevant to his success. How can that be done? That is our next topic.

VI. The Long-Run, Profit-Maximizing Price

We need a governing principle that will act as a standard, integrating all the facts that affect the firm's choice of a price, both the general kind of facts that we have looked at, and facts that are specific to individual cases. That principle, the ultimate standard of price when someone sets the price, is *the long-run, profit-maximizing price*.

A. The Meaning of Long Run and Profit Maximizing

There are two aspects to this principle:
1. Profit maximizing
This is obviously the principle of self-interest applied to the operation of a business. In the most general terms, it is the principle of "doing the best you can for your life." With that meaning, the principle of self-interest applies to everyone in a capitalist economy, not just to businessmen and entrepreneurs. Consumers act on this principle when they look for the best product at the lowest price. Workers act on this principle when they look for the highest wage for their labor, train for higher wage

jobs, and work hard to get ahead. Most people think that businessmen are the only members of the economy acting on the profit motive. This represents an enormous misunderstanding.

2. Long run

This also is the principle of self-interest. In the life of a rational man, a long-run perspective integrates all of his actions with the goal of maintaining and enjoying his life. Short-run action means action on impulse, unguided by reason or principles. Someone who acts on that basis does not know whether he is acting for his life or against it, which means that in principle his life is in danger; he is acting on the premise of death.

How long is the long run? Since life is what is at stake in the long run, for an individual human being, the long run is the time span of an individual human life, his own life, for as long as he lives. In politics and government, the long run is the lifetime of the country, which means that in principle it exceeds the life of any individual human being. A man who wins the responsibility for a country's life has to consider the consequences of his actions, not just on the next election, but on the next generation.

The long run in business is like the long run in politics. The long-run perspective embraces the whole life of the business, which means it does not have any definite end point; entrepreneurial decisions look to the indefinite future. As in the long run for an individual and a country, the ultimate value at stake in every business choice is the business's survival. Consequently, *no action taken today should bankrupt the business in the foreseeable future.* That is the minimum requirement for all business decisions, not just pricing decisions.

B. The Long-Run, Profit-Maximizing Facts

The principle of long-run profit maximization is the principle maximizing the business's chances of long-run survival. Reduced to essentials, long-run profit maximization is the means; long-run survival is the end. Rationally, the firm cannot do better than to maximize its long-run profits.

This principle is also the implicit foundation for the facts we have identified as the basis for creating prices. Long-run profit maximization integrates and validates the relevance of those facts.

A businessman focused simply on profit maximization without regard to time would not deal with demand, cost, and competition in the manner I have described. Average cost would be relevant only as a starting point. Since consumers interpret high prices as indicating high quality, the businessman could raise his prices above the range of his competitors' prices and advertise that his product quality was higher. Alternatively, the businessman could secretly undercut his competitors' prices and try to pick off their best customers. Both of these policies might increase profits for a week or two.

The facts of interest to a price leader also are relevant only over the long run. It takes time for competing firms to accumulate enough capital to challenge a price leader, and even more time for new firms to enter an industry. Short run, there is no reason for a price leader to be concerned with these things.

C. Short-Run Profit Maximization Is a Nullity

In business, short-run profit maximization means death, the death of the business, in a manner much more obvious and immediate than the death short-run action leads to for an individual man.

The beginning of part V (p. 109) noted that the standards of price setting cannot include the fact that the price should yield a profit. Sometimes businessmen deliberately set a price at which they know they will take a loss. But if their goal were short-run profit maximization, they would go out of business rather than lose money.

Businesses that sell primarily to other businesses often could raise their price and increase their short-run profits. Over time, businessmen build up a relationship with their customers, an important element of which is trust or confidence. If a businessman raised his price, and told his customers that there was a good reason ("our costs have risen"), his customers would believe him. They would assume that the costs of other suppliers also had risen and that they were raising their prices too. When they found out that was not true, the businessman would have lost his customers' trust as well as his customers.

Finally, most businesses could raise their short-run profits by cutting their costs. In manufacturing, businesses could substitute inferior materials, parts, or ingredients in the production of their products, eliminate quality controls, and end investment in research and development. Service firms too could stop improving their products. For many businesses, the cost savings generated by such measures would be substantial and could increase their profits for a year or two.

All the methods by which a businessman might increase his short-run profits are self-destructive over the long run. This is conclusive evidence that in reality, over the long run, businessmen do not try to maximize their short-run profits. Strictly speaking, short-run profit maximization is a contradiction in terms—the short-run perspective turns this principle of self-interest into a policy of self-destruction. Short-run profit maximization is irrational. It would not deserve any serious attention if it were not the dominant theory of modern economics.

D. The Alternatives to Long-Run Profit Maximization

There are two alternatives to long-run profit maximization as the standard for price-setting by businessmen: (1) No standard. It is not true that everyone maximizes or optimizes something. These businessmen do not maximize anything; they are non-optimizers. (2) Some definite standard for setting prices other than long-run profit maximization. These businessmen are maximizers. The question is, what do they maximize?

1. No standard

Warren Haynes (1962) and his associates conducted in-depth interviews with the owners of local, small businesses. Their primary purpose was to determine how and why these businessmen set the prices they set. According to Haynes, several of them did not maximize profits (pp. 49-52). In fact, most of these cases are open to the interpretation that they *were* maximizing *long-run* profits. Nevertheless, it is certainly true that there are businessmen in the economy who do not set their prices to maximize long-run profits. Paraphrasing a former associate of Ayn Rand's, the idea of universal long-run profit maximization pays businessmen a compliment that they do not deserve (*The Objectivist Newsletter*, September 1962).

Such non-maximizers are not widespread, but they appear here and there throughout a capitalist economy. They are not restricted to any particular size of business, but the form in which they eschew maximizing varies with the size of the business in which they work.

At the upper levels of big corporations, high executives occasionally are caught "cooking the books." These men use accounting subterfuge to report profits that exceed the profits the business made—and sometimes to report a profit in place of the loss that actually occurred. Since this tactic cannot succeed beyond the short run (a few years at most)—since such measures are always discovered at the price of destroyed careers for all the parties involved—such policies are ruinous. The thinking of such executives resembles that of an embezzler who continues to gamble embezzled funds on the premise that with a little luck, he can pay it all back.

The other type of non-maximizer is restricted to retail stores, and probably to retail stores in small towns. These non-maximizing businessmen are satisfied to just "get by." They prefer "a quiet life" (Haynes 1962, 120) and want to avoid stress. Others believe in a policy of "live and let live" (pp. 51 & 93) or are morally opposed to profit maximization. They consider charging what the market will bear as the equivalent of "gouging the public" (pp. 50, 109–11). Everyone knows people like this. The idea that they are really maximizers, maximizing something like "quiet" or "lack of stress," is silly.

However, it is safe to say that most non-maximizers, both big and small, do not want their businesses to fail. If so, this severely limits their price-setting, because their prices must meet the other criteria we have identified if they are to stay in business. The non-maximizer has to charge a price that takes account of demand and the value his customers place on his good or service. His price has to fall within the range charged by his competitors and it has to reflect the quality of his product relative to their products. At an absolute minimum, his price has to be low enough to generate revenue sufficient to cover his fixed costs.[4] If he fails to do any of these things, his business will fail. Since these are the same facts considered by businessmen deliberately maximizing their long-run profits, it is doubtful that the prices set by non-maximizers can differ much from long-run, profit-maximizing prices.

An ambitious local retailer will consider the same things in setting his long-run, profit-maximizing prices as the local retailer who is looking for a quiet niche in which to stagnate. If they are in the same line of business, their prices may well be the same. If their prices differ, they cannot differ by much because their prices reflect the same facts. Similarly, the corporate executive who is cooking the books will look at the same facts in setting his prices as his honest and upright competitors.

The main difference between the two types of retailers will not be their prices. Instead, the long-run profit maximizer will be continuously, actively thinking of ways to improve his business. He will scour the market looking for new products to offer his customers. He will advertise special services, sales, promotions and guarantees. He will be eager to help his customers and work hard to satisfy them. Over time, he will expand the scale of his operation, perhaps adding additional stores to a growing chain. The non-maximizer will do none of these things, and if he is in competition with a long-run profit maximizer, he probably will be driven out of business. In this way, one might argue, the long-run profit maximizers will come to dominate the market over time. However, this process seems unlikely to occur in small towns, though a national chain store entering the market may have the same effect.

On the other hand, the book-cooking corporate executive may pursue profits just as aggressively as his competitors. Indeed, his pursuit of profits may be even more intense because destruction is staring him in the face. This is not a context that is conducive to rational decisions. He is likely to become more and more focused on the short run, since he must have profits *now* if he is to escape the financial hole he has dug for himself. Now and then, the end of this process is splattered all over the business pages of the country's newspapers.

2. Alternative standards

Over the last sixty plus years, economists have conducted a number of empirical studies (including Haynes 1962 above), by interview or questionnaire, with the goal of finding out (among other things) how businessmen decide what price to charge. One cannot say that they have found any consistent answer. The businessmen interviewed have cited many standards other than long-run profit maximization.

Weston (1972) argued (in by far the best work on this subject) that the evidence had been "confounded" because the questions posed entailed a long-run context while economists interpreted the answers in the context of their theory of short-run profit maximization (pp. 2–5). Another endless source of error has been modern economists' automatic recourse to pure competition with all of its fantasy spin-offs.[5] Nevertheless, the evidence clearly indicates that many businessmen use explicit standards, goals, and methods other than long-run profit maximization as the means to determining their prices. My hypothesis here is that these standards are not alternatives to long-run profit maximization, but the means to it.

The standard "long-run, profit-maximizing price" offers little practical guidance. Basically, it says "think about the long-run effect on profits of current prices." This is not completely unhelpful. Following this rule surely would have saved some firms from bankruptcy. But obviously, it is not enough to solve a real problem.

Large firms tend to need more detailed guidance than small firms because they tend to have many more products for sale in many more markets. Consequently, they have evolved intermediate goals for their pricing, goals which in some cases may appear to be, but are not, ends in themselves. (See Weston 1972 for a similar statement [p. 2].)[6] These goals include the following:[7] setting prices to achieve (1) a particular market share, (2) a target profit rate on sales or costs, (3) a certain mark-up over total unit cost, (4) a target rate of profit on investment, (5) meeting competitors' prices, (6) an adequate cash flow, and (7) maximum sales revenue. In different contexts, the same firm may use two or more of these goals. A price that is set to achieve any of them will reflect the facts of demand, cost, and competition, as well as potentially many other facts specific to the individual businessman's market.

Other goals are sometimes used, but the preceding seven are the most important ones, and the ones with clearly the most potential value. That value is as the means to long-run profit maximization. For example, in Lanzillotti (1958), it is clear[8] that the businessmen interviewed used the goals they cited to maximize their long-run profits. The few cases that did not conform to this standard were the consequence of businessmen's fear of antitrust prosecution, an issue Lanzillotti raises explicitly (pp. 936–37).

Sometimes, the economist-commentator suggests that long-run profit maximization may be the motive for a particular practice.[9] Other times, the relation of a practice to long-run profit maximization is obvious without comment. For example, Jobber and Hooley (1987) report that a common tactic in entering a new market is "penetration-pricing" to achieve market share, after which the firm adopts "a profit oriented objective" (p. 167).[10] But both parts of this strategy are directed at the goal of long-run profit maximization. Pursuing market share, (1), is not an alternative to long-run profit maximization but a form of it.[11]

Let us consider the relation to long-run profit maximization of the other six goals. In what follows, I take long-run profit maximization and long-run survival as equivalent standards, because the first is the means to the second.

(2) A target profit rate on sales or costs, narrows the standard for price setting from general profit maximization to a specific profit rate. This focuses attention on a narrower set of facts and makes it easier to figure out the price.

(3) A certain markup over total unit cost takes the pricing decision out of the hands of lower management, whose judgment may not be the best. By naming a certain markup (for example, ten percent), upper management makes sure that the business's price is the best price they think they can get.

The relation of (4), a target rate of profit on investment, to long-run profit maximization is transparent. The explicit target of a rate of profit sets a goal for the firms' management, not just in setting prices, but in selecting the new long-term investments the business will undertake. If that target rate is to do its job, it will be the highest rate of return that the businessman thinks his firm can achieve.

We have already identified the role of meeting competitors' prices, (5), in long-run profit maximization (p. 108 above).

Achieving an adequate cash flow, (6), is an absolute necessity for the survival of all firms. Failure to achieve it represents a particular danger for smaller businesses, who Jobber and Hooley found use this standard more often (p. 169). A firm can be doing very well in terms of orders and sales and still be bankrupted by an absence of cash to pay its creditors.

(7) Maximizing sales revenue is the most dubious of these intermediate goals. Jobber and Hooley found that firms using this goal had a poorer profit record than firms using other goals (1987, 171). Nevertheless, if long-run investments have been committed, maximizing sales revenues means maximizing sales which means maximizing output which will maximize utilization of the firm's capacity (Weston 1972, 8) and minimize the unit cost associated with that capacity.

In sum, the goals that businessmen have cited as alternatives to profit maximization are the means to long-run profit maximization. As we noted above, a businessman cannot do better than to maximize his long-run profits. Achieving this goal is the way the businessman best insures the long-run survival of his business—the precondition for the continuation of his livelihood, and in many cases, a necessity for securing his fortune. This perspective is not likely to be news to any businessman.

E. Creation of the Long-Run, Profit-Maximizing Price

How does a businessman determine his long-run, profit-maximizing price? Mathematically, long-run, profit maximization means maximizing the present value of a stream of annual profits over an indefinite number of years in the future. (Silberston 1970, 531-33; Weston 1972, 2) If one knows or can estimate the amount of each future annual profit, there is a well-known formula for measuring the present value. What it would mean to maximize that formula with respect to price is not clear. In any case, businessmen do not and cannot proceed on that basis.

The general answer to how businessmen reach their long-run, profit-maximizing price is at once too simple and too complex. In principle, what a businessman does is look at the facts we have discussed, plus all the facts that are specific to an individual industry and its competitive conditions (there may be a myriad of issues under this latter heading), plus whatever intermediate goals the businessman has chosen. Then, having weighed all these considerations, the businessman selects the profit-maximizing price under those conditions, given the long-run perspective. There is no mathematical formula that gives the businessman an automatic and effortless result.

Sometimes determination of the long-run, profit-maximizing price is very easy—given the competitive conditions, there is only one price the businessman can charge if he wants to stay in business. Sometimes the market situation is enormously complex and interconnected, involving other markets and the products of competing businesses and many different versions of the business's own product. In such cases, the businessman can only make his best, most informed and intelligent guess, and then be prepared to change the price if it does not work out. The latter case is most likely for large, multi-product businesses, producing many models of the same product for different market segments, in different markets, in different parts of the country, and in different countries of the globe, where they meet widely varying competitive conditions (Weston 1972, 7). These are also the businesses most likely to have chosen an intermediate goal or goals.

The fundamental issue involved in determining the long-run, profit-maximizing price is the network of facts that set the market context in which the business functions. Essentially, a businessman's profits turn on how accurately he grasps, interprets, and forecasts those facts. Each businessman makes his best possible estimate and sets his price. The businessmen who make the best estimates, and set prices that most accurately reflect the facts, will succeed over the long run, other things equal—where success is measured by their long-run profits.

Nevertheless, "other things equal" in the last sentence subsumes issues of major significance. Setting proper prices is not the only thing a businessman does that affects his business's success. Harder, and more important, are improving the quality of his business's products over time, and improving the efficiency of his enterprise. We see the importance of price, however, in the fact that a wrong price can obliterate the profits the business should have received for its successful efforts at raising product quality or cutting costs.

F. Altruism versus the Profit Motive

We noted above (p. 116) that Lanzillotti found clear cases in which fear of antitrust prosecution had undermined businessmen's pursuit of long-run profits. This was bad for them and it was, and is, bad for their customers as well. We would all be better off if businessmen's pursuit of profits were unimpeded in any way. The remainder of this book demonstrates this point.

There is another, deeper way in which the profit motive is undermined in the modern world. The altruist moral code of selflessness and self-sacrifice, which was virtually dead in 19th century America, has been relentlessly growing in power and influence over the last 200 years. Tocqueville (1835) tells us that when Americans help others, they justify it as "self-interest properly understood" (Tracinski 1999, 21). Today, when Americans act in their self-interest, they justify it as service to others. Thus, modern businessmen justify their pursuit of profits by their contribution to economic progress, by their charitable activities, by their service to the poor and the environment—by anything except the right of a human being "to live and progress and do the best he can for his life for the time he has on this earth" (Buechner 1981, 12). The profit motive in the modern world is almost universally regarded as immoral, not just by religious leaders, intellectuals, and politicians, but also by businessmen—who do not have a moral leg to stand on.

This cultural atmosphere damning self-interest certainly has affected the exercise of the profit motive. Corporations routinely give huge funds to not-for-profit institutions, including universities, apart from and against the interest of their stockholders, who dare not protest. Frequently these recipients of corporate largess, including universities, are working day and night to destroy what remains of the capitalist economy and replace it with some form of dictatorship. Corporate officers and other employees come under enormous pressure to surrender some portion of their income to charity—any charity. Even more egregious, they are required to devote some of their free time, their personal time, to altruistic activities. Sometimes their employer helps by putting these activities on company time, paying the employee's regular salary for the equivalent of emptying bedpans. Then the business brags about it in television commercials.

This only scratches the surface of the frenzy of self-sacrificing rising in our culture. The premise underlying it is, *if you do not serve others, you do not have the right to exist.* If the altruist ideology is not reversed, it ultimately will damn capitalism, damn western civilization, damn human life on earth and bring on a new Dark Age (all three of which damnations are already entrenched in our universities). Hopefully, that end is still many years in our future and will be prevented by the spreading influence of Objectivism. At the time of this writing, however, the cultural influence of altruism is enormous and the influence of Objectivism is small. How then does the cultural dilution of the profit motive affect my theory?

That question has to be answered on two levels. First, to the extent that the moral cloud of altruism causes businessmen to pursue profits less energetically than they otherwise would, the economy does not work as well as it otherwise would. New buildings and construction projects take longer to complete, goods wear out sooner, services are not as good, the rate of innovation is diminished, progress is slower, people die younger and in more pain, jobs are harder to find and pay lower wages, and so on. But this book is primarily a theory of price and while it is probably true that altruism makes businessmen less motivated to identify the long-run, profit-maximizing price, this is not where altruism has its primary effect. Altruists are untroubled by a profit-maximizing price as long as the product is given away free to the needy and disadvantaged, and as long as the producers do not feel they have a right to their profits. Consequently, I think it is safe to conclude that the prices businessmen set for their products are still overwhelmingly long-run, profit-maximizing prices.

Second, regardless of altruism's effect on the profit motive, in the following chapters, I will assume that effect does not exist—that in all their business actions, businessmen are untroubled by the morality of self-sacrifice—that they pursue their long-run profits with as cool an intelligence, with as clear a vision, by as rational a thought process as they are capable of—and that they do this without qualification or guilt. The sole motive I will assume for all the economy's participants is self-interest in the exact meaning that Ayn Rand defined, that is, *rational* self-interest. The point is to show that self-interest does not need to be modified, diluted, inhibited, or enlightened in order to create economic abundance in a free economy—that in fact, any such modification, dilution, inhibition, or enlightenment of this fundamental motive reduces its positive effect. Rational self-interest is the principle of life. Set it free, and man will create his heaven here on earth.

The next chapter takes up the other four methods by which men create prices in a capitalist economy and concludes by considering the facts affecting the creation of wage rates.

CHAPTER SEVEN

THE OTHER METHODS
OF PRICE CREATION

I. Negotiated Prices

The most important cause of the price that results from a negotiation is the two parties' relative bargaining power. Bargaining power is primarily the product of the constellation of facts surrounding the negotiation. (The force of personality of the negotiators may also affect a negotiated price, a factor that is not subject to economic analysis.) When the facts are on his side, the seller has more bargaining power and can negotiate higher prices. When the facts are against him, the seller has less bargaining power, and he has to negotiate lower prices. Of course, it is exactly vice versa for the buyer. The facts that affect bargaining power are in large part the same facts chapter 6 identified.

A price may be negotiated in two different contexts: (1) a price for a single item, or (2) a contract which sets a price for many items.

A. Facts Affecting the Negotiated Price of an Individual Item

The price of a single item may be negotiated by two businessmen, when one of them is selling a piece of equipment, or a factory, or an entire business. Some prices are negotiated between an individual and a businessman, for example, when a man is buying a new or used car from a dealer, or an antique chair from a store. Prices of used houses usually are negotiated between individuals, as are the prices of used furniture and the bric-a-brac found in yard sales. Let us consider the facts that enter into the price in such negotiations.

(1) The seller's side

A seller will not accept a price below the best price that he thinks he can get elsewhere, and he will not accept less than the value of the good for his personal use. These two facts establish the limits within which the seller negotiates.

The seller can increase his bargaining power if he can estimate how important the good is to the buyer. This will depend primarily on the alternatives the buyer has—the relative quality of those alternatives, their cost, and how hard or easy they may be to find.

If the seller recently has spent money on the item, or if he still owes money on the item, he is likely to resist any price that does not at least cover his costs. His ability to resist, and his bargaining power, will depend on whether he can afford to wait for a higher price. His bargaining position in selling a house will be quite different if this is the third week his house has been for sale, or the third year. Normally, the seller's desire to sell increases with time and the likelihood of an alternative buyer decreases with time.

(2) The buyer's side

The buyer will not pay a higher price than the lowest price he can pay elsewhere for the same good, and he will not pay a price above the value of the good for his personal use. His estimate of the lowest price he can pay elsewhere is based on what he knows about the relative quality and price of available substitutes. The better the available substitutes, the greater his bargaining power.

The buyer may also consider the alternatives of the seller. If the buyer knows this house has been on the market for three years, he has more bargaining power than if the house has been on the market for three weeks. The likelihood of another buyer appearing depends on how high a price the seller is asking. If the buyer thinks the price is high, he can bargain harder than if he thinks the price is low.

B. Facts Affecting the Negotiated Price of a Contract

Let us assume that two businessmen are negotiating a long term contract under which one of them will sell and the other will buy a stream of goods.

(1) The seller's side

If the businessman regularly negotiates the price of his product, he may negotiate a different price with each of his customers, and he is selling many more items than he personally could ever use. Consequently, there is no "best price" he can get elsewhere, and the value of the good for his personal use is irrelevant.

The businessman considers the quality and prices of his goods relative to competing goods and their prices. If his goods are superior, his negotiating position is enhanced and the reverse if his goods are inferior. Normally, he can assume that his customers know the relative quality of his products as well as he does.

The businessman usually considers his cost of production. His goal is to negotiate a price at which he can make a profit, but if he cannot, the bottom line for the business, the lowest price he will accept, is a price that covers his variable costs. The lowest acceptable price also is affected by the business's level of capacity utilization. A seller utilizing 90% of his capacity is in a better bargaining position than a seller utilizing 20% of his capacity. The high excess capacity of the railroads was a major factor in the low freight rates that John D. Rockefeller was able to negotiate in the 19th century.

If the terms of the contract are likely to become known, then the seller must consider how the price will affect his ability to negotiate with other customers. He also may have to think about how competing businesses will respond to the price.

The seller will not accept a price from which he does not benefit over the long run, and the price he negotiates is the best price he can get, given the facts of the market. In this sense, the price that a seller negotiates with a buyer is the seller's *long-run, profit-maximizing price*.

(2) The buyer's side

The highest price the buyer will agree to is the lowest price he thinks he can negotiate elsewhere for equivalent goods. To identify that price, the buyer must be familiar with the relative quality and prices of substitute goods.[1]

The profitability of the buyer's business may affect the negotiated price. If his business is highly profitable, the buyer may not want to take a chance on interrupting or slowing his business's operations—he may decide that it is more important to close the deal right away than to negotiate the lowest possible price. For the owner of an unprofitable business, the reverse is true. He is likely to push the seller as long and as hard as he can if the price affects his ability to avoid bankruptcy.

Often there are cost savings associated with large scale production. Consequently, the greater the quantity that a business wants to buy, the lower the unit price the seller can charge and still benefit from the buyer's order. The buyer knows this and his negotiating position is correspondingly improved. The enormous quantity of business Rockefeller had to offer the railroads was another element in the low rates he negotiated.

The importance of the good to the buyer's business also can affect the negotiated price. If the good is very important, if the firm cannot function without it and acceptable substitutes are not available, the buyer's bargaining power is undercut. To the extent that the good is less important than this and/or acceptable substitutes are available, the buyer's negotiating position is improved.

Usually the value of a good to a business cannot be measured in money. This is obviously true of all those nonhuman factors that do not contribute directly to a firm's output or reduce its costs, such as office furniture and equipment—what might be called "overhead" capital (Ackley 1978, 73). In addition, the contribution to revenue of materials, parts, and ingredients cannot be separated from the contribution of the men and machines that work with them or on them.[2] The output of a business has to be understood as the product of the business as a whole (p. 46 above).

Most of the time, a businessman has to estimate the value of a factor to his business by the functions the factor will perform and how performance of those functions will help his business. The value of a new copy machine for the office staff, for example, is estimated on precisely this basis. This value is not a money value; it is an estimate of relative importance to the business as a productive enterprise. If the item is objectively necessary for the business to function, the businessman will pay the best price he can negotiate. As an upper limit, in the context of the alternatives he knows, the businessman will not pay a price that reduces his profits. This is why small businesses get their copying done at copy shops.

There are cases when a calculation can be made. For major pieces of machinery and equipment, a discounted present value often is calculated on the basis of the estimated revenue or the cost savings the equipment will add over future years. Such estimates are necessarily uncertain and are only one of the things a businessman considers in deciding to buy a new machine.

II. Sealed Bid Prices

Sealed bids are probably used more frequently for construction than for any other product,[3] but they are also the primary method of pricing in the electrical equipment industry, and undoubtedly other industries as well. Under this method, all the bids for a project are submitted in sealed envelopes as of some date, and all the bids are opened together. Usually the lowest bid wins.

A. Why Price by Sealed Bids?

Why would a builder ask for sealed bids, rather than ordinary bids? (By builder, I mean the business that puts out the project for bids and hires the contractor.) Why not just ask contractors what price they would charge, the way a homeowner gets bids on remodeling a kitchen?

Projects that are priced by sealed bids are typically large, complicated, time-consuming, expensive projects—in the multimillion dollar range. Consequently, figuring out what to bid on such projects is expensive. Significant time and work are involved in estimating the contractor's costs. In addition, usually there are subcontractors who have to estimate what they will charge and whom the primary contractor sometimes has to compensate for their estimates. Consequently, contractors do not want to bid on a project without assurance that the competition is fair. The sealed bid context gives them that assurance. It eliminates the possibility of the builder playing them off against one another, pressuring one contractor to reduce his price in order to win the job from another contractor whose bid is slightly lower. It also eliminates the possibility of a builder telling a contractor what another contractor has bid so the first contractor can underbid the second.

From the builder's perspective, the sealed bid context creates a formal competition in which contractors know that the low bid probably will get them the business.

B. Deciding Whether or Not to Bid

Before a contractor bids on a project, he has to decide whether or not it is worth the expense of putting a bid together. In principle, the contractor wants to bid only on those projects that he has a good chance of winning and on which he can make a profit. Monroe (1979, 225–6) lists eight factors that contractors consider, which I have adapted below.

1. What labor skills and engineering capability are required? Does the contractor have the requisite skills and capacity? If a major extension of skills is required, what will it cost? Monarch Construction calls this "the complexity of the project" (see note 3).

2. How much plant capacity does the contractor have available? If the contractor is operating at 90% of capacity, he cannot bid on a project that would require 50% of his capacity. If the new project would have to be given priority, how would that affect the contractor's regular customers? On the other hand, if the contractor is operating at 50% of capacity, another project might be an unqualified blessing.

3. If the contractor wins this bid, what will be the effect on follow-up orders? For example, a contractor winning a government contract to develop a new defense system will have a competitive edge in bidding to supply components for the system. In some instances, there is an announcement effect of winning a big contract; the announcement makes other builders aware of the contractor's capability.

4. If the project has low design content, that means there will not be much work for engineers. A design-oriented company has to keep its engineers busy and consequently will be less interested in such a project.

5. How many competitors are likely to be bidding for this project, and who will they be? The more competitors there are, and the tougher they are, the lower is the contractor's chance of winning.

6. How competent is the contractor in this kind of project, and how good is his reputation? Reputation is an important factor in winning bids. The builder does not have to take the lowest bid, and is unlikely to take it if the low bidder has no reputation in the area. To preserve this option, many builders use the term "best value" instead of "lowest bid" in their biding documents.

7. Can the contractor deliver the project on time? The federal government will invalidate a bid if officials judge the bidder will not be able to meet the delivery requirement.

8. What cost savings will this project generate for other projects? An increasing production volume may reduce the unit costs for similar products, making the contractor more competitive in other markets.

C. Deciding What Price to Bid

Sealed bid pricing involves a trade-off: the higher the bid, the higher the profit, but the higher the bid, the lower the chance of winning. As a result, probability theory can be used to give a formal definition of the problem. Monroe gives the following example (1979, 224): Suppose the contractor estimates the cost of completing the contract at $50,000. He also estimates that if he bids $60,000, the probability of winning the contract is 0.70, and if he bids $90,000, the probability of winning is 0.40. In this case, the second bid maximizes the contractor's expected profits (0.40[$90,000 - $50,000] = $16,000 versus 0.70[$60,000 - $50,000] = $7000).

Estimating the probabilities, of course, is the difficult part of this approach, a difficulty increased by the fact that many competing bidders do not know their costs.[4] However, estimates can be made and are made. The considerations that go into them are things like the prospective number of bidders on a contract, the reputation of the contractors expected to bid, what these firms bid on previous projects, the relation of what they bid to the cost of those projects, specific advantages these contractors have, their current rate of capacity utilization, the winning bid on previous projects of this kind, and so forth. In deciding what to bid, a contractor is likely to have much hard information of this kind, plus current trade rumors, and what he can reasonably guess. Depending on what information the firm has, there are methods by which the contractor can determine the bid that maximizes his expected profit (Monroe 1979, 228-235). The probability of winning is the most important fact affecting the contractor's bid.

A second major consideration in sealed bid prices is the contractor's current rate of capacity utilization. A firm's capacity consists of its plant and equipment, including its offices, office staff and equipment. A contractor will not bid a price that does not cover his *variable* costs, but contractors frequently bid prices that do not cover their *total* costs. Construction companies have high fixed costs (overhead) and their owners typically think of the value of a contract in terms of its contribution to overhead and profit, not to profit alone. Companies often submit bids that contribute something toward their overhead but do not yield a profit. This is more likely when a company has more unused capacity. In addition, with a lot of unused capacity, maximizing the expected contribution to overhead and profit may be less important to a contractor than submitting a bid that has a good chance of winning. In such cases, the contractor may deliberately choose a bid with a lower expected profit but a higher chance of being the low bid (Monroe 1979, 234–5). On the other hand, a contractor operating with high capacity utilization may want to win a bid only if the bid would yield an actual profit.

III. Auction Prices

This section considers only those auctions where the price is set through a process of competitive bidding—where each party bids a price higher than the previous high bid until no one bids higher, and the high bid sets the price. Within this general context, we can distinguish two types of auctions:

Auctions to individuals. In this case, the item is purchased for personal use. This is the type of auction with which people are most familiar. Very expensive items like art works and antiques are sold to the highest bidder. When a bank forecloses on a house or a car, the house or car may be auctioned off so the bank can recover, as much as possible, the money it is owed.

Auctions to businesses. In this case, a businessman purchases the item for investment or resale. When a business goes bankrupt, its assets may include new, unused goods the business produced for sale. These goods are frequently sold at auction, as liquidation sales of merchandise, to raise money for the business's creditors. Used producer goods and perishable products like fish also are sold at auction to other businesses.

A. Auctions to Individuals

(1) The seller's side

The seller's role in creating an auction price is choosing *the reserve price*. The reserve price is the minimum price below which he will not sell. This is different from the starting bid announced by the auctioneer. In New York State, the starting bid cannot exceed the reserve price, but the reserve price is kept a secret between the auctioneer, the auction house, and the seller.

Normally, the seller decides on the reserve price in consultation with the auction house. There are potentially two relevant facts: (1) The personal value the good has to the seller. The seller thinks, "If I cannot get at least this much for it, I would rather keep it myself." (2) The estimated market value of the good. This is the primary fact, and the fundamental reason for the existence of reserve prices. The auction house chooses the reserve price based on its knowledge of what items like this are selling for. A reserve price is placed on the item so that if "the wrong crowd" is at the auction, the seller can come back and try again.

If a bank is auctioning off a foreclosed home, they may set the reserve price equal to the amount of money they are owed. They want to get their money back; any money in excess of what they are owed goes to the borrower. For similar reasons, an individual seller may set the reserve price equal to the amount of money he owes on an item. He does not want to be making payments on a piece of property that he no longer possesses. Chapter 8 takes up these cases in the context of nonobjective prices.

One might think that the best price a seller has been offered by an individual buyer could be a basis for setting the reserve price. However, if a seller has a reasonable offer, he is unlikely to go through with an auction because the auction house takes a significant portion of the auction price (twenty-five to thirty percent or more).

(2) The buyers' side

The buyer will not pay more than the lowest price he would have to pay elsewhere for an equivalent item. However, auction items often are unique, in which case there is no equivalent item elsewhere. Suppose this is the perfect item in the buyer's eyes—exactly what he has been looking for. Should he keep raising his bid?

The fundamental consideration for an individual in an auction setting is what he can afford. "What I can afford" is the universal standard, used by everyone, including economists, for evaluating their purchases, but it is not part of economic thought. What does it mean? There is more involved here than the individual's income.

Consider the following: I cannot afford a $10,000,000 co-op apartment in New York City. A bank would not loan me the money, and if it did, I could not make the payments. I cannot afford a new Mercedes automobile, but a bank would loan me the money and I could make the payments. I cannot afford to pay $200 for a bottle of wine, but I could pay for it out of my current cash balance. And sometimes I put back on the shelf an item costing just a few dollars on the grounds that I cannot afford it. The reader can add his own examples. The point is that there are many purchases we reject on the grounds that we cannot afford them when our financial solvency or credit is not at stake. "I cannot afford it" does not mean, "This purchase would bankrupt me," or that one literally could not make the payments. Then what does it mean?

One might argue for the popular interpretation like this: "Of course, this purchase alone would not bankrupt me, but it would bankrupt me if I regularly made purchases like this. So actually, my financial solvency is at stake." But if that is the issue, why can I not buy just one, just this one time? Then the answer is that one has to live by principles, which is true. But what is the principle here?

Buying one unusually expensive item in the supermarket does not in any way threaten a man's financial solvency, and yet, he does not want to do it. He feels that it would, in fact, be bad for him. And this is not because the item is something he has no taste for or that he thinks is overpriced, because if he had double his current income, he would buy it. What is going on here?

In human action, everything is values. All action is "for the sake of" some value. When one refuses to buy something because he cannot afford it, for the sake of what value does he do that? For the sake of the values he could not buy instead, the goods that he values more highly than the good he cannot afford. The proper definition of what one can afford is *the amount one can spend without giving up higher ranked values.*

The basic principle for maximizing one's economic welfare is: "buy all the things you can afford and only the things you can afford." This is the principle on which rational people make their consumption choices, and thus integrate all their purchases to the ultimate end of sustaining and enjoying their lives. Properly considered, one cannot afford to act on any other basis.

This is a further development of the analysis we began with the meaning of price in chapter 3, and continued with the theory of economic choice in chapter 4. A price is a sum of money. The meaning of the sum is its purchasing power, that is, the alternative products that can be bought with that sum, as grasped by men who buy and sell with that money. The basic rule of economic choice is: purchase those items, and only those items, which are ranked higher than their price. Now we can see that by following that rule, one purchases only those items that do not cause one to give up a higher ranked item. Suppose that in the total context of all the variables that affect his economic values, a man values a hoe above a pound of nails and if he buys the nails, he will not have enough money to buy the hoe. Then he cannot afford the nails.

The meaning of a sum of money in one's mind is not its general purchasing power, but the specific purchasing power that affects one's life. That specific purchasing power does not reflect the prices of the whole universe of products, including goods which one does not know or care about. Rather, it reflects only the prices of the goods and services that one would or could buy with that sum. For each individual, every sum of money is tied directly to his life and what that sum means in his life—as measured by the prices of the goods and services he might buy with it. If the meaning of a sum of money to an individual were its general purchasing power, that meaning would not be helpful to him. It would not tell him what he personally could afford to spend on any item.[5]

So how, in principle, does the buyer at an auction decide how much to bid? He considers his current income and what he can reasonably expect to earn in the future. Then he considers the claims against that income in the form of interest and mortgage payments, food, clothing, entertainment, insurance, and so forth. Then he bids the most for an item that he can afford, that is, an amount that will not cause him to give up more highly ranked values. Usually he does not have to figure out consciously what he can afford. His mind keeps a running total without conscious effort, on the basis of a standing order such as "Pay attention to the prices you pay. Watch what you spend." As a result, most people have a pretty clear grasp of what they can afford and what they cannot afford. For unusually expensive purchases, however, such as a house, they may have to actually "run the numbers."

B. Auctions to Businesses

(1) The seller's side

We will restrict our attention to liquidation sales of merchandise. These auctions do not have any reserve price. In such sales, the creditors want as much money as possible right away; they have no interest in coming back and trying again for a higher price.

(2) The buyers' side

The winning bidder in this case is a businessman with the standard business motivation. His main concern is whether he can resell the merchandise at a profit, so usually he makes an estimate of that resale price. This in turn depends on the price and quality of competing goods, with which he also needs to be familiar.

How soon he will be able to dispose of the merchandise is likely to be another major concern. The longer he thinks he may have to hold onto the merchandise, the lower the price he is willing to pay. There is an implicit interest consideration here, just as there is for any investment in physical goods. If he has borrowed the money to bid on the goods, interest on his debt continues to accumulate until he sells the goods and repays the money. If he has invested his own money, that money could be in the bank earning interest.[6]

IV. Brokered Prices

As chapter 4 noted, brokered prices are established when the price bid by a buyer and the price asked by a seller originate independently of each other and are the same price. The buyer and seller normally do not know each other, and they may not even be in the same country. Each of them must hire a third party to find someone to buy from or to sell to. That third party is a broker. In order to fulfill their function of mediating exchanges, brokers meet at what are appropriately called "exchanges": stock exchanges, bond exchanges, mercantile exchanges, commodity exchanges, and so forth. This section focuses on the stock market. Chapter 11 takes up bond and commodity markets.

The brokers act as agents for the buyers and sellers. They conclude exchanges on orders from their customers who tell them to buy or sell specific quantities at specific prices. A price is set when two brokers make contact who represent two individuals, one of whom wants to buy and the other of whom wants to sell the same stock at the same price. The actual mechanics are more complicated, but this is the essence of the process. What used to be physical meetings and exchanges are all in the process of becoming electronic. This does not change the fundamentals of the price-setting procedure and we pass over the electronic details.

For our purposes, the important point is that there are two individual minds behind every brokered price, just as there are two individual minds behind every negotiated price. There is no difference in principle, only a difference in procedure—negotiated prices are negotiated directly by the concerned parties; brokered prices are reached by agents. In neither case are there any "impersonal market forces" at work. There are only individual human beings using their individual minds to reach their individual decisions and then reaching agreements with other individual human beings. This is the substance and content of all so-called market forces. This is a major point on which I differ from modern economists, so I repeat: *there are no impersonal market forces.*

There are two different approaches to deciding when to buy or sell a stock. One school, the fundamentalists, believes in looking at the facts of the business's operation. *The* fundamental issue is the business's long-run, expected profits, and the business's management is widely recognized to be the first cause. A fundamentalist also is concerned with the quality of the management of competing firms, the quality of the company's products relative to its competitors' products, the prices the company charges, its costs per unit relative to its competitors' costs, its reputation, its current sales and profits, its market share, how each of these facts is likely to change in the future, and many other facts that are relevant to specific industries.

Many thousands of people work fifty, sixty, seventy-hour weeks analyzing these details for insurance companies, pension funds, mutual funds, banks, brokerage houses, and other institutions that invest in stocks. Each analyst is responsible for a relatively small number of companies defining a particular economic sector, such as automobiles or soft drinks. They talk to companies' management, employees, competitors, and customers, read annual reports and other reports, collect all kinds of data, and analyze all the information they can find. Their purpose is to identify the fair market value of a company's stock, and hence to determine whether, at the stock's current price, the company is fairly valued, overvalued, or undervalued.[7]

The other school that analyzes stocks is the technicians. Technicians look at the pattern of stock prices and volume of sales over time, as well as an unlimited number of other statistical series, looking for patterns that presage rising prices and falling prices. Technical analysts, also, are employed on a full-time basis.

As a final indication of the role of facts in brokered prices, consider this description of the foreign exchange market by Evan Picoult (January 1998).

> Foreign exchange traders all over the world (in Tokyo, Hong Kong, Singapore, Frankfurt, London, New York or wherever) sit next to terminals which display the most current prices at which currencies have been traded. The terminals also display information about other markets, about macroeconomic statistics, about corporations and about political events. Corporate treasurers and investors, who need to hedge their foreign exchange risk, have access to the same information. So do so-called hedge fund (actually speculative fund) traders who try to make money by searching for relative inefficiencies in market prices or patterns of change in market prices. Some market participants take extra effort to obtain additional information (e.g., historical) or to build complex proprietary software to process information to evaluate trading or investment opportunities.

> Market participants process all this information and make different decisions depending on their objectives (e.g., whether one is hedging, speculating or simply being a market maker), their time horizon (e.g., short term trading versus long term investing), their assumptions about the significance of the information they see and their ability to integrate the information they have.

V. Someone Sets or Negotiates the Wage

Wages and salaries are the prices paid for human services. Since wage rates are prices, and are either set or negotiated, strictly speaking this subject belongs in chapter 6 and part I of this chapter. We are discussing wages separately because many of the facts that are relevant to wage rates are not relevant to the prices of nonhuman factors or to the prices of goods and services. Wage rates are also distinctive in that when someone sets the wage, usually it is the buyer.

What are the relevant facts for a business that is seeking a new employee for a particular job and has to decide what wage to offer him? How does a businessman decide whether to increase or decrease the wage of a current employee and when to do it? The following are some of the relevant facts:

(1) The worker's product

This is the fundamental fact. The employee makes some contribution, large or small, to the functioning of the business, to maintaining the business as a productive enterprise. If the employee's job description is accurate, it sums up this contribution. A businessman does not hire an employee unless that employee is needed for the business to operate or to operate better. I made this same point in part I (p. 124) with respect to nonhuman factors. A businessman estimates the value of an employee to his business by the functions the employee will perform and how performance of those functions will help the business.

For example, if a business wants to hire a new secretary, there is a definite reason. One of the current staff may have retired or resigned, or management may be adding another secretary to the current staff. Whatever the background context, the business is looking for this employee because there is work that needs to be done that the current secretarial staff cannot do. That work has no direct, physical connection to producing the firm's product, but it is just as necessary for the firm's continued existence as the work performed by the men on the assembly line.

(2) The importance of the worker's product

Given that the worker is objectively necessary, how necessary or how important he is to the business often enters into his wage. Importance to a business takes many forms, but the fundamental standard is the impact of the worker's work, and most importantly, the impact of his choices and decisions, on the business's profits. A bad decision by an assemblyline worker or a clerk may ruin a day's work. A bad decision by the CEO may ruin the business.

A worker's importance frequently is measured by the number of workers who report to the employee, directly or indirectly. This is one reason why CEOs are paid more than clerks. But this relative importance usually cannot be measured in money. The firm has no way to determine what an assemblyline worker or a clerk adds to the business's revenues.[8] Further, the relative importance of many employees cannot be distinguished either by the impact of their decisions or by the number of employees who report to them, for example, accountants, lawyers, engineers, scientists, computer programmers, and so forth. Chapter 9 explains how their wages are determined.

(3) The going wage for this type of labor

Given that the worker has an objective value to the business, the most important fact the businessman faces is the current wage for this type of worker—that is, what other businesses are paying for this kind of work. Usually, this is all the businessman needs to know. He offers a prospective employee the prevailing wage and, other things equal, the employee is happy to accept the job on that basis.

After he is hired, the worker's wage constitutes the firm's estimate of the worker's monetary value to the business. This is because, normally, the worker's current wage is the price for which he can be replaced.[9] Then, on the basis of his specific performance, his superiors judge the worker's value as being more or less than his wage. That judgment takes the form of deciding whether this man's work is inferior or superior to that of a man they could hire in his place at the same wage. If inferior, he is let go. If superior, eventually he is given a raise, and perhaps promoted.

In some cases, a business may decide that the current wage is too high and that they will get along without that employee. The reasoning is identical to that which motivates some businesses to use copy shops while others buy copy machines. A small business may not be able to afford a particular kind of worker because his wage would cut into the business's profits. For example, a small retail bookstore needed an editor for some books it wanted to print and sell to a narrow market. To hire an editor would have reduced the firm's profits, so one of its current employees learned how to be an editor.

What determines the current wage in the first place? This is the fundamental question, and the main subject of chapter 9.

(4) The quality of labor the firm wants

Usually, there is no public, average wage of a particular amount for workers of a particular kind. The current wage is usually a range, with the highest quality labor of that kind receiving wages at the high end of the range. If a businessman wants higher quality workers than is the norm for that type of job, he has to offer a wage at or above the high end of the range in order to attract workers away from other employers. A businessman who does that either has or is expecting unusually high profits. In 1914, the Ford Motor Company raised the wage rate of its workers from $2.34 for a nine-hour day (26 cents an hour) to $5.00 for an eight-hour day (over 62 cents an hour). The announcement of this wage attracted workers from all over the country. At the same time, Ford's profits skyrocketed.

On the other hand, a business may need work done that is physically hard, but easy to learn, requiring only unskilled labor. A low turnover rate may be no advantage to the business because virtually no training is required. In that case, the business may offer a below average wage and accept the high rate of turnover as workers continually leave to take higher paying jobs.

(5) The alternatives available to the worker

Unskilled workers, and most skilled workers, normally have many alternative jobs available to them offering approximately the same wage. Consequently, to hire and keep such employees, an employer has to pay the current wage, and he has to raise his workers' wages when the current wage goes up.

In contrast, a highly specialized worker may have few or no good alternative jobs available to him. In that case, it is also likely that his employer will have no good alternatives to that worker. Professional athletes are a case in point. Before the era of free agency, when Babe Ruth was playing baseball for the New York Yankees, his best alternative job might have been as an unskilled worker. At the same time, the New York Yankees had no good alternative to Babe Ruth. As a result, Babe Ruth was hardly underpaid, earning more than the President of the United States at the time.

(6) The rate of return on capital invested

If the business is making a high rate of profit on its investment, the business can afford to err on the high side in its wage payments, and probably will choose to do so. When a business is doing well, it does not want to take a chance on losing its best workers. Such a business is also likely to be looking for high quality labor, as per (4) above.

If a business is making a low rate of profit or actually losing money, it is likely to err on the low side. Unless the business sees prospects of a turnaround in its economic condition, it may be willing to see its best workers leave over time.

High-profit businesses normally can out-compete low-profit businesses for the best employees, and indeed, for all factors. Firms making relatively high profits can pay a price that low-profit firms cannot afford. This is an important principle to which we return in chapter 9.

(7) What the worker adds to the business's total revenue

Modern economics' theory of wages is that a worker's wage equals the addition he makes to a business's total revenue. There are many problems with this doctrine, but the most glaring is that it is almost always impossible to measure the revenue a worker adds.[10] In many cases, even the idea of an addition to total revenue makes no sense. What does a new secretary add to a business's revenue? She adds nothing. She is not hired to add to the business's revenue. She is hired to do a job because completion of that job is necessary to the business's continuation as a productive enterprise.

However, when it is possible to estimate a worker's contribution to total revenue, that estimate has an unavoidable effect on the wage rate a business offers to pay. The clearest case is that of professional athletes. When Pete Rose left the Cincinnati Reds for the Philadelphia Phillies in 1979, the Phillies offered him a salary of $3.2 million for four years ($800,000 a year). Before the Phillies made that offer, the Philadelphia television station agreed to add $600,000 a year to what it paid the Phillies to carry their games—if the Phillies signed Pete Rose. The Phillies' management expected that the addition of Rose to the team also would bring many thousands of additional fans to the games, which would cover the remaining $200,000 a year—which is what happened.

Professional sports teams are an unusual case because for many modern owners, the team is partly a consumer good. The owner's first interest is winning; his interest in making profits is secondary. But for those owners who are concerned with profits, the kind of estimate the Phillies made regarding Pete Rose has to be made all the time in this era of free agency, as businesses compete for players when they become eligible to leave their current team.

Chapter 9 takes up in more detail many of the topics raised in this section on wages. This has been a preliminary overview. Its purpose has been to demonstrate that businessmen decide what wages to pay (and workers decide what wages to accept) by reference to the economic facts.

CHAPTER EIGHT

THE THEORY OF
OBJECTIVE PRICES

I. The Extent to Which
Market Prices Are Objective

Chapter 5 (p. 92) began this investigation with two questions: (1) How do prices at which exchanges are made come into existence? (2) Are those prices objective? Chapter 5 began the answer to these questions by identifying the five methods by which prices are created in a free economy. Chapters 6 and 7 completed the answer by elaborating each of these methods, in each case pointing out the economic facts of demand, cost, and competition that the parties to the price consider in figuring out the price. As a result, my initial proposition, "most prices are objective," now has real content. I asked, "How many are most?" Now we see that "most" means "almost all," that prices at which exchanges are made are overwhelmingly objective, certainly constituting more than 99 percent of all prices.

The objective theory of price is that prices reflect the relevant economic facts grasped by the men who exchange at that price. Prices set this way are objective prices, in the full meaning of Ayn Rand's concept of objective. Prices are the product of a relation between a conceptual consciousness and the facts; they are the result of volitional processing by man's mind of the evidence of reality given by his senses. Prices are not forced on man by some intrinsic aspect of reality. They are not dictated by God, or supply and demand, or the labor embodied in a good, or the cost of production. But neither are they the result of the businessman's arbitrary feeling. Prices are the result of a human consciousness grasping economic facts.

II. Nonobjective Prices

Now we take up the question of nonobjective prices, first raised in chapter 5 (p. 89). We have to consider whether any market prices are nonobjective, and what it means if they are.

First, let us note that there are no intrinsic prices. There is no element in reality that forces itself on one's mind and makes a man set or accept a particular price, apart from his choice to grasp the facts and act accordingly.

Nonobjective prices are subjective prices. The only alternative to economic facts as the basis for price in this world is someone's feeling, wish, or desire; that is, someone's subjective emotion. The essence of the subjectivist view is captured by the popular complaint: "Businessmen set any price they want." Since subjective prices are created without reference to economic facts, subjective prices are arbitrary. Thus, nonobjective prices, subjective prices, and arbitrary prices all mean the same thing.

Are any market prices set independently of the facts? To answer that question, let us review the five methods of price setting.

A. Someone Sets the Price

The prices set by this method include consumer goods and services, some used consumer goods, many producer goods and services, many used producer goods, and the wages of most employees. In every case, it would be very strange for the price of such a good or service to be set arbitrarily. In most of these cases, the price of the good or service directly affects the profits and ultimately the survival of the business producing the good or service. In the case of employees, the price directly affects the business's existence as a productive entity—if the wages the business offers are too low, the business will be unable to hire anyone. In addition, the business's wage rates determine the standard of living of the employees, who have good reason to make certain they are being paid the going wage. In the case of worker services sold to households (housekeepers, painters, carpenters, and so forth), the price determines the standard of living of the worker who sets the price. The price of a used producer good may be of less than urgent interest to the seller, but even here, there is no reason that a rational man should just make up a price, or accept less than what the market will bear.

This does not mean that in each case, the price will be the long-run, profit-maximizing price. Case 3 in chapter 5 (p. 91) describes a major capital equipment manufacturer whose prices were being set by its distributors. The prices the distributors were setting were certainly objective prices; that is, given the facts of the competitive conditions, the distributors set the prices that they judged were necessary to get the business. But the distributors' implicit standard for setting prices was maximizing current sales, not maximizing long-run profits. If the company wanted to maximize its long-run profits, the price-setting function had to be taken out of the hands of the distributors, and that is what was done. The firm's management took control of its price setting, raising prices and accepting lower profits over the short run in order to reestablish the firm's reputation as a high-quality supplier.

The U. S. Steel case (p. 90 above) is also one of set prices. Does average cost pricing yield an objective price? The answer is no. Average cost pricing takes no account of the market. An objective price reflects the relevant economic facts. The conditions of demand and competition are certainly among those facts. Indeed, they are priority items.

For U. S. Steel, average cost pricing would have meant that in recessions, when average costs rose due to falling volume, the corporation would have raised its price. In boom times, it would have lowered its price as average costs fell on an increasing volume. U. S. Steel did neither of these things (Kaplan, Dirlam & Lanzillotti 1958, 18–19). In fact, the record is clear that U. S. Steel did not follow average cost pricing, except as a kind of preliminary guideline. There were always variations in the prices of its products reflecting differing market conditions of demand and competition (Kaplan, Dirlam & Lanzillotti 1958, 170–75).

Let us note as well that identical delivered prices from all the steel manufacturers were an objective requirement of the market, originating in the economic facts. The steel products of the various steel producers were indistinguishable to their customers. Any steel firm with a slightly lower price would have taken all the business. Consequently, the steel firms' prices had to be the same, and it was natural that U. S. Steel, being the largest and therefore having the most sources of market information, would determine the prices for all.

B. Negotiated Prices

When prices are set by negotiation, the price will be affected by who is the better negotiator. If the seller is the better negotiator, the price will be higher. If the buyer is the better negotiator, the price will be lower. What is the relevance of a theory of objective prices?

First, we saw in chapter 7 that the bargaining power of a negotiator reflects the economic facts. Second, there are definite limits both to how high a price a buyer will pay and to how low a price a seller will accept. Those limits are objective; they are determined by the relevant economic facts. Those facts do not fix a price independently of the negotiation process, but the impact on the price of differences in negotiating skills usually is small.

The selling price of a doctor's practice normally is negotiated, so let us consider the methods of determining the asking price discussed in case 2 of chapter 5. (1) The net worth method would not yield an objective price because it leaves out the most important asset of the doctor's practice, his patients.[1] (2) The gross income method is essentially arbitrary; there is no necessary connection between the gross income of a practice and the value of a practice. (3) The distress sale method, as described, does yield an objective price, although those conditions must be unusual. Both (4) the debt capacity method and (5) the present value method yield objective prices, because they are both thoughtful, sophisticated attempts to measure the essential facts and reach an objective value. This is true even though the prices reached by the two methods are not the same. The defining condition of objectivity is method. The method by which one reaches a result makes the result objective or nonobjective.[2]

However, some doctors price and sell their practices by the gross income method. What does that imply for a general theory of objective prices? Or, consider this case: The owner of a small antique store was completely unnerved by the process of negotiating the price of an item with an overbearing, aggressive customer. The next time that customer asked what the store owner wanted for an item, the owner told him to take it and pay whatever he thought it was worth. How can that be reconciled with a general theory that prices are objective?

C. Sealed Bid Prices

The contractor's livelihood depends directly on the accuracy of his bid. The prices bid by contractors are the prices in the economy least likely to be set arbitrarily.

D. Auction Prices

Auctions are the most likely places to find nonobjective prices. People get carried away at auctions, bidding more than they planned and more than they can afford and regretting it later. This means that the price they bid is not objective, that it does not reflect the facts they know. By how much does the price exceed an objective evaluation?—by the difference between the winning bid and the preceding bid (provided that the person who made the preceding bid did not also lose his head).

What about banks that set a reserve price on a house equal to what the bank is owed on the mortgage, or a seller who sets a reserve price equal to what he owes on an item? This practice is common, but such prices have no necessary connection to the economic facts. There is nothing in a free market that requires other men to value a good at least as high as the money owed on it. Such prices are not objective, and if the reserve price exceeds the market price, no one will buy the good.

More important, auctions and auction prices are a side issue for a free economy. The products sold at auction are primarily consumer goods, most of them used. They are not goods that are currently being produced or being used in production. Consequently, for the rational functioning of the economy, it is essentially unimportant whether the prices of these goods reflect economic facts. This is in stark contrast to those goods that are currently being used in production. For such goods, a nonobjective price would mislead every producer about its economic value. If the nonobjective price overvalued the good, producers using it productively in less profitable pursuits would give it up, and some of it would go unused. If the nonobjective price undervalued the good, some producers would use the good where it was essentially wasted; others would be unable to acquire a good whose value to them exceeded its (objective) price. In both cases, the good would be diverted from its most valuable uses—the uses consistent with an objective price.[3]

E. Brokered Prices

Putting aside full-time, professional analysts, there are many investors in the stock market who do not always go by the facts. Particularly, small investors may invest on a hunch or a feeling or a rumor. Some consult their horoscopes (disgracefully, not just small investors), and some invest in Disney because they had a childhood affection for Bambi. Nevertheless, the prices to which such people are a party are objective.

Investors in the stock market, professional and nonprofessional, focus overwhelmingly on the facts. The objective investors' orders to buy and sell are so great in a normal market that they swamp whatever impact the nonobjective investor's orders might have. This means that, with trivial variations, the objective investors determine the brokered prices for everyone. The price paid by a subjectivist for stock is like the price paid by him for any product. He pays an objective price, not due to his grasp of the economic facts, but due to the grasp of everyone around him.

What about mass nonobjectivity? What about a general irrational enthusiasm or panic selling? Man's free will consists of the freedom to think or not, to be rational or not, to focus on the facts or not. Since human beings have that freedom, one cannot rule out that many of them will choose not to think at the same time. A rising price may lead people to invest in a stock in the belief that it will go on rising, not because of the economic facts, but because everyone else thinks it will go on rising. On the other side, panic selling is a real phenomenon, and not necessarily irrational. Because the market is falling, people think it is going to go on falling, and everyone tries to save their money by selling at the same time. These things happen. Usually their duration is brief. More important, the crash of 1987 (25% in a single day, the worst fall ever, worse than Black Tuesday in 1929) showed that a stock market crash is of no consequence for the health of the economy if the government stays out of the way.

F. Nonobjective Markets

There is no market where nonobjective prices are the rule, a market where a rational grasp of the facts is consistently absent. In the modern world, such a market could not survive. If businessmen always set the price too high, no one would buy. If they always set the price too low, rational buyers would purchase all their goods and they would have nothing to sell. Nonobjective prices, that is, prices independent of the cost of production and/or the value of products to customers and/or the competitive conditions of the market, are self-eliminating. They eliminate the businessmen who set such prices.

What about the price of nonobjective values, like psychic hotlines, love potions, and divining rods? Their prices are exactly what are *not* nonobjective about them. Their sellers set prices that reflect the facts of their markets.

G. Conclusion

I conclude that nonobjective prices are very unusual in a free market. In principle, the reason that nonobjective prices are exceptional is that it is in the long-run self-interest of everyone that prices be objective, and a free economy sanctions self-interest. Objective prices are in the interest of man the producer so he can buy and sell and sustain his business. Objective prices are in the interest of man the consumer so he can buy and sell and sustain his life.

However, exceptional does not mean nonexistent. We have seen that it is possible for people to make exchanges at nonobjective prices. A seller intimidated into total surrender in a negotiation, a doctor who misprices his practice, a homeowner who misprices his house, a buyer who bids too much at an auction—these are real cases. In addition, there are probably occasions when a businessman sets his price too high and finds someone to buy who is equally ignorant of the going market price.

Chapter 5 said, "A theory of objective prices has to be in the form of a general proposition, that is, a proposition . . . incorporating the word 'all'." Ninety-nine percent is not all. One more step is required to reach that general proposition.

III. Market Prices and Objective Prices

Economics has no interest in and can say nothing about nonobjective or subjective or arbitrary prices, because such prices are set without reference to the economic facts. The only point economics can make about nonobjective prices is that they cannot endure.

With respect to pricing, the technical name for the subject matter of economics is "market price." Market prices are frequently thought of as prices at which an exchange is made. That conception of market price does not name the essential fact. Exchanges are made at market prices, but that is because market prices are consistent with the facts of their markets.

In markets where repeated exchanges are possible, the market price generates regular, continuing, repeated exchanges over time, often numbering in the millions, hundreds of millions, and billions (for example, automobiles, boxes of Cheerios, and cans of beer). This is because market prices reflect the existing market conditions.[4] By contrast, the cases we discussed at the end of the preceding section make clear that exchanges also can take place at nonmarket prices when the parties to the price are ignorant or weak willed or emotion driven. Further, there are market prices at which exchanges are *not* made, like asking prices for houses, offers and counteroffers in negotiations, and limit or stop orders in the stock market.

A market price should be defined as *a price that reflects the facts of the market,* specifically, the facts of demand, cost, and competition. Given that definition, we can state the theory of objective prices as a general proposition: *all market prices are objective prices.* All market prices reflect the relevant economic facts as grasped by the parties to the price. Market price and objective price are two different perspectives on the same price. A market price is the price seen from the perspective of the relation of the price to the facts of the market. An objective price is the same price seen from the perspective of its origin in a human mind grasping the economic facts—the same facts in relation to which the price is the market price.

The proposition that all market prices are objective prices cannot be reversed. It is not true that all objective prices are market prices. People can make mistakes. A man may select a price based on his best, rational evaluation of the facts available to him and still be wrong. To be wrong in this context means that the price he selects is not a market price, even though he reaches the price by an objective process. If his price is not a market price, he will be unable to buy, or unable to sell, or unable to sell enough, or sell too much, and he will have to change the price.

IV. Evaluation of the Theory

Now let us identify the appropriate standards for evaluating a theory of price and apply them to the theory of objective prices.

A. The Answers to Three Questions

To start with, we want a theory of price to answer three elementary questions: (1) *Why is each price what it is?* We want to know what causes each price, what economic conditions define or delimit each price. We want an answer in principle to questions such as: Why does a half gallon of 1% lowfat milk cost $2.49 in the local supermarket? Why does the lamb chop special at the neighborhood restaurant cost $33.00? Why does it cost $482 a month to garage a car in midtown Manhattan? (2) *Why do prices change?* When a price changes, what causes it to change? Rationally, this question is inseparable from (1). If we cannot explain what causes prices to change, from what and to what, we cannot explain why they are what they are. (3) *When a price changes, what causes how much it changes?*

In answer to (1), the theory of objective prices holds that each price is what it is because it reflects the relevant economic facts in the judgment of the men who establish the price. When someone sets a price, or negotiates a price, or selects a price as a sealed bid, the price thus created reflects the current and prospective economic conditions in the judgment of the parties to the price. Usually, therefore, the price is the long-run, profit-maximizing price. Auction prices and brokered prices also originate in the economic conditions grasped by the men who ask and pay the price.

In answer to (2), prices change because there is a change in the judgment of the men who set and/or pay the price. Usually this is because there has been a change in the current or expected economic facts. But it is also possible that some fact is noticed that was not noticed before, or a new director of pricing has different ideas about how it should be done, or the same director has a new idea, and so forth.

As for (3), in the light of the answers to (1) and (2), how much prices change is obvious. It depends on how much men's judgments change and how much economic conditions change.

B. A Causal Explanation

The second standard of evaluation is that a theory should provide a causal explanation. The theory should identify the relation of cause and effect that necessarily brings the price into existence. Without this explanation, a theory is empty. There is no reason to believe the price has the characteristics ascribed to it by the theory.[5]

The cause of objective prices is an integral part of the theory. The theory says that every market price is the product of the economic facts grasped by the parties to the price. *Every price is set by someone.* Some individual human being chooses every price (sometimes two individuals, as in negotiation). The cause of the price is the man or men who set the price.

On a deeper level, the first cause in all human affairs is the individual's choice to think or not. Objective prices are the product of the choices of the men who choose to think. In a modern industrial economy, when one's economic welfare is as clearly at stake as it is when one chooses a price, most people do choose to think and be guided by the facts in selecting a price.

C. A Universal Explanation

The third standard of evaluation is that a theory of price should be a general or universal theory. It should apply to all the prices that appear in a market economy. It should explain every price that is subject to explanation, that is, every price that is not arbitrary or subjective. If the theory is not universal, then it has exceptions, and it is not a theory of price, but only a theory of some prices.

Economics has never had a universal theory of price. The closest it has come is the labor theory of value. However, apart from being false, the labor theory applied only to reproducible items and could not explain the prices of goods like old masters and unimproved land. Nevertheless, the labor theory was closer to being a universal theory than any of the theories of modern economics.

Clearly, the theory of objective prices is a general theory. We have examined all the prices of a market economy and we have seen that all of them are based on a grasp of the facts by everyone who sets and pays those prices, that every market price is an objective price. A price theory cannot be more general than that.

D. An Explanation of How Prices Reflect Economic Facts

The last standard of evaluation is that a valid theory of price should explain how prices coordinate all the actions of all the people who participate in a free economy. In explaining how prices come into existence, how they come to be what they are, such a theory should explain exactly how and why each price reflects all the relevant economic facts, so that men, in deciding to pay or not to pay that price, take those facts into account. "[I]t is said that the market price embodies everything that buyers and sellers need to know about the commodity in question" (Blinder and others 1998, 283). A valid theory of price should explain how and why every market price reflects that knowledge.

This feature is transparent in the theory of objective prices. Every price reflects all the relevant facts of the market for a product because those facts are the basis on which the parties to the price set and agree on the price. Nevertheless, there is much more to say on this subject. In particular, Chapters 10 and 11 show how businessmen change prices when the facts change and how those changes in price change the economy.

E. The Theory of Objective Prices Is Not Circular

Let me try to forestall the charge that I have presented a circular argument. The theory of objective prices says that businessmen create prices by reference to the relevant economic facts, and those facts include other prices. Demand in part reflects the businessman's price in relation to the prices of his competitors. The costs of production are a joint product of the price and quantity for every factor a businessman hires. Competition includes competitors' prices and whether and how they might change their prices when the businessman changes his. In significant part, my theory of price explains prices by the price-setters' consideration of other prices.

The circularity charge depends on imagining that the chain of cause and effect underlying my theory is this: Price A causes price B which causes price C which causes price A. If that was my argument, then it would be circular. But that is not my argument. I do not claim and I do not think that prices are the first cause in the economy. The first cause in the economy is man's reasoning mind. There are many prices a businessman may take into account in creating his own price: the prices of his competitors, the prices of his factors, the price he is currently charging, the price of products that complement his own, and his expectations concerning all those prices. But the price he sets is his choice, given those other prices and all the other economic facts I have discussed. Nothing forces him to choose one price rather than another. It is his responsibility to grasp the facts and to choose. If he chooses well, his business will survive and prosper. If not, not. There is no circularity. In every case, there are only the relevant economic facts grasped, weighed and considered by a man who then decides, given those facts, what price will maximize his long-run profits.

Other prices have no effect on the price one chooses to set until the mind of a rational man processes those prices. In my theory, prices do not cause other prices. Prices by themselves cause nothing until a man evaluates their significance. My conception of man as a being of free will who chooses in his economic dealings to be guided by reason—*that* is what keeps the theory of objective prices from being circular. To repeat, in my theory the first cause is man, and qua economic actor, man is a free agent.

F. Price *Is* the Value versus Price *Measures* the Value

Which of the following expresses the correct view? The price *is* the value of a good or service or the price *measures* the value of a good or service. I struggled with this issue for many years. I leaned toward the view that the price is the value. If the price measures the value, I thought, that implies that the value exists prior to the price and is something distinct from the price. This seemed to imply an underlying intrinsic value in goods that is measured by the price. But on the other hand, if the price *is* the value of a good, to whom and for what is that value the value?

I found the answer to this dilemma in *Ayn Rand's Marginalia* (1995). In *Human Action*, Mises says "The prices are not measured in money, they consist in money" (1966, 217) In a marginal comment, Ayn Rand wrote "They are, and do, *both*." (p. 131; her emphasis).

The context of my problem is a little different, but that observation by Ayn Rand gave me the solution. Every price both is the value of the item and measures the value of the item. In this respect, price is exactly like many other measurements. Thirty feet is the length of the room; thirty feet also measures the room's length. Two tons is the weight of the car; two tons also measures the car's weight. There is nothing to be gained by arguing over which conception of length, weight, or price is right. In each case, both conceptions are right. With reference to price, I will use *is* and *measures* interchangeably.

In conclusion, every price is, gives, measures, and reflects the objective economic value of the good or service of which it is the price.

V. Objective Economic Value

Chapter 2 concluded (pp. 34 and 37–38) by establishing the concept of objective economic value. An economic value is an item, a thing, an object, or an action (a service) that is bought and sold. An *objective* economic value is an economic value that supports human life and originates in a rational grasp of the facts.

The price of a product also is its objective economic value. This is the concept of value as ranking in a hierarchy, the second concept of value identified in chapter 2 (p. 34). We saw in chapter 3 (p. 50) that each price exists in a network of other prices and derives its meaning from its relation to that network. That network is the market's hierarchy of values. Objective economic value adds to that conception the idea that every price in the hierarchy reflects the facts as grasped by the parties to the price, that as the measure of economic value, prices are objective.

Economic value is the issue of what people are willing to pay or to accept in exchange. As we have seen, the willingness to pay a price reflects the value of the good to the buyer; the willingness to accept a price reflects the value of the good to the seller. A product's price identifies what the product is worth, in the market and to the market, that is, to everyone who is willing to buy and/or sell at that price.[6] In some cases, like auctions, it may be that only one person is willing to pay the price—but somebody must pay it—and when a business is producing a product, people must pay the price in sufficient numbers to make production profitable over the long run.

As the objective economic value of a good, the price does not necessarily imply anything about the objective merit of the good in question. The subject here is market value, not aesthetic value nor political value nor philosophical value nor personal value nor any other kind of value. An art gallery asks high prices for pieces of junk. People pay to hear a speaker who is a dangerous fraud. Parents pay tuition to a university that destroys their child's self-esteem. But barring mistakes, the price is the product's objective economic value.

Businessmen determine the prices of their products in the total context of their market—as a means to their long-run profits and the survival of their companies. Sometimes they are wrong, but nothing is more objective than that judgment—the rational judgment of an individual man—that, in the context of the facts of his market, this price is good for his business.

Businessmen judge the value of their employees in the context of their specific, individual businesses—as means to the success of their productive enterprises. Sometimes they are wrong, but nothing is more objective than that judgment—the rational judgment of an individual man—that in the context of his business, this man is worth the price.

No less objective is an employee's judgment that his wage is worth the work he is hired to do or a consumer's judgment that a product is worth the price.

This is the theory of objective prices: every market price is and measures objective economic value—the price people are willing to pay and accept based on their grasp of the relevant economic facts. Whether it is the prices of consumer goods or producer goods, the prices of consumer services or producer services, the wages of day laborers or the salaries of business executives, their prices are their objective economic value. You cannot get under, over, around, or through that value. The only thing more fundamental is the mind of the rational man who makes that judgment. Objective economic value is the rock on which an economic system is built.

CHAPTER NINE

THE FACTORS OF PRODUCTION

I. The Original Factor of Production

The original factor of production is the reasoning human mind. In the fundamental sense, there is no other factor. Apart from the discoveries arising from the application of reason to the problem of man's survival, there would be no human beings. The survival of even the most primitive tribal communities depends on some tools discovered at some time by some individuals. This basic fact is wiped out by the standard list of the factors of production as land, labor, and capital. Of these three, only labor is human and, following Marx, modern economists implicitly take labor as the physical ability to move things by muscle power. Qua contribution to production, economics treats creative human intelligence as if it did not exist. Of all the deficits of modern economics, this is the greatest. Consequently, in this book I have avoided and will continue to avoid the term labor with all of its Marxist connotations. Instead, I use the terms workers, employees, human beings, people, and men.[1]

Man's faculty of reason is the origin of all economic activity. There is no principle in economics that is more important than this. It should be the featured fact at the beginning of every economics text.[2] It is the foundation for explaining all the prices in the economy, including the prices of all the factors of production. Indeed, everything since chapter 5 has shown how man's reasoning mind grasps the facts and makes the choices and takes the actions that bring about the prices that integrate all those facts, choices, and actions. (Chapters 10 and 11 show how all these come together to make the economy work.)

Whenever I use the terms worker or employee, therefore, I mean the productive power of human beings, the foundation of which is reason. Even the least intelligent worker must be able to understand what he is asked to do. Then, as we move up the scale of productive contribution, more and more thought, judgment, and intelligence are required as the guide to productive action, until we reach the top of the productive pyramid: the president, the chief executive officer, the entrepreneur.

Historically, economists have classified the factors of production according to the different theories of price that apply to each class. I agree with this practice. Consequently, I do not distinguish between land and capital goods as factors because the same theory explains both of their prices. Whether the price is set or negotiated, the market prices of land and capital goods originate in a rational grasp of the relevant economic facts by the buyer and the seller.[3]

However, it is not true that land and capital cannot be distinguished (as Frank Knight claimed; Buechner 1976). Broadly, capital is augmentable and land is not, as Kaldor pointed out (1937, 174). This is not an absolute distinction. Additions have been made to the land mass of Manhattan and Hong Kong. But it is a distinction sufficient to allow us to talk meaningfully about land and capital, as we have been doing. There are other differences between land and capital. As the site for private homes, land is often a consumer good, and capital never is. The relative price of land increases with the increasing demand arising from economic progress while the relative price of capital falls. But the relative price of collectibles and the wages of workers also rise with economic progress. There is no reason in economic theory to distinguish land from capital as a factor of production.

The fundamental distinction between the factors of production is between human and nonhuman factors. The difference is that human factors have the faculty of reason and the power of choice, and nonhuman factors do not. The economic difference that follows from this is that the theory of employee prices (wages and salaries) is a special case, a subdivision, of the general theory of objective prices.

There are other fundamental differences between human and nonhuman factors of which economics must take account. Human beings create the nonhuman factors (capital) or bring them into the economic realm (land). The human factors are the producers; land and capital are the means with which they produce. The prices of all the nonhuman factors originate in the minds of the human factors. The human factors cannot be sold and the entire economic system is for their sake. These differences are important. Indeed, they are so important that it is potentially misleading to treat human beings and nonhuman factors under the same heading as "factors of production." The nonhuman factors are the factors; human beings produce and then use those factors in order to create economic values.

Nevertheless, it is a universal fact that some men employ other men to create economic values. Human beings are responsible for the operation of every business and for the production of every product each business produces. In exchange for wages and salaries, men participate in, contribute to, direct and control the entire productive process. Performance of these functions by human beings has value to business owners who are willing (in fact, eager) to pay prices for their performance.

The prices of employees in conjunction with the prices of the nonhuman factors put both factors on the same footing in the productive network, allowing businessmen to compare the cost of men with the cost of nonhuman factors and determine the lowest cost method of production. Some methods of producing a particular product require relatively more workers and workers of particular kinds. Other methods of producing the same product require relatively more capital and workers of different kinds. Which should be used? There was a time when every elevator had an elevatorman. That time has passed. It passed when it became less expensive to install and operate automatic elevators than manually operated elevators.

The integration of human work into the production choices of businessmen is essential to the rational functioning of the economy. Consequently, economic theory has to treat human beings as a distinct factor of production. We can nullify the danger in this by keeping clearly in mind the special status of that factor as the one whose sustenance is the goal of every other factor.

II. The Law of Demand for
Factors of Production

The law of demand for factors of production is one of the foundations for understanding an economy as it changes through time (the subject of chapters 10 and 11). It is also a foundation for the theory of wages. Consequently, let us prove the law of demand for factors of production.

Businessmen create the prices of nonhuman factors by all the methods we have discussed: The prices of some factors are set by their sellers or by their buyers. The prices of many factors are negotiated. Sealed bid prices probably apply exclusively to factors of production. The used equipment and tools of a bankrupt firm frequently are sold at auction, as are the new goods which a bankrupt firm had produced for sale. Finally, all the basic commodities bought and sold at brokered prices on commodity markets are factors of production (for example, wheat, corn, oats, scrap iron, oil, and coal). Thus, the analysis of chapters 6 and 7 covered the creation of prices for all the factors of production in the economy.

Chapter 7 rejected the traditional explanation of the law of demand for factors of production (pp. 124, 135, and 137 above), that is, the amount of money an additional unit of a factor adds to a business's total revenue (what economists call marginal revenue product [p. 298 below]). This alleged addition to revenue is a chimera; marginal revenue product is almost always irrelevant to the decision of whether or not to hire another unit of any specific factor.[4]

There are two interconnected causes of the law of demand for factors. Each cause depends on the effect of changes in factor prices on businessmen's long-run profits. Consequently, the underlying premise here is the one chapter 6 established: that businessmen buy, hire, lease, rent and build factors as the means to long-run profits.

A. The Rate of Profit on Investment

Up to this point, this book has used the concepts of profit and rate of profit interchangeably. Now we need to distinguish them. Profit is the difference between a firm's total revenue and its total cost. Suppose Excel Menswear has $110 million in total revenue, $100 million in total costs, for a profit of $10 million, while New World Furniture has $10 million in total revenue, $5 million in total costs, for a profit of $5 million. New World Furniture's profits are half those of Excel Menswear.

The rate of profit is measured by dividing the businessman's total profits by his total cost.[5] Excel Menswear has a rate of profit of 10% while New World Furniture's rate of profit is 100%. In the competition for cloth, either to make clothes or upholster furniture, the manager of New World Furniture will be willing to pay more because he makes a 100% return on the money he spends on his business while the manager of Excel Menswear makes only 10% on the money he spends.

The rate of profit governs the operation of the economy. Industries with high rates of profit tend to grow rapidly as capital flows into them from all over the world. Industries with rates of profit that are just average do not attract much outside capital. Some maintain their plant and equipment; others grow slowly or shrink slowly over time. Industries and businesses with below average rates of profit or losses are in a constant struggle to survive. Investors shun them and eventually they go out of business. A business's or an industry's rate of profit is the motivating force for the flow of capital.

In gauging the significance of the law of demand for factors, it is important that we conceive of the business the way it actually is—which is the way its managers and directors experience it. A business is a dynamic, changing, evolving entity moving through time in a dynamic, changing, evolving economy. The real economy in which businessmen operate is one of continuous change, changes in the conditions facing the business and changes in the business itself, including changes in the business's profits. The managers of a business have to constantly anticipate and respond to these changes.

Let us survey the economy's businesses from the perspective of their sensitivity to changes in the prices of factors. Across the economy, the size of businesses varies in a virtually continuous range, from single proprietorships with no employees to multibillion dollar corporations with tens of thousands of employees. For the purpose of analysis, we can roughly divide up these businesses into small, medium, and large companies. Within each of these three subdivisions, on average, over the business cycle, there will be businesses that are growing rapidly with high rates of profit on investment, businesses with average rates of profit that are not growing or growing slowly or declining slowly, and businesses with low rates of profit or losses that are struggling to survive. Again, the distinction between high, low, and average rates of profit is an analytical device. It would be surprising if the variations in businesses' rates of profit were not virtually continuous within each size category.

The sensitivity of businesses to changes in the prices of factors is not determined by their size, but by their rate of profit on investment. The fundamental thing determining the purchase of factors is the profits the entrepreneur expects in the future. If a businessman's rate of profit is average and the demand for his product is constant or fluctuating within a narrow range, he sees any additional expense as a subtraction from profits. But if a business's rate of profit is high and profits have been growing rapidly, the entrepreneur rationally views an additional unit of a factor as adding to his future profits. Businessmen whose businesses are growing therefore are the ones most likely to adopt a new technology or

raise wages or buy additional factors. Managers see expenditures of this
kind as contributing to the business's growth and they expect the cost of
a new factor to shrink relative to profits over time as profits continue to
grow. Businesses with the highest rates of profit are the least price sensitive, and the higher the rate of profit, the less price sensitive they are.
The most profitable, fastest growing businesses will buy any factor that
contributes to the operation of the business. Any reasonable price is
worth paying because the factor will add to the company's profits.

When a factor's price rises, businesses with average rates of profit
are most likely to give up the factor; when a factor's price falls, they are
most likely to start using it. Consider a business with an average rate of
profit and constant demand. The owner may want to adopt a new technology, like computerizing his offices. But in his economic circumstances, an investment of this kind cannot be justified unless the computers save more than they cost. In this case, a relatively small change in
price per computer may be the deciding factor. Alternatively, there may
be a change in technology that increases output. But such a change is
senseless if the demand for the business's product is unchanging—unless
the new technology also reduces costs, permitting the businessman to sell
the additional output at a lower price.

The manager of a stable or slowly growing business cannot afford to
buy just any factor that would contribute to his operation. Since his rate
of profit is just average, he has to consider the effect of the price of the
factor on the business's future profits. Depending on the price, the businessman may decide that he can afford the factor or that he cannot. The
relevant standard is long-run profits.

A major purchase of machinery or equipment or plant may be subject
to a money evaluation (p. 125 above). The calculation may show that the
purchase will contribute to short-run profits when the long-run prospects
for the business are in doubt. The decision in such a case is difficult and
may be altered by a change in price of the factor. However, even when a
monetary calculation is possible, it may be irrelevant. The calculation
may show that a major investment will reduce the business's profits for
the foreseeable future, but the businessman must make this investment to
match the quality of his competitors' products. Any businessman that
does not keep up with his competitors will be out of business in the short
run, not the long run. On the other hand, even the prospect of bankruptcy
may not justify an investment that merely postpones the inevitable.
When a business's overall financial condition is less than good, a factor's

price is likely to be a major consideration in the decision of whether or not to employ it, and often the deciding consideration.

Now, consider those businesses with a low rate of profit or losses whose main concern is trying to avoid bankruptcy. In his 1964 study, Lanzillotti documented a number of small firms (250 employees or less) that could not afford to buy or hire needed factors (pp. 40, 47, 63). This study was restricted to the state of Washington, but any large economy has many low-profit firms like this. Furthermore, businesses in this position need not be small. The phenomenon is well-known of large companies that get into trouble and the order comes down from top management: "no more hires."

Businesses with low rates of profit or losses are more or less price sensitive depending on their individual circumstances. Sometimes there is no realistic price reduction that would cause the businessman to buy a new factor. His profits may be so low that he has no retained earnings and is unable to borrow funds for capital improvement. Other businessmen, however, though still struggling, can afford to hire an additional unit of a factor if the price is low enough.

Let us put aside businesses that are growing rapidly with high rates of profit. Then, an increase in the price of a factor means higher costs and lower long-run profits for the businessmen employing that factor. By the same token, a decrease in price of a factor increases the long-run profits businessmen derive from hiring that factor. The basis of the law of demand for factors of production is that as a factor's price falls, employing that factor contributes to the long-run profits of more and more businesses. As a factor's price rises, hiring the factor fails to contribute to or reduces the long-run profits of more and more businesses.

B. Relative Importance to the Businessman

Businessmen vary in the importance they attach to the same factor. This is a second cause of the law of demand for factors.

A factor may be a prerequisite for a business's continued functioning, that is, the business cannot exist without it. Or a factor may be incidental to the business's existence; it may make the product a little better, or reduce average cost a little, or improve the flow of information a little. Or the importance of the factor may fall anywhere between these two extremes; for example, the business can get along without it, but only at a significant increase in cost.

The importance a businessman attaches to a factor affects the price he is willing to pay. If the entrepreneur estimates a factor's importance as high, he will pay a high price if he has to. If he thinks the factor is of small importance, he will be willing to pay only a low price. The psychological process parallels that of consumers when they rank consumer goods relative to their prices (chapter 4, part I). Businessmen rank factor/price combinations relative to other factor/price combinations.

The major determinant of a factor's importance is the estimated impact of the factor on the business's long–run profits. Businessmen also gauge a factor's importance in part by how easy it is to replace by an identical factor, and in part by the factor's relation to potential substitutes—how good those substitutes are and what they cost. Nonhuman factors, particularly parts, materials, and ingredients, usually can be replaced without difficulty by identical factors, at the same price from the same supplier. In these cases, businessmen value the factor at its price.[6] Human factors, on the other hand, usually cannot be replaced by an identical factor—even regarded solely from the perspective of a man's economic performance.

As the price of a factor rises, it rises above the importance attached to it by more and more businessmen; consequently, fewer and fewer businessmen buy it, and demand decreases. As a factor's price falls, it falls below the estimated importance of more and more businessmen; more and more businessmen buy it, and demand increases. These changes in demand depend in part on businessmen expecting the price change to last for some time, particularly if a costly changeover in technology is required to use a new factor or to give up an old one.[7]

III. The Worker Markets

The concept of demand used up to this point in the book has been the demand for an individual business's product or products. This is the demand that the businessman considers when he sets or negotiates his price. A different concept of demand, market demand, is the relevant concept in the creation of the wages and salaries of workers. Consequently, we begin the theory of wages by considering the meaning of market demand for workers and why that demand increases or decreases. Then we will take up the supply of workers.

A. The Market Demand for Workers

The market demand for a particular type of worker (for example, industrial engineers) is the total quantity of new hires demanded by all the businesses in the relevant geographical area over some time period (again, let us say a month).[8] For each and every worker of every different kind and type, this constitutes the demand relevant to the creation of his wage rate.

For example, the primary cause of the market demand for industrial engineers is the employment vacancies that businessmen need industrial engineers to fill. These vacancies in turn reflect the profitability of the businesses that use industrial engineers. An increase in the rate of profit on products produced by industrial engineers leads businessmen to invest in such businesses, demanding more engineers. Over the long run, businessmen add plant and equipment and still more engineers. Employment vacancies for industrial engineers also are affected by the demand for the goods and services that they help to produce. If the demand increases for goods produced by engineers, then the businessmen producing such goods need more engineers. The demand for industrial engineers also reflects the availability of substitutes for industrial engineers and the prices of those substitutes. The demand for engineers increases if the prices of substitute factors increase or if the availability of substitute factors decreases.

Demand for some kinds of employees increases as the result of general economic growth because virtually all businesses need such employees—for example, accountants, secretaries, managers, and the like. Demand also may increase because businessmen decide that they need a special type of worker, the way they did with computer programmers and web masters. There may be a change in technology that requires more workers of a particular kind or that makes those workers more important to the success of the businessmen employing them. When the typewriter was invented, workers who could type became important. When the personal computer replaced the typewriter, workers who knew how to use a computer became important.

If a type of retail store enjoys an increased rate of profit, retailers in that line will need more inventory in order to expand their stores or open more stores, both of which require more employees of many different kinds. For example, an increase in demand for electronics products will increase the rate of profit on electronics stores, motivating businessmen to expand existing stores and open more stores, requiring more clerks, more managers, more cashiers, and so forth.

Decreases in demand for a specific type of worker are the result of the opposite of any or all of the above causes. For example, in a capitalist economy, all schools would be private, profit-maximizing businesses. Then, a decrease in the demand for teachers would take the form of a decrease in employment vacancies for teachers which could be caused by a decrease in the profitability of schools, or a decrease in the demand for schooling, or an increase in the number of substitutes for teachers, or an increase in the effectiveness of the substitutes and, as a consequence of any or all of these, a decrease in the importance businessmen attach to their teaching staffs.

This overview is not intended to be exhaustive.

B. The Market Supply of Workers

The prices of nonhuman and of human factors do not affect their markets in the same way. Chapter 3 showed that at the going price, the demand equals the supply for nonhuman factors (with the exceptions of short-term shortages and surpluses). For human factors, however, the wage rate for each specific kind of worker does not equate the demand for that worker to the supply. Outside of recessions, unemployed workers remain unemployed probably for about a month on average, and individuals can look for work much longer.

Finding employment requires work, and that work is not the work for which the individual is trained. He is not a specialist in selling himself, the way salesmen and advertising firms are specialists in selling their products. The man looking for work frequently has only a partial awareness of the relevant facts. He may not know where the employment vacancies are in his field and he may be mistaken about the wage he can command from potential employers. To find a vacancy that suits his abilities, to learn what his abilities are worth to employers, to decide on a new career path, takes time, and it can take a lot of time. Consequently, there are almost always a number of workers of every skill and ability looking for jobs at any point in time. Let us call these men and women "pools of workers." They constitute the supply of employees relevant to the creation of wage rates.

The supply of workers of any particular type is the number of workers of that type looking for jobs in the relevant geographical area over a month. The relevant geographical area is different depending on the job, expanding as the ability and salary level rise. For low-paying, unskilled work, the relevant area is local. For top executives of large corporations, the relevant area is international.

On the other side, businessmen do not know where to find the employees they need either. They advertise or go to employment agencies or hire executive recruiters or headhunters. A businessman may interview many candidates before he finds someone he wants to hire. The number of workers of a particular kind that businesses want to hire in a geographical area over a month constitutes the demand for those workers relevant to the creation of wage rates.[9]

C. Worker Pools

The pools of workers consist of the unemployed workers of every specific kind and type. Each pool is composed of men who have quit or who have been fired or who are entering the work force for the first time or who are reentering the work force after a period of time, and who are looking for work of a particular kind. They may be trained in a particular profession or skill like accounting or engineering or nursing and be looking for a job in their field. They may have a more general background in administration or management and be looking for a job in which they can apply their knowledge. They may have little or no training or background and be looking for a job in which they can learn a business, an occupation, a skill, or a trade. They may have no career ambition and be looking for any kind of work to support themselves and their families.

There are many, many pools of workers—as many pools as there are particular kinds, types, and classifications of jobs that can only be filled by workers with a particular skill or knowledge. These pools create a degree of slack in employee markets so that the demand for workers of a particular kind can increase without raising the wage rates of those workers, as long as the increased demand does not significantly shrink the pool.

For some types of worker, the supply is affected by the wages being offered. An increase in wages in a geographical area may attract workers from neighboring areas. In the case of unskilled workers (and perhaps even some types of skilled workers), an increase in wage rates pulls workers into the pool who would otherwise prefer not to work.[10] In the case of skilled workers, people may join the pool who are unhappy in jobs they already have. In all these cases, the effect is to slow down the rate at which the worker pool shrinks in response to an increase in demand for that kind of worker.

In the normal course of events (the economy is neither booming nor in a recession), newly unemployed workers looking for work join their specific pool at some rate per month, and firms that are looking for those workers hire the men they need at approximately the same rate. The pool remains roughly the same size as the number of jobs offered and filled ebbs and flows, while the going wage is unchanged. Wages change when the pool shrinks or expands to the point that businessmen find it significantly harder or easier to hire the workers they need. *The key to understanding changes in wages is the thinking of the businessman who changes his wage offer first.*

D. How Wages Rise

The pool of unemployed workers of a particular type shrinks because either the demand for those workers increases or the supply decreases. I discussed the possible causes of an increase in demand above (pp. 161–62). The effect is to increase the number of workers businessmen want to hire at the going wage. The increase in demand causes a decrease in supply as businessmen hire workers out of a specific pool at an increased rate.[11]

Suppose the pool of accountants looking for work is shrinking because of a general increase in demand for accountants. At some point, the businesses that are looking for accountants start to have difficulty finding employees they want to hire. More and more time is required to identify an acceptable candidate. Eventually, the businessman or his personnel director or some other responsible person decides that the business must offer a higher wage.

This is how wages rise. The first businessman to offer a higher wage does so because he must in order to hire the worker he needs. This higher wage has to be met by other businessmen who also are looking for accountants to hire. Further, this increase in wages, if it lasts, within a short time will redound throughout the accounting profession. Businessmen become aware that to keep the accountants they employ, they must raise their accountants' salaries to a level competitive with the going wage for new hires. Even if the new hires are all starting accountants, the higher wage will ripple up the accounting hierarchy, so the wages of senior accountants keep pace with the higher wages of starting accountants.

If an employee and an employer negotiate the wage, the current wage is the background context for the negotiation. The prospective employee will not want to take less than the current wage, but if he is a poor negotiator, or if the firm evaluates him as average, or if workers are easy to find in his particular labor market, he may negotiate less than the current wage. On the other hand, if the prospective employee is a good negotiator, or if the firm evaluates him highly, or if workers are hard to find in his particular labor market, he may negotiate more than the current wage. Usually the employee and his potential employer will negotiate something close to the current wage.

This is how businessmen *compete* for employees: They offer to pay the going wage, they offer a higher wage when necessary to hire the workers they want, and they raise the wages of their current employees when the going wage rises. They do this *because they must* in order to get and keep the workers they need.

This is also how real wages increase with economic progress. More and more businessmen find they have to offer higher wages to keep their workers and to add new workers when they need them. Eventually every employer has to raise his wages or lose his employees.

In an economy afflicted with price inflation, money wages rise in the same way and for the same reason they rise with economic progress. As price inflation goes on year after year, it becomes routine for businessmen to raise the wages of their employees every year to keep up with the inflation rate. They do this because if they do not, they will lose their best employees to other employers. From the perspective of relative prices (chapter 3), wages that increase at the same rate as the rate of price inflation are neither increasing nor decreasing. Wages rising less than the rate of price inflation are really falling; the men earning those wages can buy less and less each year. Only wages rising faster than the inflation rate represent real increases in wages.

E. How Wages Fall

The pool of unemployed workers of a particular type expands because the demand for those workers decreases or the supply increases. Demand may decrease for the reasons given in part A. However, recessions are the most familiar cause of decreases in demand. In a recession, the number of workers demanded at the going wage decreases for almost every type of worker. Supply simultaneously increases during recessions as workers are laid off.[12]

A businessman experiences an expansion in the pool of unemployed workers as an abundance of workers available at the going wage. Potential employees, in response to an advertisement, besiege the business, or word-of-mouth about a job vacancy brings in a surfeit of applicants. In such circumstances, the business may offer less than the going wage, or prospective employees may offer to take less, and the going wage for that type of employee falls. In 1982 and 1983, the average union wage rate fell as unions negotiated lower wages in order to avoid layoffs. In the Great Recession of 2007–2009, skilled and unskilled workers alike accepted lower wages.

In the modern economy, it is unusual for businessmen to reduce the wages they pay because of their concern for worker morale (Howitt 2002). But that is a product of recent history—of the fact that there has been no general decrease in money wages in the United States since the 1930s—and consequently, workers view a decrease in money wages as the equivalent of a violation of natural law. In contrast, in the general deflation following the Civil War, money wages fell (and rose and fell) continuously.[13] In an inflationary economy, as we have just seen, the money wage rate does not have to decline in order for the real wage rate to fall, and the American economy has been more or less inflationary for most of the last eighty years. Consequently, real wages can and do fall when money wages do not keep up with the rate of price inflation.

Finally, let us note that the supply of and demand for workers affect wages in the form of the facts faced by each businessman and each worker. The businessman's grasp of those facts (the going wage, how long he has been looking for a particular worker, the number of applicants for a job, and so forth) determines the wage he decides he must pay. The unemployed worker's grasp of those facts (the job offers he has had, how long he has been looking for a job, the jobs and salaries his friends are getting, and so forth) affects the maximum wage he thinks he can command in the market. The role of supply and demand in the creation of wages is through their effect on the facts faced and grasped by individual human beings.

F. Supply and Demand and Relative Scarcity

A change in the supply of or the demand for a particular kind of worker is simultaneously a change in the relative scarcity of workers of that kind. As a consequence, the salary of each kind of worker measures his scarcity relative to the scarcity of other worker types. Let us see why.

Over time, the going wage roughly equates the number of workers entering a worker pool to the number of workers hired out of that pool. If the number of workers hired out consistently exceeds the number of workers entering the pool, eventually the wage rises for that kind of worker. Put in terms of supply and demand, this means that if the demand for a specific kind of worker increases relative to the supply of that kind of worker, their wages rise. Alternatively, if the number of workers entering regularly exceeds the number of workers hired out of a pool, eventually the wages fall for that kind of worker. In terms of supply and demand, this means that if the supply of a specific kind of worker increases relative to the demand for those workers, their wages fall.

Changes in supply relative to demand or in demand relative to supply are changes in relative scarcity. The same changes in supply and demand that change objective wages and salaries are simultaneously changes in relative scarcity. If the supply of engineers increases relative to the demand for engineers, that is a decrease in the relative scarcity of engineers and their wages fall. If the demand for secretaries increases relative to the supply of secretaries, that is an increase in the relative scarcity of secretaries, and their wage rate rises. The wage rate of every worker, of whatever kind or type or skill or training, reflects the scarcity of that type of worker relative to all other worker types.

Taken altogether, the array of annual wages and salaries of all the employees in the economy is a hierarchy reflecting the relative scarcity of every kind and type of employee. Workers with higher salaries are relatively more scarce than workers with lower salaries. The same hierarchy ranks all the different kinds and types of workers according to their value to their employers. Employees with higher wages and salaries have higher value. The businessman chooses to pay the wage required by a worker's relative scarcity only when he thinks the worker is worth it.

Consider, for example, a scientist working in the research and development department of a large corporation. The scientist contributes nothing to current output; he has no role in reducing current costs, in marketing the corporation's products, in improving communications, or in facilitating management control. His contribution is entirely prospective and uncertain. Yet management chooses to pay him a very high salary, perhaps on the level of a vice president. Why? First, his scarcity value is such that they must pay him that salary to retain his services. Second, his work is judged to be essential to the future of the company—because while his contribution is prospective and uncertain, it is a certainty that the corporation will fail without him (that is, without research and development).

The fundamental principle governing the creation of wages and salaries is that businessmen pay workers what they have to pay them in order to employ them. What they have to pay them reflects the conditions of demand and supply in each worker's particular worker pool—that is, the worker's relative scarcity. Then, given what the businessman must pay, he decides whether his long-run profits will be served by paying that price.

When a businessman decides to pay a worker's wage, he becomes part of the market demand which, in conjunction with supply, causes that wage. Here is how demand and supply interact: Consider, for example,

the market for people with new Master of Business Administration de-
grees (new MBAs). Businessmen weigh the relevant facts and decide
how many new MBAs they want to hire. If something raises the rate of
profit of the businesses hiring new MBAs, or makes new MBAs more
valuable, the rate at which businessmen hire new MBAs increases. This
is simultaneously an increase in demand for and a decrease in supply of
new MBAs at the going wage. If the pool of new MBAs shrinks sufficiently, businessmen have to offer higher wages to hire the new MBAs
they want. As the going wage for new MBAs rises, businessmen with
lower rates of profit withdraw from or do not enter the new MBA market. This represents a decrease in demand at the higher wage and simultaneously a reduction in the rate at which the supply of new MBAs decreases. The wage stops rising when businessmen draw new MBAs from
the pool at approximately the same rate at which new MBAs enter the
pool.

G. Executive Compensation

Now, let us consider the determination of the compensation of top corporate executives, with particular attention to chief executive officers
(CEOs).

Suppose that over a year, the going wage in every worker market
was unchanging and was not under any pressure to change. This would
mean that the rate at which workers were entering each specific worker
pool would approximately equal the rate at which businesses were draw-
ing them out. If these conditions were universal across all worker pools,
it seems likely that businessmen would be able to replace every worker
of whatever type or skill with roughly the same degree of ease or difficulty.

The occupations for which this would *not* be true are the upper levels
of management. At those levels, there usually are few or no men in the
pool of unemployed. This means that the market for CEOs is by far the
tightest worker market in the economy. This is why corporations fill executive positions, almost without exception, either by promotion from
within the business or by hiring executives away from other corporations. Almost all executive positions are filled by people who are already
employed.[14]

Compensation for CEOs is based on the grasp of the relevant economic facts by the two parties to the price: the candidate for CEO and the
men who must agree to his compensation, usually the corporation's
Board of Directors. The relevant facts include the size and type of the

corporation, its current state of profitability, its prospects in the future, the primary characteristics the Board wants in a new CEO, the caliber of this candidate, the going rate of compensation for CEOs of this size and type of business, and so forth.

If a CEO is being promoted from within the corporation, the Board has to offer him compensation that is comparable to what CEOs in similar corporations are earning. If a Board is hiring a new CEO away from another corporation, usually the Board must offer him more than he is currently making.[15] If the Board is looking for the rarest kind of CEO, a turnaround expert whose job will be to restore an unprofitable business to profitability, the new CEO may require an extraordinary level of compensation. In all these cases, the compensation eventually becomes more or less public and the remuneration negotiated for the last CEO hired becomes one of the relevant economic facts for the negotiation between the next company and its prospective CEO. Undoubtedly, there are cases where a hard-bargaining candidate persuades a Board of Directors to pay him more than it should. But that is not why the salaries of CEOs are high. They are high because those salaries reflect CEOs' relative scarcity—the demand for CEOs relative to the supply.

The demand for CEOs is like the demand for old masters—in both cases, the quantity demanded is one. Consequently, in both cases, demand has to be understood as the highest price someone is willing to pay. A change in the demand for business executives does not consist of a change in the number of executives whom businesses want to hire. It consists of a change in the price that Boards of Directors are willing to pay.[16] The demand for CEOs differs from the demand for old masters in that the compensation for CEOs is negotiated.

The CEO is the most important factor of production in the corporation; in the economy, such men are the scarcest factors. When a corporation starts looking for a new chief executive, the supply may be zero—no one is available with the required characteristics. Consequently, many corporations start the search for a new chief executive as much as two to five years before the current CEO is scheduled to retire.

From the corporation's point of view, it is hard to overpay the right man for the job. The price he is paid is a direct reflection of his relative scarcity—of the demand relative to the supply of one—in the judgment of the men who decide what to offer him, and in his own judgment of the maximum price he can command in the market—if and when they reach agreement. Salaries at lower levels of responsibility are reached in the same way, only the requirements are less demanding, the candidates are not as scarce, and the resulting compensation is lower.

How does a Board of Directors or a candidate estimate his value as a prospective CEO? The same way one estimates the value of an old master or a secretary or an engineer. The standard is: how much people are willing to pay. Usually that amount is how much they *must* pay, as determined by the demand relative to the supply, that is, by relative scarcity. The number of men qualified for top level executive positions in large corporations is very small, perhaps 50,000 men out of a world population of seven billion (7,000,000,000). Very few people have the required characteristics of rationality, intelligence, creativity, confidence, judgment, independence, acumen, and energy. Those who do often would rather start their own businesses.

As with all other wages and salaries, CEO compensation rises over time when a Board of Directors discovers that it must offer more to hire the candidate it wants. This happens when the Board cannot find an appropriate candidate at the compensation it is offering, or the candidate it wants will not work for that compensation. Sometimes, a Board has to offer more in competition with another corporation for the same candidate.

We hear everywhere today cries of shock and anger about the compensation received by CEOs. The anger often is an expression of envy, particularly when it comes from our egalitarian intellectuals who do not want anyone to make more than a bare pittance. But the average man may also be shocked because he does not understand how important and how scarce are the men capable of being CEOs.

III. Conclusion

At this point, we have the knowledge necessary to look at the economy in action. We know that all market prices are objective prices and we know that businessmen create their prices in consideration of the facts, usually including demand, cost, and competition. We have had a preliminary look at the way in which these facts affect price. We have grasped the law of demand in relation to both consumer goods and producer goods. We have looked at the creation of the prices of all the factors of production, including the human factors, concluding in this chapter with the causes of increases and decreases in wages.

The next step is to see how businessmen change prices, including wages, when the facts change, and how those changes in price affect the actions of other businessmen and consumers. Our goal is a bird's-eye view of the economic system—a vision of how all the actions of all the participants in the economy are tied together by prices into a unified, noncontradictory whole—and how this is brought about by men concerned with nothing but their financial self-interest and the economic well-being of themselves and those they love.

CHAPTER TEN

CHANGES IN OBJECTIVE PRICES I
THE EFFECT OF CHANGES
IN FACTS ON SET PRICES

I. Background Premises

This chapter begins the application of the theory of objective prices to changes in price. We will see how prices change when the economic facts change; the chain of events in the economy set in motion by those changes; and conclude with a grasp of how the economy works. The subject of this chapter is the effect on the economy of changes in the facts when someone sets the price. Chapter 11 analyzes these effects for the other four methods of creating prices.

The theory of objective prices is founded on the fundamental fact that *every price is set by someone*. If a price changes, someone has to change it, and if someone changes it, there is one fundamental cause: the choice of the price-setter(s) has changed (pp. 147–48 above). Such a change does not occur in a vacuum. Normally, a change in the facts is the cause of the change in the price-setter's choice of price. Sometimes the facts change in such a way that a change in price is not necessary. Sometimes a price-setter changes his mind about what the price should be without a change in the facts. But the most common sequence is first the facts change and then the price-setter chooses a new price that reflects the new facts.

Chapter 9 (pp. 164–65) pointed out that the key to understanding how wages change is the thinking of the businessman who changes his wage offer first. The same approach applies here. To understand changes in price, the key is the thinking of the businessman who changes *his price* first. If the other businessmen in an industry are changing their prices, it is usually obvious why a competing businessman would follow their lead. For example, suppose the other businesses are raising their selling prices to cover an increase in the price of a material or ingredient that they all use. A businessman with the same increase in costs does not have to worry about losing customers to his competitors when he raises his price, because they have raised or are raising their prices. But the businessman who goes first in raising his price *will* lose customers to his competitors if they do not follow his lead. His thinking is the thinking we need to understand.

When a businessman changes his price, he changes the economic conditions faced by his competitors. The quantity he will be able to sell depends on how his competitors respond to his price change. Suppose he lowers his price. If his competitors match his new price, the law of demand implies that they will all sell more at the lower price. If his competitors ignore his price cut, then he alone will sell more, usually much more, and his competitors will sell less. Each of his competitors could do something different: one matching his price cut, another ignoring it, another cutting further, and so forth.[1] The businessman changing his price needs to know, or at least have *some* idea, of how his competitors are going to respond if he is going to have *any* idea of how his change in price is going to affect *him*. But at first glance, there does not seem to be any way he can know that.

We can resolve this ambiguity by distinguishing between two different types of change in economic conditions: (1) a change that affects all the businesses in the industry, and (2) a change that is unique to an individual business. In principle, if all or most of the businesses in an industry experience the same change in economic conditions, the businessman going first in changing his price can expect to be followed. If the change in economic conditions is unique to the individual business, then the businessman changing his price can expect *not* to be followed.[2]

On the Origin of Changes in the Facts

Changes in cost and demand can originate within an industry or from outside an industry. For example, the costs of the personal computer (PC) industry can rise because the producers of PCs raise the wages of their workers, or because Intel raises the price of their microprocessors. Similarly, an advertising campaign by PC producers may raise the demand for PCs, or demand may increase because the industry's customers independently want more PCs.

Part II following analyzes what happens when a change in average costs originates outside an industry. Part III analyzes what happens when a change in demand originates outside an industry. These are not the only, or even the most likely, possibilities. Businessmen do not sit and wait passively to react to outside events. Successful businessmen work actively to change the facts their businesses face; they aggressively push down their costs so that they can cut their prices or meet the price cuts of others; they show their suppliers how to cut costs so they can cut their own costs;[3] they launch advertising campaigns to maintain and increase the demand for their products; they invest huge sums in research and development to improve their products and to create new products.

Most of parts II and III consider how businessmen across an entire industry react to changes in facts that they do not themselves create. We consider the consequences when businessmen act to change the facts under the heading of changes unique to the individual business. This division is somewhat artificial. Many businesses in an industry may adopt a new technology at approximately the same time. However, unusual individuals usually initiate the important changes in the economic facts of industries.

Part IV considers the long-run consequences of the changes discussed in parts II and III. Finally, part V discusses the meaning and consequences of changes in competition, including the effect on prices.

The method throughout is as inductive as I can make it. Nevertheless, there are significant deductive elements. Those deductive elements make the conclusions somewhat speculative. Someday there will be empirical evidence on these subjects. Today there is none. Where it is necessary, I have to deduce what makes sense in the context of everything else I know. This step cannot be skipped. Deduction is an essential part of the process by which we grasp the integrated functioning of the economy as a whole.

The effect of changes in average cost on price is the logical starting point.

II. Changes in Average Cost

A. Increases in Average Cost

1. An industry-wide increase in average cost

Let us begin by imagining that suppliers have increased the price of a part, material, or ingredient that all the businesses in the industry use. The increase in cost is sufficient to reduce everyone's profits and every businessman wants to raise his price to reestablish his profit margin. The businessman who raises his price first can expect to be followed, if his price increase is appropriate for the change in cost. If the businessman's competitors think his change in price is too much or too little, there may be a period in which they all jockey their prices up and down until a mutually acceptable result is reached.

This analysis assumes that an individual businessman knows that all the businesses in the industry have experienced the same increase in cost as he. Such knowledge is not guaranteed. Weston (1972) notes that

> ...it is extremely difficult to obtain information on cost accounting procedures and standard cost systems from individual firms because such information is regarded as highly proprietary and as being of great potential value to competitors. (p. 11, note 20)

If businessmen conceal their "cost accounting procedures," they certainly conceal their costs. If a businessman does not know that his competitors' costs have increased, or that their costs have increased to the same extent as his own, he will be reluctant to raise his price. Businessmen say that the primary reason they resist raising their prices is fear they will lose customers to their competitors (Blinder and others 1998, 262–63). Blinder and others also found an average time period of two to eight months between a rise in cost and a rise in price (p. 86). I hypothesize that this lag reflects primarily the time it takes a businessman to be sure his competitors' costs have gone up before he raises his price first.

Since all the businesses face the same increase in cost, a price increase that reestablishes the preexisting structure of prices at a higher level probably is acceptable to all the competitors. By price structure, I mean the range of prices from highest to lowest and the difference between each price in the range. If a price increase reestablishes the preexisting structure of prices, then the businessman who had the highest price before still has the highest price, and there is the same percentage difference between his price and the price of the business with the next highest price, which is the same business that had the second highest price before, and so forth. Other facts will be changing at the same time, so the actual results may be an approximation of this.

In other cases, a looser conception of price structure may be appropriate. For example, among pizza stands in New York City neighborhoods, it is common for each owner to raise his price by the same absolute amount, so that the business charging 25¢ more a slice is still charging 25¢ more after the increases in price.

While correct as far as it goes, the preceding interpretation of the effect on price of an increase in cost is incomplete. It is not true that an increase in price by all the businesses in an industry necessarily will increase their profits. As background for the analysis that follows, we need to understand two new topics: (a) elasticity; and (b) the cost classification of industries.

a) Price elasticity of demand

Elasticity is the responsiveness or sensitivity of one variable to changes in another variable. Price elasticity of demand is the responsiveness or sensitivity of the quantity customers buy to changes in a good's price.

The law of demand says that when the price of a good goes up, the quantity sold goes down; when the price goes down, the quantity sold goes up. Total revenue is the price (P) times the quantity sold (Q) (chapter 6, part I). Since price and quantity change in opposite directions, they have opposite effects on total revenue; whether total revenue rises or falls depends on which one changes more. If the percentage increase in price is greater than the percentage decrease in quantity, total revenue will increase. For example, suppose the price is $10, the quantity sold is 1000 units, and total revenue is $10 x 1000 = $10,000. Now suppose the seller raises the price by 20% to $12 and the quantity sold declines by 10% to 900. Then total revenue rises to $10,800 ($12 x 900). Alternatively, if the percentage increase in price is less than the percentage decrease in quantity, total revenue decreases. If the price rises by 10% to $11 and the quantity sold declines by 20% to 800, total revenue falls from $10,000 to $8,800 ($11 x 800).

The concept which captures this relationship is price elasticity of demand—for which I will use the symbol E_D. E_D is calculated as the percentage change in quantity divided by the percentage change in price ($\%\Delta Q \div \%\Delta P$). The quotient is the percentage change in quantity for a 1% change in price. If the price of television sets rises by 5% and the quantity falls by 10%, the elasticity is two (2.0)—(10% ÷ 5%)—which means that for each 1% change in price, quantity changes by 2%. Since price and quantity move in opposite directions, the sign of $'E_D$ is negative. However, economists typically ignore this, and I will too.

If the price of wheelbarrows decreases by 12% and the quantity increases by 4%, the elasticity is one third (0.33)—(4% ÷ 12%)—which means that a 1% change in price causes a 0.33% change in quantity.

If the $'E_D$ is greater than one, demand is said to be elastic; if the $'E_D$ is less than one, demand is said to be inelastic.

b) The cost classification of industries

Economists classify industries according to how average cost (cost per unit) changes as output increases. In this context, we will interpret this classification as reflecting current conditions, that is, how average cost changes for businesses over the range of output they customarily produce (p. 106 above).[4]

Industries for which average cost is unchanging or constant as output increases or decreases are called *constant cost industries*. Graph A below represents their costs with average cost (AC) on the vertical axis, quantity (Q) on the horizontal axis, and a horizontal straight line across the graph at the level of the business's average cost (AC1).

Graph A

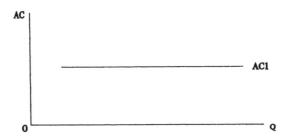

In this case, if the businessman raises his price, he sells less, but his average cost does not change. Likewise, if he lowers his price, he sells more, but again his average cost does not change.

Industries for which average cost falls as output increases are called *decreasing cost industries*. Graph B below represents their costs by a decreasing straight line (AC2).

Graph B

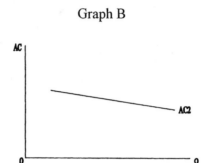

In this case, a rise in the businessman's price reduces the quantity sold and his average cost increases. If the businessman cuts his price, the quantity he sells increases and his average cost falls.

Industries for which average cost rises as output increases are called *increasing cost industries*. Graph C below represents their average cost by a rising straight line (AC3).

Graph C

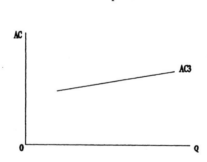

In this case, if the businessman raises his price, Q falls, and average cost falls. If instead, he cuts his price, the quantity sold increases and his average cost goes up.

In all three cases, an increase in cost *for reasons other than a change in output* is represented by a shift up in the average cost curve. We began this discussion (p. 176 above) by assuming that costs had risen because the price had risen of an input used by the businesses in the industry. If the industry is a constant cost industry, graph D below illustrates the increase in cost by a shift upward of the constant average cost curve AC1 to AC11, showing a higher average cost of production at every output level. If the industry is an decreasing cost industry, graph E represents the increase in cost by an upward shift in the decreasing average cost curve from AC2 to AC22. Graph F shows an increase in cost in an increasing cost industry, as the increasing average cost curve shifts up from AC3 to AC33.[5]

Graph D

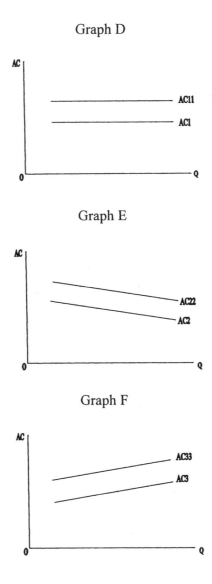

Graph E

Graph F

2. The effect on profits of increases in price

Consider the following example: one of the products produced by Acme Enterprises is electric can openers. Acme charges an average price of $100 per can opener, the average cost of each can opener is $80, and Acme sells an average of 1000 can openers each month. Thus, Acme has a profit per can opener of $20 and total profits of $20,000 per month on its can opener business. Let us assume that Acme expects the other businesses in the can opener industry to match its price change (in the price structure sense described above). Consequently, Acme's elasticity of demand[6] is equal to the elasticity of demand for the can opener industry.[7]

This is the problem: suppose Acme's average cost per can opener rises from $80 to $90. This is the shift up in the average cost curves illustrated above. As long as the price remains $100, Acme's profit per can opener falls from $20 to $10 and total profits on Acme's can opener business fall from $20,000 to $10,000 per week. The question is: can Acme raise its profits above $10,000 by raising its price if all the other can opener producers follow?

a) Demand is inelastic

If demand is inelastic, any percentage change in price causes a smaller percentage change in quantity. If price rises, the quantity falls by a smaller percentage amount, and total revenue for the industry rises. At the same time, each individual business can produce the smaller quantity for a smaller total cost and profits for the industry increase. It does not make any difference whether the industry is constant cost, increasing cost, or decreasing cost. The total cost of producing less is less because each business needs less materials and fewer employees.[8]

When an increase in average cost affects all the businesses in an industry, if the demand for the industry's product is inelastic, then an across-the-board increase in price will raise the industry's profits. The businessman who raises his price first can expect to be followed.

b) Demand is elastic

If demand is elastic, an increase in price will cause a greater percentage decrease in quantity and reduce total revenue. Whether or not profits increase depends on what happens to total cost[9], which in turn depends on the cost classification of the industry.

(1) A constant cost industry

In a constant cost industry, an increase in price reduces the quantity sold, but does not change average cost. Both total revenue and total cost fall, but there is a tendency for total cost to fall more. Total revenue is composed of both a rising element (price) offset by a falling element (quantity), while total cost is composed of a constant element (average cost) and a falling element (quantity). For example, suppose Acme raises its price from $100 to $110, all the other can opener companies follow, and Acme's sales fall from 1000 to 800. Then Acme's total revenue is $110 x 800 = $88,000. Average cost is unchanged at $90, so Acme's total cost is now $90 x 800 = $72,000. Acme's profits rise from $10,000 to $16,000.

If the elasticity of demand is very high, the fall in quantity and total revenue may be so severe that a 10% increase in price does not raise profits.[10] For example, if elasticity is 5.0, an increase in price to $110 causes a 50% decrease in quantity, from 1000 to 500 per week. Total revenue falls from $100,000 to $55,000 and total cost falls from $90,000 to $45,000, leaving profit unchanged. Since industry elasticities of demand above 3.0 are unusual, in constant cost industries, an increase in price is likely to raise industry profits. The businessman who raises his price first can expect to be followed.

(2) An increasing cost industry

In an increasing cost industry, average cost decreases with decreases in quantity. In contrast to the constant cost industry, both elements of total cost decline. This makes it more likely that the decrease in total cost will exceed the decrease in total revenue and raise profits. Again, the businessman who increases his price first can expect to be followed.

(3) A decreasing cost industry

The troublesome case is when average cost declines with increases in output, which happens in 41 percent of businesses according to Blinder and others (p. 105 above). In this case, the falling quantity that results from the price increase also raises cost per unit. The critical issue here is the steepness of the average cost curve. The faster average cost declines with increases in output, the faster it increases with decreases in output, and the more likely it is that an increase in price will not raise profit. In appendix E, I show that even here, an increase in price probably will raise profits.

Summing up, if industry demand is inelastic, an increase in price raises industry profits. If demand is elastic, an increase in price is likely to raise the industry's profits, but not necessarily. We have to allow for the possibility in decreasing cost industries that an increase in price may reduce the industry's profits.

3. Restoring an industry's profits

An increase in price usually will not restore an industry's profits to what they were before the increase in average cost. In the case of Acme, the increase in average cost reduces its profits from $20,000 to $10,000 per week. Probably there is no increase in price that will restore Acme's profits to $20,000. The reason is the law of demand. Suppose Acme and its competitors have the same costs. Should they all raise their prices by the full 10 percent (to $110) necessary to return their profit margins to $20 a unit, the fall in quantity sold would keep their profits below $20,000. In a decreasing cost industry, the profit result would be worse, because the cost per unit rises as quantity decreases. Only in an increasing cost industry is it conceivable that a return to the old profit margin might return businesses to their original total profits.

One might think that if an increase in price raises Acme's profits, then a greater increase in price would raise profits more. Not necessarily. A particular percentage increase in price may raise profits for specific values of elasticity and average cost while a greater percentage increase in price reduces profits for those same values (see appendix E, pp. 315–16).

Further, major changes in price and quantity change the elasticity of demand and average cost. A specific percentage change in price represents more money if the good is expensive. A 10% change in the price of a $30,000 car is worth $3,000, while a 10% change in the price of a $200 cell phone is worth $20. Consequently, people are more sensitive to percentage changes in the price of high-priced items, and the demand for such items is almost always more elastic than the demand for low-priced items. Thus big increases in price tend to increase the elasticity of demand, magnifying the decrease in quantity. In addition, big increases in price cause big decreases in quantity, possibly moving the firm out of its normal range of output and raising average cost (p. 105 above). These effects on the elasticity of demand and on average cost are additional factors working against the possibility of businessmen restoring their profits by large increases in price.

4. An increase in average cost unique to the businessman

Suppose the management of a business has been lax, operations have become inefficient, and average cost has risen; or the business's workers have joined a union and negotiated a higher wage; or the business has raised wages in order to discourage its workers from joining a union, and so forth. For whatever reason, this business's costs have risen while the costs of its competitors have not. The owner would like to raise his price to cover his increased costs, but he cannot. Since his competitors are satisfied with their profit margins, the businessman knows that they will not follow a price increase. To raise his price in the face of their unchanged prices would be an invitation to his customers to take their business elsewhere.

Perhaps if the business's product has unique features and customer loyalty is high, the businessman might be able to get away with an increase in price. But in that case, he could have been charging the higher price all along.

B. Decreases in Average Cost

1. An industry-wide decrease in average cost

All the businesses in an industry have experienced a decrease in their costs as the result of a fall in the price of a factor. Modern economists think that a decrease in average cost automatically reduces price. In a perverse application of this theory, they criticize businessmen for having "market power" if they do not reduce their prices when costs fall.[11] This relation is so taken for granted that Blinder and others (1998) presented it to their business executives as a foregone conclusion. "What about when costs *decline*? How much time normally elapses until you *reduce* your prices?" (their emphasis, p. 319).

The error in this view is that in the actual economy, in any industry, for any business, almost any reduction in price will reduce profits, regardless of the demand or cost conditions. Economists do not know this. Marketing professors do (for example, see Dolan and Simon 1996, pp. 17–30).[12]

2. The effect on profits of decreases in price

Continuing with the Acme Enterprises example, suppose Acme's average cost per can opener falls from $80 to $70. (The average cost curve shifts down by $10 along its whole length.) With a price of $100, profit per can opener rises from $20 to $30 and total profits on Acme's can opener business increase from $20,000 to $30,000 per week. Can Acme raise its profits above $30,000 by cutting its price if all the other can opener producers follow?

a) Demand is inelastic

If industry demand is inelastic, a reduction in price causes a smaller percentage increase in quantity sold, reducing total revenue for the industry. At the same time, the increased quantity will cost more to produce, raising total costs. A price reduction is guaranteed to reduce industry profits if demand is inelastic.

b) Demand is elastic

When demand is elastic, a decrease in price causes a greater percentage increase in quantity sold, raising total revenue. But the total cost of producing the greater quantity is greater. What happens to profits depends on how average cost changes with increases in quantity. Consider again the cost classification of industries.

(1) A constant cost industry

If average cost does not change with increases in quantity, a price reduction reduces profits almost regardless of the elasticity of demand. In the case of Acme Enterprises, a 5% reduction in price reduces profits up to a demand elasticity of 4.0; a 10% price reduction reduces profits up to a demand elasticity of 5.0 (appendix E, pp. 313–14). Again, elasticities of demand above 3.0 are unusual. There is virtually no chance that a decrease in price will increase profits in a constant cost industry.

(2) An increasing cost industry

Since average cost increases with increases in output, the effect on profits of a price reduction is worse if the industry has increasing costs.

(3) A decreasing cost industry

Only if average cost falls with increases in output is there some ambiguity in these results. Then we can imagine some conditions under which a price reduction will increase profits for the industry (appendix E, pp. 314–16).

3. Why prices fall

If demand is inelastic, or elastic with constant or increasing average cost, why would the industry's price ever fall after a reduction in average cost? Why would a businessman in such an industry reduce his price first, expecting to be followed? My hypothesis is that if the price falls (and that is not guaranteed), the explanation is competition.

The exact situation is this: A reduction in average cost raises the profits of all the businesses in the industry. If then they all reduce their prices to return to the original profit margin per unit, sales will increase, and profits will fall. But profits will be higher than they were before the decline in average cost; the profit margin per unit will be the same while the total quantity sold will be higher at the lower price.

In many cases, every businessman knows that every other businessman is in approximately the same position. Average cost has fallen, a decrease in price is consistent with an increase in long-run profits, and the businessman who does not cut price is in danger of losing market share. So even though it is true that every businessman in the industry would be still better off with no reduction in price, from the perspective of each businessman as an individual, reducing his price may maximize his long-run profits.

In addition, there is the fact that the prices charged by competitors often are not public and may be difficult to discover. Dolan & Simon (1996) warn against taking the reports of one's salesmen as the sole source of information about other businesses' prices. "Customers are selective in what they disclose about prices they are offered or paid. Some competitive 'offers' may be clouded by other terms or lost in the course of negotiations" (pp. 109–10).

When a businessman cuts his price, competing businessmen may not know right away, and the price-cutter may increase his market share and his long-run profits. Even if his price reduction is matched, the business's profits will be higher than they were before his average cost fell. At the same time, he has reason to worry that competing businessmen are cutting their prices without his knowledge. Under these circumstances, a price reduction that keeps the same profit margin per unit, or something close to it, may be the long-run profit-maximizing alternative.

In the case of retail outlets that sell many goods, which is the norm for retail stores (Andrews 1964), the motive for reducing the price of a good when its cost falls may be somewhat different. It is the kiss of death to get the reputation of being a high-priced store, unless one also gets the reputation of being a high quality store. Again, this is a phenomenon of competition; a store cannot get the reputation of being "high-priced" except relative to the prices of its competitors.

4. A decrease in average cost unique to the businessman

Suppose new management has raised efficiency and pushed down the business's average cost below the average cost of its competitors. The businessman has essentially two options under these conditions. One is to leave his price unchanged and enjoy the increased profits that his superior efficiency has made available. As long as the businessman can maintain his cost advantage, there is nothing in a free market that will eliminate such profits.

The preceding outcome is probably most likely if the decrease in average cost is not too great. But if the businessman has achieved a major reduction in average cost, he may make a significant reduction in price with the goal of expanding his market share at the expense of his competitors. In this case, the businessman establishes a new price structure for the market, as competitors must match his price or go out of business.

III. Changes in Demand

In order to avoid truly mind-boggling complications[13], we will assume that all the industries in the following analysis are constant cost industries. In addition, we will take as true what I have shown above, that industry-wide increases in price normally increase an industry's profits and industry-wide decreases in price normally decrease an industry's profits.

A. Increases in Demand

1. An industry-wide increase in demand

Businesses experience an increase in demand as an increase in the quantity sold at the current price. If businesses are satisfied with their profit margins, they increase the quantity of output to meet the increase in demand. This is possible because most businesses operate at something less than full capacity—probably 70 to 80 percent of full capacity on average.[14] This means that there is a degree of slack in the economy—the same slack we observed in employee markets in chapter 9 (p. 163), with the same beneficial result: demand can increase and decrease without causing changes in price.

Businessmen operate with excess capacity because they want to be able to satisfy an increase in demand for their products; they do not want to be forced to send a new customer to a competitor. Economists generally disapprove of excess capacity as a waste of resources. In fact, excess capacity is a positive feature of a free economy. If every business operated at full capacity all the time, every businessman would have to raise his price when demand for his product increased (or else operate with a shortage). This would require his customers to raise their prices, and their customers to raise their prices, and so forth. Neither producers nor consumers would be able to make plans based on current prices because any price could rise at a moment's notice. Contracts would be impossible.

If the demand for a consumer good increases, its producers need more materials and may need more workers in order to increase their output. The increase in demand for materials is passed back to the businesses' suppliers, who pass it back to their suppliers, and so forth. Producers draw additional employees from the pools for each particular type of worker required. If each business in the chain of production can produce the increased quantity demanded at about the same average cost, output may rise along the whole chain without any increase in price. This is the typical result of an increase in industry demand when the economy is growing normally.

For example, iron ore is a major factor in the production of steel and steel is a major factor in the production of cars. If the demand for cars increases, the car manufacturers increase their demand for steel and autoworkers. The steel producers in turn increase their demand for iron ore and steelworkers. If the iron ore mining companies can increase their output in a few weeks, or if they have large inventories of iron ore to sell, or if iron ore is available from foreign suppliers at about the same price, the quantity of steel and cars produced can increase with little or no increase in price—if additional workers can be hired at the same wage rates. Thus, the increase in the demand for cars causes an increase in the supply of cars, steel, and iron ore. The average cost of the businesses in these three industries is unchanged because the prices of their factors are unchanged. Since their selling prices are also unchanged, their profit margins per unit are unchanged while they sell more output. Everybody's profits rise.

The chain of cause and effect described above is not unknown in modern economics, but knowledge of it is not widespread either. Most principles of economics texts do not describe it. Alchian and Allen were an exception (1972, pp. 95–97). More recently, Heyne (1997) presented the same example described at greater length in Alchian and Allen.

> [I]magine a sudden and unexpected increase in the demand for hamburger. . . . The first effect will be a depletion of butchers' hamburger inventories. When butchers find their hamburger inventories low and the demand continuing strong, they will increase their orders for beef suitable for grinding. With this happening all over the country, meat packers will in turn find their inventories of beef reduced and will try to buy more cattle. But the increased demand for cattle will encounter, in the short run, a relatively inelastic [supply because the quantity of cattle is relatively fixed over the short run.]…the price of cattle will rise. The packers who must consequently pay more for cattle will increase the price to the butcher . . . (pp. 116-17).

As this example shows, an increased demand may be passed back to an industry that is unable to increase output, either because the industry is operating at full capacity or because the nature of the product does not allow an increase in quantity over a few weeks or months—for example, all commodities, hotel rooms, apartment space, commercial office space, new and used housing, commercial time on television and radio, and so forth. Since these industries are equally unable to decrease supply over the short run (p. 195 below), we will call them cases of fixed supply, although the quantity often is not literally fixed. If the product is a commodity, speculators bid up the price in futures markets. If the product is not a commodity, such as commercial office space, the owner raises his price. In either case, the average cost of the businessmen buying this product increases.

Let us return to the increased demand for cars. If other sources of iron ore do not exist, then businessmen must deal with the fact that the rate at which iron ore is mined (tons per week) cannot be increased right away. To increase the supply, more deposits of iron ore must be discovered and mined, and existing deposits must be mined more intensively, both of which require additional capital investment, additional workers, and time.

Since the steel producers want more iron ore than can be produced, the iron miners raise the price until the quantity the steel producers want to buy equals the quantity that the miners can supply. The increase in the price of iron ore reduces the quantity of iron ore that producers demand for making products other than steel, like cast iron and pig iron. This releases iron ore to the manufacturers of steel who can produce more steel even though the supply of iron ore is fixed. At the same time, the average costs of the steel producers increase due to the increase in the price of iron ore, so the steel producer who goes first in raising his price will be followed. The increase in the price of steel reduces the demand for steel for purposes other than making cars, releasing steel for the manufacture of cars. The net result *in production* is that the manufacture from iron ore of products other than steel goes down, the manufacture from steel of products other than cars goes down, and the manufacture of steel and cars goes up.

The above changes also affect prices and profits.

First, *the effect on prices*: We have seen how the price of steel rises. All the car producers face the same increase in that price. Consequently, the car executive who raises his price first can expect to be followed. Indeed, in this context, he may not care whether he is followed since he is confronted on one side by an increased demand (from customers) and on the other side by an increased cost (from suppliers)—which is also true of the steel producers. The net result is that the increase in the demand for cars causes an increase in the price of iron ore which causes an increase in the price of steel which causes an increase in the price of cars, and prices rise along the whole chain of production.

At the same time, the pools of unemployed iron miners or steelworkers or automobile workers may be small enough that producers have to offer higher wages to employ the workers they need. These higher wages constitute a further increase in average cost for these businessmen and to the extent they occur, cause greater increases in price along the chain of production.[15]

Finally, let us consider *the effect on profits*. Clearly, the profits of the iron ore companies have increased—the whole increase in the demand for cars ends up focused on the demand for iron ore, allowing the mining companies to raise their prices. If they have to offer higher wage rates to their workers, their profits rise less than if higher wages are not necessary.

The effect on the profits of the steel and car producers depends on the price elasticity of the demand for cars. If the demand for cars is very elastic, the increase in price by the car companies may reduce the quantity of cars sold back to the original level. In that case, the number of tons of steel and of cars sold is unchanged (there is no diversion of iron ore and steel from other uses), and the profits of the steel producers and the car manufacturers are unchanged.

For example, suppose three million cars a year are sold for $20,000 each, the average cost is $18,000, and car manufacturers make $2000 per car or $6 million total. Then demand increases to four million a year, average cost rises to $20,000, car manufacturers raise their price to $22,000, and sales fall back to three million a year. The car manufacturers are again making $2000 a car for a total profit of $6 million.

In fact, the demand for cars (and for most products) is not that elastic.[16] The increase in price necessary to maintain the industry's profit margin (covering the increase in the cost of steel and automobile workers) reduces the demand for cars, but the quantity sold is greater than before the increase in demand, increasing the profits of the automobile industry. The same thing is true for the profits of the steel industry for the same reason—the steel producers raise the price of steel to cover the increased cost of iron ore and wages of steelworkers, and an increase in the quantity of steel sold at the same profit margin raises the industry's profits.

Now consider the fact that an automobile manufacturer uses workers of a hundred different types and has thousands of suppliers, direct and indirect, of different parts, materials, tools, and machines, and that an increase in the demand for cars radiates back through all these different businesses and industries just as it radiates back through the steel industry. The steel producers and the iron miners too have their own labor requirements and their own suppliers of parts and tools and materials and equipment. And the suppliers of those parts and tools and materials and equipment have their own employees and suppliers, and so on and so on. The net result of an increase in the demand for cars is to alter the structure of production across a major portion of the economy to make possible an increase in the production of cars.

Over the short run (again, a few weeks or months), an increase in demand for an industry's product(s) raises the price *if average cost rises*, and average cost rises if (1) the increase in demand eventually is focused on a product whose supply cannot increase in the short run, or if (2) the requirements for additional labor can be met only at higher wage rates.

When the supply of a good does not equal the demand

This subject needs separate attention: the effect of an increase in demand on the price of products for which the supply usually does not equal the demand (pp. 44 and 189 above). They include hotel rooms, apartment space, commercial office space, retail space, new and used housing, and land.

Nobody expects a house to sell immediately; if it does, that is reason to think that the asking price was too low. There is a trade-off in selling a house between getting the highest possible price and getting it as soon as possible. The seller is better off the higher the price he can get and the sooner he can get it. But typically, the higher the price he asks, the longer he will have to wait for a buyer. If he asks too high a price, a buyer may never appear. There is no intrinsic price that best balances this trade-off. The home owner and/or the real estate agent make their best estimate given their knowledge of the local housing market.[17]

The going price for hotel rooms usually is not the price at which there are no vacancies. The hotelier wants to maximize his profits, not the number of rooms he rents. The cost of renting an additional room may be close to zero. If that is so, then his profit-maximizing price is the price that maximizes his total revenue. If he has 100 rooms, he may need to charge a price of $50 a night to rent them all ($5,000), while for $100 a night, he can rent 75 ($7,500). The hotelier charges the price that, in his judgment, maximizes his long-run profits—which usually leaves some rooms unsold. Likewise, a free market in apartment rents results in a vacancy rate that averages about 5 percent.

A rise in the demand for housing does not cause an immediate increase in selling prices. Sellers routinely ask higher prices for houses than they expect to receive on the principle that, with thousands of dollars at stake, it is better to ask more and negotiate down than to ask less than a buyer is willing to pay. When demand increases, buyers pay some of these asking prices without quibbling, while negotiated prices also are higher than expected. Real estate brokers make it their business to keep close track of housing prices and, as prices start to rise, they advise their clients to ask higher prices.

In the case of rental housing the effect of an increase in demand is more direct. The landlord finds he is all rented up and he has to turn away potential tenants, some of whom may offer to pay rents higher than he is currently charging. Under such conditions, the benefit of an increase in rent is obvious, and the landlord who raises his rent first is quickly followed. The increase in rents spreads throughout the rental housing market, so that even landlords with vacancies decide that an increase in rents will increase their long-run profits.

Hoteliers raise the price of their hotel rooms when demand increases for the same reason. A higher demand means that their guests are willing, sometimes eager, to pay the higher price, and a higher price means more profit to the hotel.

2. An increase in demand unique to the businessman

Suppose a businessman has been doing an excellent job for his customers, providing prompt deliveries, good service, and high quality products. Along with his rising reputation, his customer base is expanding. As in the case of a general increase in sales for an industry, the businessman will expand production to meet the increase in demand. However, in this case, the increased demand for labor and materials by a single firm (rather than an industry) is less likely to cause an increase in the price of the factors the business needs.

If the prices of his factors do not rise, the businessman can go on increasing output with constant average cost until he approaches capacity, when average cost starts to rise for the reasons discussed in chapter 6 (p. 106). However, even then, the businessman might not raise his price; he does not want to drive away his new customers. The increase in demand is the businessman's reward for his superior work. The way to capitalize on that reward is not with a rising price and an immediate increase in profits. The way to capitalize on it is by using the increase in demand as the base for a permanent expansion in scale. Thus the businessman is likely to absorb the higher costs, queue up his customers, and work to expand his productive capacity as rapidly as possible (Silberston 1970, 569; Haddock and McChesney 1994, 567). The increase in long-run profits achieved by the latter policy normally will greatly exceed the profits from simply raising price.

B. Decreases in Demand

1. An industry-wide decrease in demand

Businessmen experience a decrease in demand as a decrease in the quantity sold at the current price. Sales are rarely absolutely steady over a week or a month, so it may take some time for a businessman to realize that he has suffered a real reduction in demand. When he does, he reduces output to equal the decreased quantity sold.

a) When all industries in the chain of production are able to reduce supply

To produce the lower level of output, the businessman needs a smaller quantity of materials and often a smaller number of employees as well. The decrease in demand for materials is passed back to the businessman's suppliers, who pass it back to their suppliers, and so forth. For ex-

ample, a decrease in the demand for cars is passed back as a decrease in
the demand for steel from the steel producers, who reduce their demand
for iron ore. If the steel producers and the iron ore producers are able to
reduce the quantity they produce to meet the decrease in quantity demanded, output may fall along the whole chain of production with no decrease in price. At the same time, the businesses in the chain earn decreased profits or losses due to the lower quantity sold. This is a common
experience for businesses entering a recession.

If, at the same time, the automobile producers lay off some autoworkers and the steel producers lay off some steelworkers and the iron
ore producers lay off some iron ore miners, the pools of unemployed
workers for each of these different types of employee will rise. These rising pools of unemployed workers mean that employers can offer to pay
lower wages and employees may offer to take lower wages. This reduces
the producers' average costs and reduces their losses.

We saw above (part II) that decreases in price usually reduce profits.
Nevertheless, when demand decreases, and particularly in recessions, we
frequently observe competitive reductions in price by businessmen. The
iron ore producers, facing a decreased demand and reduced wage costs,
may cut the price of iron ore to the steel producers. The steel producers,
also facing a decreased demand, reduced wages costs, and now a decrease in the price of iron ore, may compete down the price of steel to the
car companies. The decrease in the price of steel and decrease in the
wage rates of autoworkers reduces the average cost of the car companies,
who may start offering rebates, interest free loans, and other forms of gi-
vebacks that reduce the price of their cars. The decreased price of cars
reduces the fall in quantity sold by the car companies which reduces the
decrease in demand for steel which reduces the decrease in demand for
iron ore. Thus, wage and price reductions reduce average cost, which
leads businessmen to compete down their prices, which reduces the decrease in output along the chain of production, which reduces the number
of workers laid off. The decrease in output caused by the decrease in demand is minimized.

b) When an industry in the chain of production is unable to reduce
   supply

Alternatively, the decrease in demand may be passed back to an industry
that is unable to decrease quantity in the short run (within a few weeks).
In addition to the products listed above (p. 189), this includes perishable
items like strawberries, fish, and passenger seats in mass transportation

(after the plane takes off, an empty seat on that flight can never be sold). For these products, price-setters are likely to compete down their prices in the face of a demand for less than the quantity they have available to sell. For example, in the summer of 2001, most of the TV networks reduced their advertising rates for the 2001–2002 season. The economy was in recession, the demand for advertising time had fallen, and they expected the decrease in demand to continue into the fall (*New York Times*, June 26, 2001, p. C1). In the 2007–2009 recession, wine wholesalers, who distribute wine to restaurants and retail stores, demanded and received price cuts from the winemakers (*New York Times*, February 17, 2010, p. D7).

If the product in fixed supply is sold at a brokered price in a commodity market, then a decrease in demand will cause the price to fall until the quantity buyers want to buy equals the quantity sellers want to sell.[18] For example, wheat is the chief ingredient in the manufacture of flour and flour is a major ingredient in the manufacture of bread. A decrease in the demand for bread from bakers reduces the demand by bakers for flour from millers, which reduces the demand for wheat in commodity markets—specifically in the cash (or spot) market for current delivery—and the price falls until the demand for wheat equals the supply.

At the same time, the bakers and millers may be laying off some of their employees, increasing their respective pools of workers, making it possible to offer lower wages to the employees they retain. The decrease in the price of wheat combined with the decrease in wage rates lowers the average cost of the millers. The millers then may lower the price of flour to the bakers, and the bakers may lower the price of bread to consumers.

Part II, B suggested this would happen. In that case, however, the businesses were making profits before the decrease in average cost and the decrease raised their profits to above normal levels. The context here is different. The initial decrease in demand from consumers reduces the profits of the bakers. Then the decrease in demand from the bakers reduces the profits of the millers. A decrease in the millers' average cost mitigates the fall in their profits, but if they cut their prices, that further reduces their profits or magnifies their losses. Thus, we would expect the millers to resist a decrease in price.[19]

All of the preceding is true of the bakers as well. The wage rates of bakers' workers may fall and the millers may reduce the price of flour to the bakers. Even so, the bakers may resist lowering their prices to avoid reducing their profits. Alternatively, the bakers may compete down their prices in pursuit of revenue to cover their fixed costs. There certainly is no guarantee that decreases in cost will cause prices to fall along the whole chain of production. *There does not seem to be any basis for predicting the effect on prices of a decrease in demand in the short run.*

The decrease in demand for bread means that there are quantities of wheat and flour previously consumed in the production of bread that are no longer needed for that purpose. In their pursuit of profits, businessmen quickly rectify such conditions. Although we have treated the supply of wheat in the cash market as fixed (p. 189 above), it is actually only semi-fixed. Speculators buy wheat at the lower price to hold in storage, hoping to sell at a higher price in the future. The fall in price also increases the quantity of wheat demanded by businesses for purposes other than making flour, such as feeding cattle or making beer. If the price of flour decreases, that decrease raises the quantity of flour demanded by businesses for purposes other than baking bread. The net result is that (1) some wheat is stored for future sale; (2) the use of wheat for purposes other than grinding flour goes up; (3) the use of flour for making products other than bread goes up; (4) the production of flour and bread goes down.

Regardless of what happens to the millers and the bakers, the major loss in profits here is on the part of the wheat farmers, who experience a decrease in price with very little offsetting decrease in the cost of materials or the wage rates of workers. The farmers of almost all other crops also use the materials and workers used by wheat farmers. Thus, the decrease in demand for fertilizer or pesticides by wheat farmers is unlikely to have much effect on the price; they are too small a portion of the total demand. The wage rates of farm workers also are unlikely to decrease much for the same reason.[20]

c) When the supply of a good usually does not equal the demand

A fall in the demand for housing does not cause an immediate decrease in asking prices. Rather, the decreased demand first is reflected in an increase in the number of houses for sale and a longer average time span between when a house first appears on the market and when it is sold. The number of houses and the time span then diminish over time as sellers come to accept the necessity of reducing their asking prices—a process that may take several years.

When the demand for housing falls, eventually the asking price for houses also falls. When the demand for rental apartments falls, landlords ask for lower rents or stop raising their rents. When the demand for hotel rooms falls, hoteliers lower their prices. But in none of these cases does the price fall to the point that no houses, no apartments, and no hotel rooms are available. The markets for these products are like the markets for workers in that there is almost always a pool of hotel rooms for rent, a pool of apartments for rent, and a pool of houses for sale.

2. A decrease in demand unique to the businessman

Suppose a businessman has been doing an inferior job, providing poor service while producing a low quality product. In such cases, the businessman is very likely to suffer a decrease in demand to which he may respond by laying off some workers and cutting his price. The businessman sees the price reduction as necessary to maintain his market share while he does something, if he can, about his decline relative to his competitors. The price reduction also may be necessary to bring the price into line with the reduced quality of the business's product. Under these conditions, usually the businessman can reduce his price without fear of retaliation from his competitors because they are unlikely to regard the price reduction as a threat to their sales or profits. Their attitude will be, "Acme Enterprises has to cut their price because they are doing so poorly. We don't need to do that." And they don't. In 1997, in the face of a declining share of the market, McDonald's cut the price of their sandwiches to 55¢ each. At the same time, Burger King was charging $2.99 for a meal. Burger King ignored McDonald's price reductions and McDonald's soon gave them up (*The Wall Street Journal*, June 4, 1997, p. B7).

IV. Long-Run Results

Now let us consider the long-run results of the changes in price we analyzed above, focusing on the response to industry-wide changes in average cost and demand.

A. When the Rate of Profit Rises

We have seen two causes of an increase in industry profits: (1) a fall in the average cost of production; (2) an increase in demand for the industry's product.

   If an increase in industry profits raises the rate of profit on investment sufficiently above the average rate in the economy, additional capital flows into that industry. The established companies reinvest their profits in additional plant and equipment, new entrepreneurs enter the industry looking for a high rate of return, and businesses acquire human and nonhuman factors of all kinds to support the new enterprises. Over time, the total productive capacity of the industry expands and the quantity supplied to the market increases. This may take a year, two years, or more—(seven years to build a new oil refinery, twelve to fifteen years to build a nuclear power plant)—depending primarily on the time it takes to construct and install the capital equipment needed to produce the industry's output.

The first businessman to get additional capacity up and running must lower his price in order to sell the extra quantity he puts on the market, and his competitors have to match his price reduction. As additional businessmen continue to produce additional output, they may have to offer higher wage rates to workers and/or pay higher prices for nonhuman factors, and they must continually reduce the price of their output in order to sell a greater quantity. This goes on until the industry's price has fallen to the point, or the prices of factors have risen to the point, or some combination of both, that the rate of profit on investment in the industry no longer attracts additional capital.

If the increased profits are focused on an industry with a short-run fixed supply, then the additions to capital begin in that industry. For example, in the iron ore industry, mining companies purchase new heavy machinery and equipment; they hire additional workers to operate the new equipment; they invest resources in finding new deposits of iron ore; they mine existing deposits more intensively; they start mining deposits which at lower prices were too poor to be mined profitably; and they hire additional workers to do all these things. In the cattle ranching industry, cattlemen expand their herds, entrepreneurs start up new cattle ranches, and both of them hire additional workers. In the wheat farming industry, wheat farmers plant more acres of wheat and new wheat farmers appear.

The resulting increases in supply can only be sold at lower prices, so over time the rate of profit on investment falls, even if the prices of the human and nonhuman factors of production do not increase. At the same time, businessmen who are customers of the expanding industry can see what is happening in the iron ore industry or in cattle ranching or in wheat farming. They can anticipate rising profits for their businesses as the result of falling prices for the factors they buy from these industries. New investment in steel does not have to wait for the price of iron ore to fall. Eventually, capital flows into all the industries in the chain of production. The process stops when all the industries have expanded to the point that prices have fallen to the point that the rate of return on investment no longer attracts additional capital.

Two general conclusions follow from this: (1) Whether or not businessmen cut their prices when average cost falls, the rate of profit rises. Consequently, over the long run, capital flows into the industry, supply increases, prices fall, and the rate of profit falls back toward its original level. The long-run effect on price depends on whether the industry is an increasing, decreasing, or constant cost industry (pp. 178–79 above). If average cost increases with increases in industry output, the long-run price will be higher than the original price. If average cost decreases, the long-run price will be lower. If average cost is constant, the long-run price will be the same as the original price. The important conclusion for understanding how the economy works is that there is a profit motive for businessmen to increase the supply of a product when its cost of production falls.

(2) Whether or not businessmen raise price in response to an increase in demand, the rate of profit rises. Consequently, the long-run result is the same as when average cost falls. When their customers increase their demand for products, businessmen increase their profits by increasing the supply.

B. When the Rate of Profit Falls

We saw above that when average cost rises in an industry, businessmen raise the price of their products and their profits fall. We also saw that when demand decreases, the price may or may not fall, but profits fall along the whole chain of production if there is no factor in fixed supply. If there are factors in fixed supply, the decrease in demand is focused on the businesses producing those factors. Their profits decline, and probably also the profits of the businesses to whom they sell (pp. 195–96).

If a recession causes the decrease in demand, demand recovers when the recession ends and the industry goes on as before. In an economy experiencing price inflation, if there is an increase in average cost, businesses often can raise their selling price and maintain their profits.[21] However, if a decrease in demand is not caused by a recession or average cost rises when businesses cannot raise their selling prices, the resulting decrease in profits causes long-run changes in the industry.

These conditions characterize a declining industry. All or most of the businesses are losing money, or if they are making profits, the profits are too low to justify the investment necessary to maintain the businesses' plant and equipment. Under these circumstances, capital flows out of the industry. The least efficient businesses, the businesses making the greatest losses, go bankrupt. The capital of other businesses shrinks, their capital goods deteriorate, and they reduce their work force. Still other businesses sell off their plant and equipment and invest their capital elsewhere. The resulting decrease in productive capacity eventually reduces the total quantity offered for sale. This will take some time, but normally, much less time than is required to construct and install capital equipment when an industry is growing (p. 198 above).

The decrease in total quantity allows the remaining businesses to raise their prices, and in this context, there is no question that higher prices will raise their profits (or reduce their losses). Supply has decreased because businesses have left the industry and the customers of those businesses have to buy from the businesses that remain. Thus, the remaining businessmen can sell the same quantity they were selling before at a higher price—the price necessary to reduce demand to equal the reduced supply. This process continues until the price has risen to the point that the remaining businesses are making a rate of profit sufficient to maintain their capital—in an industry shrunken in size.

If the decreased profits are focused on an industry with a short-run fixed supply, then the withdrawal of capital begins in that industry. For example, the least productive iron ore mines close down and the least efficient producers go out of business; or some cattlemen go bankrupt while others reduce the size of their cattle herds; or some wheat farmers sell their farms to developers while others plant crops other than wheat. The resulting decline in supplies allows the remaining producers to raise their prices or, in the case of wheat, causes speculators to bid up the price in commodity markets. The increase in price reduces the losses of the producers that remain.

At the same time, the customers of these businesses are already losing money from the same decrease in demand or rise in average cost that depressed their suppliers. Now they have to anticipate further losses as the result of rising prices for the factors they buy from those same suppliers. They do not have to wait for their costs to increase to begin disinvesting. Eventually, capital flows out of all the industries in the chain of production. The process stops when the industries and their output have shrunk enough, and prices have risen enough, that the businessmen remaining in those industries are making a rate of profit sufficient to maintain their capital.

There is no guarantee that this point will be reached. The decrease in demand may be so severe and/or so protracted that there is no quantity the industry can sell at a profit. In that case, the product and the industry disappear, as has happened to many industries since the Industrial Revolution—for example, the industries that produced sailing ships, horses, harnesses, carriages, steam engines, dirigibles, plows, scythes, kerosene, kerosene lamps, milk bottles, ice boxes, wood-burning stoves, typewriters, radios, and so forth. Some of these things are still produced, but not in an industry.

Again, two general conclusions follow: (1) If an increase in average cost significantly reduces profits or creates losses, capital flows out of the industry over the long run, supply decreases, prices rise, and the rate of profit rises until the remaining firms can maintain their capital. The long-run effect on price depends on what happens to average cost as output shrinks. The important conclusion for understanding how the economy works is that when the average cost of a product rises, there is a profit motive for businessmen to reduce its supply.

(2) A decrease in demand for a product reduces industry profits. Consequently, the long-run result is the same as for a rise in average cost. The important conclusion for understanding the economy is that when the demand for a product declines, there is a profit motive for businessmen to reduce its supply.

Comment on the preceding in relation to modern economics

Much of the long-run adjustment process of industrial expansion and contraction described above is well known to economists. However, the theory on which their knowledge is based (appendices A and B) has no counterpart in the real world. Consequently, modern economists have no way to explain, and many do not believe, that high rates of profit lead to increases in output, falling prices, and falling profits (and the reverse for losses).

The theory of objective prices explains prices by focusing on the processing of the facts by the mind of an individual human being. *Men's economic actions flow from their understanding of the economic facts*—that is the principle underlying the theory of objective prices. Unusually profitable industries and unusually unprofitable industries present facts that must be faced by the people in those industries, facts that pertain directly to their immediate, economic self-interest—facts which businessmen are eager to grasp in the context of high profits, and facts which they dare not evade in the context of losses. Since men generally do face the facts when their immediate self-interest is directly and obviously at stake, we can conclude that the process of adjustment described above applies to the industries of a capitalist economy that are making high profits or losses.

V. Changes in Competition

Chapter 3 defined economic competition as "the activity of two or more businesses pursuing the same customers' dollars by offering the highest values in exchange." A change in competition is a change in this activity of *value-offering*. A change in competition means a change in the competitive effort exerted by businessmen, a change in the energy, thought, and sense of purpose with which businessmen *act* to create higher values to offer, including the money they commit to research and development. As chapter 3 said, "The issue is how hard they are working and succeeding at offering higher values" (p. 58).

Competitive effort implies an intention and then the corresponding thought and action to achieve the intended result. Competitive effort can be directed at figuring out the long-run, profit-maximizing price, working out a pricing strategy, doing customer research, lowering the business's average costs, improving the business's product, conducting an advertising campaign, identifying competitors' costs, prices, and pricing strategy, and many other things. The two primary forms of competition are price competition and quality competition.

A. An Increase in Competition

1. Price competition

A businessman engages in price competition when he initiates a price reduction, or when he does not raise his price when other businessmen are raising theirs, or when he raises his price less than other businessmen raise theirs, or when he cuts price to meet a price reduction by a competitor. But a businessman also is engaged in price competition when neither he nor his competitors are changing their prices. Price competition does not require continuously lowering prices. If it did, there would be no price competition, because a continuously declining price is absurd on its face. The absence of a price war does not mean that there is no price competition.

Every day, businessmen engage in price competition by keeping their prices within range of their competitors' prices and at a level that reflects the relative quality of their products. A policy of meeting competitors' prices, of underpricing competitors, of not allowing anybody to charge less ("We will not be undersold!"), or even of being the high-priced (and high-quality) supplier—each of these is a commitment to continuous competitive action, whether the price is changed or not.

From a different perspective, continuous action is required to keep costs down, and a businessman requires the lowest possible costs if he is to offer his products at competitive prices. The competitive pressure on businessmen to reduce costs means that every day, average cost is as low as the businessman can make it. This means that the price he charges is also as low as possible—that is, as low as is consistent with long-run profits sufficient to maintain his capital—which means as low as is consistent with continued production of the product. For an industry, prices and profits above that level are short run, the result of an industry-wide decrease in costs or increase in demand (pp. 198–99 above).

Now consider what happens to price when price competition increases. When a businessman achieves significantly lower costs than his competitors and cuts his price to increase his market share (p. 187 above), there is a clear change in purpose and an increase in the intensity of price competition. The producer intends to drive other businesses from the market and thus increase his sales and long-run profits.

Another clear case of increased price competition is a price war. A price war often throws the competitors into a whirlpool of falling prices from which nearly everyone loses. Perhaps for this reason, in today's economies, price wars usually seem to originate in some irrationality by one of the warring parties and are infrequent. By contrast, in the early 19th century (roughly 1825–1840), price wars were virtually continuous between competing steamboat companies plying New York Harbor and the Hudson River (Renehan 2007, 121–38). It is certain that price wars would be much more frequent in a laissez-faire economy than they are now under the threat of antitrust prosecution.

Now, consider the charge of "dog-eat-dog" or "cutthroat" or "destructive" competition. An individual businessman sometimes makes this complaint when he is being beaten by a superior competitor. More often, it is voiced by business owners when all or most of the businesses in the industry are losing money. The implication is that they are losing money because the competition is too intense.

There are three reasons that most of the businesses in an industry may be losing money: (1) There has been an increase in the industry's cost of production; (2) There has been a decrease in demand for the industry's product; or (3) Too many businessmen have invested in the industry in pursuit of above average profits. Losses by businessmen may spur more intense competition, but that is not the cause of the losses. The cause is that, under the existing demand conditions, the total quantity the industry has to sell can only be sold at a price below average cost. The reason these businessmen are losing money is the law of demand, not competition. The closest thing to dog-eat-dog and cutthroat competition are price wars, which are infrequent and good for customers while they last.

2. Quality competition

An increase in quality competition takes the form of product innovation. Quality competition is much more important than price competition. Quality competition is the source of new and improved goods and services. Consequently, it is the source of economic growth and a rising standard of living over time—the leading characteristics of a capitalist economy.

Producer sovereignty

The beginning of this chapter stressed that businessmen usually do not wait to act until their costs or demand change (p. 175 above). Changes in the structure of production normally do not originate with changes in demand by consumers. Capitalism is a producer-driven economic system, and the sweeping changes in production and consumption that characterize its history originate with and are created by the producers. It is the producers who create a continuous, relentless, and constantly increasing flow of new and better products. It is the producers who grasp and create all the changes in the structure of production that are necessary to produce and market those new and better products. Furthermore, a great portion of those new products are producer goods (new machines, tools, equipment, parts, materials, ingredients, factories, office buildings, and so forth). The customers for these goods are other producers.

When the customer is the consumer, his role is essentially passive. He does not create; he does not initiate; he does not change anything. He only responds; he says "yes" or "no." This is all there is to so-called "consumer sovereignty"—no consumer good can succeed if consumers refuse to buy it. But most of the objective values that flow from the creative energy of the economy's entrepreneurs eventually are welcomed by consumers as additions to their economic welfare. They say "yes." Even then, that "yes" sometimes is reluctant and occurs only after the producers have invested money, time, and effort in educating consumers about the virtues of new and unfamiliar goods and services. All the initiative is on the producers' side. At root, capitalism is a system of producer sovereignty, not consumer sovereignty (Rand 1966, 18).

As a system of producer sovereignty, production comes first in a capitalist system. In every market, both buyers and sellers are producers. Children and people living on charity are exceptions. The seller must produce in order to have something to sell. The buyer must produce in order to acquire the means to buy. If the buyer borrows his means, the loan is based on either his past production (collateral) or his future production (income).

Logically, production must come before consumption. One cannot consume what has not been produced. Capitalism enacts and enforces this principle by granting men the ability to consume to the precise extent of their production. Chapter 9 showed that men's wages and salaries reflect the relative scarcity of their work. The employees in a capitalist economy receive income and the ability to consume in exact proportion to the value of their production, as estimated by their employers, who chose to pay them their scarcity value. A man's wage is the objective measure of his productive contribution.[22]

Now let us consider the effect of quality competition on price. When an entrepreneur innovates a significantly improved version of an industry product, he may increase his price, whether or not his costs have increased. The quality improvement will prevent the loss of customers. The higher quality may even attract new customers, despite the increase in price. In any case, the entrepreneur need not worry about what competing firms will do. The quality improvement gives him a decisive competitive advantage. Competing firms may do nothing, or they may try to remain competitive by cutting their prices.

Alternatively, the innovating entrepreneur may keep his price unchanged, or even reduce it, in order to maximize the increase in his market. In that case, his competitors are under much greater pressure to reduce their prices, even though that decreases or eliminates their profits. The writing is on the wall for these businessmen. Their only hope to stay in business is to look for some way to match their competitor's innovation.

For the above reasons, innovating entrepreneurs make above-normal profits, often greatly in excess of what is required to maintain their capital. As long as the innovation represents a superior product, nothing in a free market can take those profits away—except that a free market is characterized by continuing innovation and competitors usually surpass any specific product improvement relatively quickly. To keep his above-average rate of profit, the entrepreneur cannot just innovate, he must *repeatedly* innovate—he must continually improve his products faster than his competitors (Reisman 1998, 176). The businessman who can do that can make above-average profits indefinitely. Consequently, high rates of profit are often associated with high rates of innovation.

Quality competition increases when innovation increases, when businessmen offer new and better products more frequently. Quality competition is most intense in those industries where new and better products are offered at the greatest rate. These include many industries that economists frequently have attacked as monopolistic, such as pharmaceuticals, automobiles, and computers. Such attacks are perverse; they can be understood only as delusions caused by a false economic theory (perfect competition) and a worse ethical theory (altruism) (appendix B).

Quality competition includes the introduction of entirely new products, like steamboats, trains, automobiles, electricity, radio, television, computers, and information technology.[23] World-changing products like these typically require the creation of an entirely new primary industry plus a whole network of supporting industries throughout the economy. Consequently, the introduction of significant new products is usually gradual, taking a decade or longer to be integrated into the economy. The course of prices over this period cannot be predicted with certainty, but we can observe that historically, innovating entrepreneurs have continuously reduced their prices in order to maximize the rate of expansion of their market. Henry Ford's role in the automobile industry is the outstanding example.

Innovation on the level described in the preceding paragraph is not motivated by competition. The man who creates a whole new product or industry is not competing with anyone. He is out there alone, recreating the world in the image of his own values and vision. His motive is best understood in the terms of the youthful idealist. He wants to "change the world," to do something great, to reshape the earth to reflect the one that he sees in his mind. These are the men of exalted vision; pride is their leading virtue. To a great extent, the history of capitalism is their history—the history of the great men who, in changing the world to bring their ideas into reality, transformed the lives of their fellow men.

B. A Decrease in Competition

A decrease in competition in any industry, in whatever form, is an invitation to outside entrepreneurs to profit. If prices drift upward over time because of a loss of focus and a consequent loss of efficiency, if businessmen adopt a policy of live and let live, an ambitious newcomer can take over the market by producing with low costs and charging low prices. If the rate of innovation slows down or stops, any entrepreneur who will innovate can take substantially all the business. In both these cases, the laggard businessmen's only hope is to cut their prices while they totally reform their management.

For example, in the 1950s and 60s, the banks in a southern city enjoyed a comfortable status quo with comfortable profits and a tacit understanding not to hire each other's employees. An outside businessman grasped the profit potential in the situation, bought one of the banks for twice what the management thought it was worth, and proceeded to make profits—and to make the competitive environment the opposite of comfortable.

VI. Conclusion

This chapter has shown how businessmen change prices in response to changes in cost, demand, and competition. In addition to adding to our understanding of how the economy works, this application of the theory of objective prices is additional evidence for its validity—that prices are set by human beings based on their grasp of the relevant economic facts.

For industry-wide changes, we have seen that competition is the active cause of falling prices when average costs fall (p. 186 above). In addition, if the price falls when demand falls, often the cause is falling average costs and the price falls because businessmen compete down the price (p. 194 above). Competition is also the reason that an individual businessman does not raise his price if average cost for the industry has *not* increased—if he raised his price, he would lose customers to his competitors. Demand, cost, and competition are interdependent in their effects on price. For most businessmen, competition is the active, motivating force. For the great creators among them, the motivating force is pride.

The understanding reached in this chapter also allows us to begin to grasp the role of supply and demand in changing prices. We now can see more clearly why the law of supply and demand in its traditional interpretation is weak. That interpretation is that prices always change in some specific, predictable way when either supply or demand changes. That is not true.

The law of supply and demand says that when industry supply increases, the price falls and when industry supply decreases, the price rises (pp. 198–201 above). That is true, but it is because of the law of demand. Larger quantities can only be sold at lower prices and smaller quantities can be sold for higher prices.

The law of supply and demand also says that increases in demand cause increases in price and decreases in demand cause decreases in price. That is not true. When demand increases, businessmen do not raise their prices if they can increase supply to meet the increased demand. When demand decreases, businessmen do not cut their prices if they can reduce supply to meet the decreased demand.

However, there is an important connection between changes in price and changes in the relation of supply to demand. As an introduction, we can express that relation in each of the following three equivalent statements.

(1) If businessmen cannot increase the supply of a product to equal an increase in demand, they raise the price. If they cannot reduce the supply of a product to equal a decrease in demand, they cut the price.

(2) Businessmen raise the price of a product when the demand for the product increases relative to the supply. Businessmen reduce the price of a product when the demand decreases relative to the supply.

(3) The price of a product increases when the product's relative scarcity increases. The price of a product decreases when the product's relative scarcity decreases.

As a first approximation, relative scarcity is the quantity demanded relative to the quantity supplied. Prices are a measure of relative scarcity. Products with higher prices are relatively more scarce than products with lower prices.

Chapter 12 has much more to say about the meaning of relative scarcity and its relation to price. For now, let us note that the case for holding that prices are a measure of relative scarcity is far from complete. Chapter 9 showed that wage rates measure the relative scarcity of the employees who receive those wages. The analysis of this chapter pertains only to set prices. We have yet to consider the cases of changes in negotiated prices, sealed bid prices, auction prices and brokered prices. Those cases are the subject of chapter 11. There we continue with the main theme of this chapter, the implications of the theory of objective prices for how prices change. We also continue with the two themes this conclusion has introduced: 1) the role of supply and demand in the theory of objective prices, and 2) prices as a measure of relative scarcity.

CHAPTER ELEVEN

CHANGES IN OBJECTIVE PRICES II
THE EFFECT OF CHANGES IN
FACTS ON OTHER PRICES

I. Negotiated Prices

When the facts change, there are three differences between the effect on negotiated prices and the effect on set prices.

1. The idea of an industry price structure is fuzzier for negotiated prices because businesses negotiate different prices with different customers. An individual business's price has to be thought of as an average price and the price structure as an array of the average prices of all the businesses in the industry.

2. The relative bargaining skill of the negotiators is an additional factor affecting a change in negotiated prices. Consequently, when a new business with a new negotiator enters a growing industry (or the reverse for a declining industry), there may be a greater change in negotiated prices compared to set prices under the same circumstances.

3. The most important difference is that there is no announced price for a product, so no businessman can go first in announcing a price increase or decrease. Consequently, negotiated prices differ from set prices in how prices change.

In what follows, we will suppose that Ohio Machine produces machine tools and negotiates the price with its customers, on the premise that the results in the machine-tool industry can be extended to other industries where prices are negotiated.

A. Changes in Average Cost

1. An increase in average cost

Imagine that the producers of machine tools need a specialized metal to produce their products and the price of that metal increases. As time goes by, knowledge of the increase in cost becomes general in the industry. All the producers feel pressure to negotiate higher prices to maintain their profit margins, and they know that every other producer feels the same pressure. At some point, a customer who refuses to negotiate a higher price with Ohio Machine finds that the next producer also is resolved to negotiate a higher price. Eventually, this resolve becomes general and higher prices are negotiated across the board.

2. A decrease in average cost

After a cost decrease, the machine tool firms feel less pressure to negotiate high prices because their profits are still high at lower prices. The company which goes first in negotiating lower prices creates pressure on others also to negotiate lower prices as news of falling prices is spread by their customers. If Ohio Machine continues to push for the previous prices, the company will lose contracts to competitors who settle for less. As we saw with set prices, if negotiated prices fall after a cost decrease, the cause is competition.

The indirect procedure by which negotiated prices change implies that, compared to set prices, negotiated prices change more slowly when average costs change. Blinder and others (1998) found a great range of time lags between changes in cost and changes in price—from immediate changes in price to lags of a year or more (p. 87). I hypothesize that longer lags are more likely for industries with negotiated prices.

B. Changes in demand

1. An increase in demand

It is possible that negotiated prices rise faster than set prices in response to an industry-wide increase in demand. We have seen that businessmen who set their prices increase output without raising price until they approach capacity. However, the bargaining power of companies who negotiate their prices is affected by their capacity utilization independently of rising average cost.

For example, an increase in the demand for machine tools may increase the capacity utilization of Ohio Machine sufficiently to increase the company's bargaining power before its average costs begin to rise. In general, allowing for negotiated prices may mean that prices increase sooner and therefore average cost increases sooner along the chains of production described in chapter 10. If this is true, then Ohio Machine's prices will rise more rapidly than if its prices were set, when demand increases.

In addition, as we saw with set prices, the effect of an increase in demand on price depends on whether the machine tool companies are able to increase their output to meet the increase in demand. If they are, then the relative scarcity of the product is unaffected and the price does not change. If demand increases, and the industry is not able to increase supply, then businessmen will negotiate higher prices reflecting the increase in relative scarcity.

2. A decrease in demand

By the same argument, a decrease in demand for machine tools lowers the capacity utilization of Ohio Machine, undermining the company's bargaining power. This may cause faster price reductions and faster decreases in average cost along the chain of production than in the case of set prices, so that a decrease in demand for machine tools leads to a more rapid decrease in their prices.

If demand decreases and the businesses in the industry are unable to decrease supply to meet the decreased demand, then they are under competitive pressure to negotiate lower prices. The decrease in prices reflects the decrease in relative scarcity.

C. Long-Run Results

1. An increase in supply

Chapter 10 showed that long-run changes in price in an industry are caused by changes in supply—increases in supply if the businesses in the industry are unusually profitable, decreases in supply if the businesses in the industry are losing money. In an industry where prices are negotiated, an increase in market supply puts pressure on sellers to negotiate lower prices. First, the law of demand means that lower prices are necessary to sell the increased supply. Second, sellers' negotiating positions are undercut by additional sources of output from old and new competitors. Third, capacity utilization decreases as some of a business's customers patronize those new sources of supply. The negotiating position of the buyers is improved by these same changes. An increase in supply lowers negotiated prices, just as it lowers set prices.

2. A decrease in supply

When market supply decreases, the smaller supply can be sold for higher prices. In addition, businesses leaving the industry reduce the sources of supply and increase the capacity utilization of those remaining. Thus, the bargaining power of the sellers increases, that of the buyers declines and negotiated prices rise.

3. Conclusion

If the firms in an industry are making unusually high profits, the long-run effect on prices is the same, whether someone sets the price or negotiates the price. Capital flows into the industry, total capacity rises, supply increases and prices and profits fall. The long-run effect on prices of losses also is the same: Capital flows out of the industry, productive capacity falls, supply falls, and prices rise; losses diminish and are replaced by profits.

II. Sealed Bid Prices

A. Changes in Average Cost

1. Industry-wide changes in average cost

An increase in the average cost of contractors raises sealed bid prices because, like all other businessmen, contractors have to make a profit over the long run to stay in business. An industry-wide decrease in average cost reduces sealed bid prices because competing contractors have to lower their bids in order to have a chance to win the contract.

2. A change in average cost unique to the contractor

If a contractor tries to submit higher bids to cover an increase in his average cost, he is unlikely to win any contracts, because his competitors' bids will reflect the fact that they do not have higher costs to cover. On the other hand, a decrease in average cost may enable a contractor to win contracts and make profits by submitting bids on which his competitors would lose money.

B. Changes in Demand

A change in demand unique to a contractor is not a meaningful idea.

An industry-wide change in demand

The meanings of demand, supply, and price are different in the context of industry-wide changes in demand for construction projects. The relevant concept of demand in this context is the total value of the construction projects that builders want to undertake over some time period (let us say a year). The total value of construction projects includes projects already under construction and projects currently put out for bid. We have to conceive of this value as measured by an amount of money, even though for any individual project, that amount is not precise until someone wins the bid.

The relevant concept of price in this market is the *average* percentage markup over cost of all the winning bids—that is, the *average* percent the winning contractors add to their bids to contribute to their overhead and profit. If Jones adds seven percent, Smith adds ten percent, and Anderson adds thirteen percent, the price is the average of these three markups, that is, ten percent. If the price is ten percent and the contractor's cost is $100 million, then the winning bid would be $110 million. The higher the average percentage markup, the higher is the cost to the builder of any individual project. Thus, an increase in the average percentage markup reduces the demand by builders for construction projects because it increases the total cost of each project. Similarly, a decrease in the average percentage markup reduces the total cost of each project and increases the demand by builders for construction projects. This is the law of demand in the context of construction projects.

Supply consists of the total capacity to build projects of all the contractors in the construction industry. Suppose at full capacity, one contractor can handle projects worth $100 million, another can handle $85 million, another can handle $130 million, and so forth. The total supply of the industry is the total value of all the projects that all the contractors can handle at full capacity—for example, $1,500 million.

Chapter 7 showed that one of the important facts affecting contractors' choices of what to bid is the current rate of capacity utilization, both the contractor's own rate and his estimate of his competitors' rates. Other things equal, low rates of capacity utilization result in lower bids and high rates result in higher bids. In the construction industry, changes in supply and demand first affect capacity utilization, and then the price.

For example, an increase in the total value of construction projects builders want to undertake is an increase in demand. It causes an increase in the industry's capacity utilization and as a consequence contractors add higher markup percentages to their bids—that is, the price rises. At the same time, contractors increase their demand for the factors necessary to carry out the increased projects. Those factors whose supply cannot be increased over a few weeks or months rise in price, raising the costs of contractors, further raising the average winning bid (though not the price) and reducing the demand for construction projects in the future. A decrease in demand has the opposite effects.

C. Long-Run Results

A decrease in costs or an increase in demand will increase profits in the construction industry, just as in other industries, and the long-run consequences are the same. If profits are high enough to attract new capital, existing firms will expand and new firms will enter, increasing the total capacity of the industry (supply), decreasing the rate of capacity utilization, lowering the average winning markup, and over time lowering the industry's profits. An increase in costs or a decrease in demand will reduce profits with opposite long-run effects.

Over the long run, a rough relation exists between the capacity required for the projects builders want to build (demand) and the capacity of contractors to build projects (supply). If supply exceeds demand by too great an amount, some contractors will not get enough work to stay in business.

D. Changes in Competition

1. Price competition

The intensity of price competition in a sealed bid context reflects the factors identified in chapter 7 (p. 127)—primarily the rate of capacity utilization.

2. Quality competition

A contractor with a superior reputation can win a contract with a bid that is not the lowest submitted. By the same token, a contractor with no reputation or a poor reputation in a particular area can lose the contract even if his bid is the lowest.

In a free market, an entrepreneur who devised a method to build better structures would be able to win contracts with bids that exceeded those of other contractors. He might not have to bid at all as builders sought him out. However, today's construction industry, and particularly the erection of buildings, is so heavily regulated as to make this impossible.

E. Conclusion

Like set prices and negotiated prices, sealed bid prices change with changes in cost, demand, and competition. Sealed bid prices reflect the conditions of supply and demand in the industry, but supply and demand do not create the price. Prices are created by the businessmen involved, governed by their grasp of all the facts relevant to their businesses, including the industry's supply and demand, their own costs, and the intensity of competition.

Both supply (the industry's total capacity) and demand (the total value of current construction projects) affect sealed bid prices. Demand affects prices over the short run as it increases and decreases relative to supply. Supply affects prices over the long run as it increases and decreases in response to the industry's profits. There is no tendency for the demand to equal the supply, except in the very rough sense described at the end of part C above.

F. The Meaning and Measure of Scarcity When Pricing Is by Sealed Bids

There are two components to a sealed bid price: The greater part consists of the cost of all the materials, parts, machines, tools, equipment, and construction workers that are necessary to complete the project. The prices of factors are set by the buyer or the seller, or they are negotiated. Regardless of how they originate, the prices of factors reflect their relative scarcity. Chapter 9 showed this for workers wages and salaries. Chapter 12 shows this for the other factors.

A separate part consists of the contractor's markup for contribution to his overhead and profit. This is his price. Increases in demand and decreases in supply reduce capacity utilization and contractors raise the percentage markup. Decreases in demand and increases in supply lower capacity utilization and contractors lower the percentage markup. Contractors' markups (prices) reflect the relative scarcity of the industry's productive capacity to carry out construction projects.

III. Auction Prices

In this section, I pass over liquidation sales of merchandise and focus on the auction of collectibles, particularly art works such as old masters.

Auction prices are widely described by economists as determined by supply and demand. Economists attribute rising prices of art works sold at auction to a rising demand in the face of a fixed supply. But the rising demand that raises the prices of collectibles is *not* an increase in the quantity that collectors want to buy.

The meaning of demand when the quantity is limited to one is important in fields much more widespread than individual works of art. Chapter 9 applied this concept of demand to the market for corporate executives (pp. 168-70). Demand when there is only one unit also pertains to individual real estate sites, in any case where equivalent sites do not exist. For homes, for apartments, for buildings, for building sites in cities, the relevant concept of increasing demand is *not* an increase in the quantity people want to buy.

When the demand is for a single unit, the proper conception of demand is not a quantity, but a price—the price at which the single unit is demanded by only one party. A change in demand is not a change in quantity at the same price, but a change in price at the same quantity, that is, the quantity of one. To the best of my knowledge, this concept of demand has not been recognized before, so I want to stress its value and validity. In the context of a single, unique unit, this is the change in demand that changes the price.

Increases in demand, defined as increases in the prices offered for a unit, explain the rising prices paid at auction for old masters during times of inflation and prosperity. The cause is that men or institutions with more money to spend enter the competition. They have more money in part as a result of the economic growth and price inflation since the last time an art work of this kind was offered for sale. Decreases in demand during recessions and depressions take the form of falling prices or the failure of prices to rise. The price necessary to secure an old master is lower because there are fewer competitors with smaller fortunes to spend.

The law of demand is still true. At a price lower than the price that wins the bid, a greater quantity would be demanded. To be precise, the greater quantity would be a greater number of men and/or institutions willing to buy the one unit. If the price were low enough, perhaps thousands would want to buy it. But the change in demand that raises the price is not a change in this number.

The price settled on at auction equates the quantity demanded to the single unit supplied. Consequently, the price is an exact measure of the relative scarcity of the auctioned item, where scarcity means the demand relative to the supply—where demand is understood in the sense relevant to a market for a single unit, that is, the price which only one buyer will pay.

IV. Brokered Prices

Brokered prices are the prices most frequently thought of by people as determined by supply and demand. This section analyzes the meanings of supply and demand that are relevant for the stock market and then applies those conceptions to show how supply and demand affect the prices of stocks. Then we consider the same subjects in connection with commodity markets.

A. The Role of Supply and Demand in Stock Markets

At any point in time, the demand for a stock is the number of shares in buy orders (bid for) at market. For example, "the demand for IBM is 5,600 shares" means that buyers have placed orders with their brokers to buy 5,600 shares of IBM at market "At market" means the best price available at this time—which may be a little higher or a little lower than the last price at which an exchange was made. An increase in the demand for IBM is an increase in the number of shares in buy orders at market and a decrease in demand is a decrease in the number of shares in buy orders at market.

The supply of a stock is the number of shares in sell orders (offered for sale) at market. For example, "the supply of IBM is 5,600 shares," means that current owners have placed orders with their brokers to sell 5,600 shares of IBM at market. An increase in the supply of IBM is an increase in the number of shares offered for sale at market and a decrease in supply is a decrease in the number of shares offered for sale at market.

1. The law of demand for stocks

The basis of the law of demand for stocks is the concept of "fair market value." The fair market value of a stock is the value of the corporation divided by the number of shares the corporation has issued. If the company is worth $1 billion, and it has issued 100 million shares, the fair market value of each share is $10. The calculation is easy. Estimating the value of the company is hard.

The value of a corporation is determined by its long-run expected profits (to be exact, the present value of those long-run expected profits). Fundamentalists estimate those expected profits by looking at the facts listed in chapter 7 (pp. 132–33): the quality of the company's current management, the quality of the management of competing firms, the quality of the company's products relative to its competitors' products, the prices the company charges, its costs per unit relative to its competitors' costs, its reputation, its current sales and profits, its market share, how each of these facts is likely to change in the future, and possibly many other facts as well.

Analysts are paid to estimate the fair market value of stocks on the premise that over time, the price of a stock will tend to equal its fair market value. If the analyst is right in his estimate of fair market value, more and more investors will come to recognize that value and the price of the stock will change accordingly. If investors believe the market price is below the stock's fair market value, the stock is said to be undervalued or underpriced. Investors who believe this, offer to buy more shares (demand increases) while investors holding the stock offer to sell less (supply decreases), or ask for a higher price. This causes an excess demand for the company's stock—the number of shares investors want to buy exceeds the number investors want to sell at the current price. This causes the price of the stock to rise. (Part 3 below shows how that happens.)

Alternatively, if investors come to believe the current price of the stock is above its fair market value, the stock is said to be overvalued or overpriced. Investors who believe this want to sell their shares, while other investors want to buy less or none at all. Thus, the number of shares investors offer to sell increases while the number of shares investors offer to buy falls. This creates an excess supply of the company's stock and causes the price of the stock to fall.

Thus, the rule governing the purchase of a stock is this: If the price is above the fair market value and you own it, sell. If the price is below the fair market value and you own it, hold, and if you do not own it, buy. However, successful investment in the stock market is not that easy.

The estimation of a company's long-run profits is *not* easy. It is very hard. Every such estimate is an instance of "telling the future." Businesses that invest in stocks, or that advise others on buying stocks, hire many thousands of men who work full time estimating the fair market value of all the stocks in the economy. Because these estimations are difficult, analysts' calculations of fair market value vary over a range for any individual stock.

The basis for the law of demand in the stock market is that as the price of a stock rises, it rises above the estimated fair market value of more and more analysts, and fewer and fewer recommend purchase of the stock to their customers or employers. Alternatively, as the price of a stock falls, it falls below the estimated fair market value of more and more analysts, and more and more of them recommend its purchase. Consequently, the demand for shares of a stock goes down as the price goes up and the demand goes up as the price goes down. This is the law of demand in the context of stock prices.

Changes in the number of shares demanded of a particular stock are not caused primarily by changes in price. Any change in investors' estimates of a company's fair market value change demand. Good news for the company implies an increase in the fair market value of its stock. Announcements of things like a merger, or hiring a new president with a good reputation, or a quarterly earnings report that is better than expected cause an increase in demand—bids to buy at the current price go up. Bad news for a company causes decreases in demand—things like a quarterly earnings report that is below expectations or the announcement of a new product by a competitor. These facts imply a decrease in the fair market value of the company's stock, and investors act accordingly—bids to buy at the current price go down.

2. The rule of supply for stocks

The rule of supply is that as the price rises, the number of shares offered for sale increases, and as the price falls, the number of shares offered for sale decreases. In other words, the relation between the price of a stock and its supply is direct. Price goes up and supply goes up; price goes down and supply goes down.

The rule of supply is a rule rather than a law because the relation between price and supply is a minor phenomenon compared to the relation between price and demand. The law of demand is a universal fact of an exchange economy. It applies anywhere and everywhere across the economy, as we have seen. We have not encountered the rule of supply before because it has no meaning in the context of set prices, negotiated prices, sealed bid prices, or auction prices. The rule of supply is a rule only in the context of brokered price markets. In this context, it is important. Without it, we cannot understand changes in brokered prices.

Like the law of demand, the rule of supply is rooted in the concept of fair market value and the fact that analysts' estimates of that value vary over a range. Thus, as the price of IBM rises, it rises above the estimated fair market value of more and more analysts, and more and more of them advise their customers or employers to sell their shares of IBM, which increases the supply. As the price of IBM falls, it falls below the estimated fair market value of more and more analysts, who advise their customers to hold IBM, and the supply of IBM falls.

Like demand, supply changes primarily for reasons other than changes in price. Good news for a company decreases supply at the going price and bad news increases supply at the going price.

3. Supply, demand, and the price of stocks

Now let us see how supply and demand cause changes in the prices of stocks.

If the number of shares bid for at market exceeds the number of shares offered for sale at market, the price of the stock will rise. The mechanism that brings this about is different in different stock markets. In the New York Stock Exchange, for example, it is in the hands of the specialist, who acts as an agent for the brokers. There are several hundred specialists on the New York Stock Exchange. Each stock listed on the Exchange is assigned to a single specialist, and each specialist is responsible for a small number of stocks (an average of perhaps six). A broker who wants to buy or sell a particular stock for a customer goes to the specialist responsible for that stock.

Small orders to buy and sell at market are matched electronically by the specialist's clerk—continuously, and at amazing speed—less than a second per order. If the quantities to buy and sell at market are the same, the price does not change.

The specialist keeps a record of limit orders for his stocks. Limit orders are orders to buy at prices below the current market price and orders to sell at prices above the current market price. Under normal circumstances, he executes limit orders when the market price reaches the customer's limit price. The specialist also manages the execution of large orders left with him by a broker. The Exchange allows him, and often requires him, to reduce price fluctuations by buying for his own account when the price is falling and selling from his own account when the price is rising.

If the orders to buy at market exceed the orders to sell, the specialist may sell from a limit order above the last market price. Alternatively, the specialist may sell at a higher price from his own account. In either case, the market price rises. If the orders to sell at market exceed the orders to buy, the price falls as the specialist buys for limit orders below the last price, or he buys for his own account at a lower price. This is how the specialist handles relatively small imbalances in supply and demand.

Now let us consider a large imbalance. Suppose a large order to buy AT&T at market comes in to a broker. A large order is an order for 100 thousand shares or more. Orders for millions of shares are not unusual. The broker takes the order to the AT&T specialist. Sell orders are coming in at the same time, but at the last market price, the quantity demanded of AT&T now greatly exceeds the quantity supplied. The price of AT&T rises. How does it rise? (1) The specialist may sell from his own account at a higher price. (2) The specialist can execute limit orders to sell at higher prices to help fill the order. However, under normal circumstances, the Exchange does not allow the specialist to complete an order by working his way up the limit orders, which would push the price straight up. (3) Usually the broker leaves the order with the specialist, who puts the order "on the book." (The book is a log of all orders left with the specialist for execution, including limit orders.) Then, over time, new sell orders come in, in response to the rising price. As the day goes on, the specialist fills the order with the new sell orders in combination with limit orders and perhaps sales by the specialist from his own account. Sometimes this process can stretch over more than one day. In this way, the specialist minimizes the increase in price caused by the large order and minimizes the price the buyer has to pay.[1]

The same mechanism operates to lower the price in response to a large order to sell: (1) The specialist may buy for his own account at a lower price. (2) He executes limit orders to buy at lower prices to help fill the order. (3) Over time, new buy orders come in, in response to the lower price. In these ways, the specialist fills the order to sell while minimizing the decrease in price and maximizing the price the seller receives.

4. Excess demand and excess supply

Based on the preceding, we can abstract the essential roles of supply and demand in the determination of the price of stocks. In order to broaden this analysis beyond the New York Stock Exchange, let us put the specialist aside.

In explaining the reaction of investors to undervalued or overpriced stocks, section 1 above showed that in both cases, the actions taken by investors change demand and supply in opposite directions at the same time. The result is that investors create an excess demand for the stock, causing its price to rise, or an excess supply of stock, causing its price to fall. Good news and bad news for a company have the same effect. Section 3 showed the mechanism by which an excess demand raises price and by which an excess supply reduces price.

What we have observed is the norm in stock markets. The immediate cause of all changes in the prices of stocks is either excess demand for a stock or excess supply of a stock. Many things can lead to an excess demand or an excess supply. These consist, after all, of bids to buy and offers to sell by investors, and news that affects the demand and supply of investors often causes demand and supply to change in opposite directions. Changes in facts that make some investors more eager to buy a stock, causing an increase in demand, also make other investors more reluctant to sell the stock, causing a decrease in supply—and vice versa for changes that make a stock less attractive.

Thus it is that all the news of changes in facts that leads investors to raise their estimates of a stock's fair market value creates an excess demand for the stock. If the news of changes in facts lowers analysts' estimates of a stock's fair market value, it creates an excess supply of the stock. This is not to deny that often the news is ambiguous and investors may disagree about its implications for a stock's fair market value. But unambiguous news changes demand and supply in opposite directions.

When there is an excess demand for a stock, the price rises until the excess demand is absorbed. It is absorbed by the execution of limit orders to sell at higher prices, by some investor's placement of new orders to sell at the higher price, and by other investor's withdrawal of orders to buy. When there is an excess supply of stock, the price falls until the excess supply disappears. It disappears as limit orders to buy are executed at lower prices, as some investors place additional bids to buy as the price declines, and as other investors withdraw their offers to sell.

Now let us consider explicitly the law of demand in this process. For falling prices, the law of demand takes the form of limit orders to buy and the placement of new orders to buy. For rising prices, the law of demand takes the form of the withdrawal of existing orders to buy and of orders to buy that are not submitted. We cannot observe the orders to buy that are not submitted, but they exist nonetheless. These are investors for whom the price has risen above their estimates of fair market value. When the price of a stock rises, the number of shares demanded is less than it would have been if the price had not risen.

This phenomenon also occurs in markets for goods and services sold at set prices and negotiated prices. It is not unusual for the price of a product and the quantity sold to rise at the same time or to fall at the same time. For example, rising costs as he approaches capacity may induce a businessman to raise his price at the same time his customers are demanding more of his product. Or he may raise his price to take advantage of the rising demand for his product. Or, trying to keep up volume, he may lower his price in the face of a decrease in demand. Or falling costs may motivate him to lower his price at the same time demand is falling. In all these cases, the law of demand is valid—at the higher price, the demand is less than it would have been if the businessman had not raised his price, and at the lower price, the demand is greater than it would have been if the businessman had not lowered his price—because as the price of a good rises, it rises above the ranking of more and more people (p. 71 above).

As the price rises, the rule of supply takes the form of limit orders to sell at higher prices and of the placement of new orders to sell. For falling prices, the rule of supply takes the form of the withdrawal of existing orders to sell and of orders to sell that are not submitted. We cannot observe the latter when the price falls, but we know they exist as the response of investors for whom the price falls below their estimates of fair market value. When the price of a stock falls, the rule of supply says that the quantity supplied will be less than if the price had not fallen. (Unlike the law of demand, there is no counterpart to the rule of supply for goods and services.)

Thus, the continuous movement of the prices of stocks up and down are the product of constantly changing demands for and supplies of each stock. These constantly changing demands and supplies in turn reflect the constantly changing evaluations of the buyers and sellers of stock, based on their grasp of the constantly changing relevant economic facts, all of which are relevant because they affect the fair market value of the corporation.

5. Fundamental analysis versus technical analysis

In all of the preceding, I have ignored the implications of technical analysis for the demand and supply of stocks. Technical analysts do not estimate the fair market value of corporations as the basis for predicting the movement of their stock prices. Rather, technical analysts chart statistical series looking for statistical patterns foretelling the rise or fall of a stock's price. Since I have known people who have made a lot of money using technical analysis, I assume that it has some basis in reality. Here we will resolve an apparent conflict between technical analysis and both the law of demand and the rule of supply.

Technicians sometimes take an increase in price as foretelling further increases in price, which implies further increases in demand or decreases in supply. Technicians sometimes take a decrease in price as foretelling further decreases in price, which implies additional increases in supply or decreases in demand. This analysis seems to contradict both the law of demand and the rule of supply for stocks. It seems to imply that a rising price may cause both an increase in demand and a decrease in supply, and a falling price may cause both a decrease in demand and an increase in supply.

Suppose that the fundamentalists calculate that the stock's price exceeds its fair market value, but the technical analysts predict the stock's price will rise, and both estimates are right. The technicians' forecast may reflect the fact that a rising price leads people to think that the price will keep on rising; they want to get on the bandwagon, and demand will continue to increase. This does not contradict the law of demand. People are buying today because they think the price will be higher tomorrow. In other words, demand increases because people think today's price is low—*relative to tomorrow's price*—and the real price is the relative price (pp. 49–53 above).[2]

A falling price may increase supply for the same reason: people want to sell now because they are afraid the price will be lower tomorrow. In other words, relative to tomorrow's price, today's price is high. This is exactly the thinking that lies behind a stock market panic or a crash. An increase in demand when the price is rising does not contradict the law of demand nor does an increase in supply when the price is falling contradict the rule of supply.

6. Relative scarcity and the price of stocks

In stock markets, the price of a stock rises when the quantity demanded exceeds the quantity supplied at the market price. This may be caused by (1) an increase in demand and a decrease in supply; (2) an increase in demand when supply is unchanged; (3) an increase in demand that exceeds an increase in supply; (4) a decrease in supply when demand is unchanged; (5) a decrease in supply that exceeds a decrease in demand. The relation reflected in these relative changes in quantity supplied and quantity demanded is scarcity. Each of these five changes in demand and supply represent an increase in relative scarcity, and the corresponding increase in price measures that increase in relative scarcity. Similarly, a change in the demand or the supply of a stock that results in the quantity supplied exceeding the quantity demanded represents a decrease in relative scarcity and the corresponding fall in price measures that decrease.

Changes in the price of a stock reflect a change in the quantity demanded of its shares relative to the quantity offered for sale. The resulting price is the price that is necessary to equate the quantity demanded to the quantity supplied. Consequently, the price of a stock reflects the scarcity of its shares relative to the scarcity of the shares of other stocks. Stocks with higher prices per share are more scarce than stocks with lower prices per share. Compare Berkshire Hathaway with Microsoft or a penny stock. The relative scarcity of those stocks is given by their prices, that is, the prices required to equate the quantity demanded of the stock to the quantity supplied—where both the quantity demanded and the quantity supplied reflect analysts' estimates of fair market value.

But what is the point of a higher price for a scarcer stock? Unlike the consequences of high prices for goods and services, economizing on high-priced stocks is meaningless. Shares of stock are not factors of production and their prices do not directly affect the distribution of the factors of production.

Shares of stock are shares of ownership in a corporation. As such, they are shares of ownership in all the resources owned by the corporation. The price of a stock affects the distribution of resources through that ownership. A high price for a company's stock encourages its management to raise capital for investment by selling more stock. The company then uses that money to claim more resources (more workers, machines, plant and equipment), expanding the range of the company's productive effort.[3]

B. The Bond Market

Essentially the same principles that determine the prices of stocks are at work in the bond market. The bond market is the market for debt. Every bond is a promise to pay the holder a certain interest rate on a specified principal, and a promise eventually to repay the principle itself. If a company chooses to finance its expansion through the sale of bonds, the interest rate on the bonds is the price the company pays. An economy has some average interest rate at any point in time. The interest rate on a company's bonds varies from the average depending on the company's prospects for making profits, in the judgment of the analysts who follow the company. The better the company's prospects, the lower the risk associated with its bonds, and the lower the interest rate the company has to pay. These prospects are reflected in the interest rate currently earned in the bond market by whatever bonds the company previously sold. If the company is selling debt for the first time, the interest rate it has to pay reflects the underwriters' estimate of the company's prospects.

C. The Role of Supply and Demand in Commodity Futures Markets

In commodity futures markets, speculators make contracts to deliver and receive commodities on some future date. For example, in January, John may reach a contract with Mary to deliver 5000 bushels of wheat in

March for $3.00/bushel. By the contract, John obligates himself to deliver the wheat and Mary obligates herself to accept delivery and pay the agreed upon price ($15,000). The quality of each commodity in a futures market is standardized and the contracted delivery is to the same site on the same date. Each exchange rigidly defines each commodity in order to make price the only variable.

Contracts are made through commodity brokers on the floor of the various mercantile exchanges, like the Chicago Board of Trade (CBOT). The brokers signal and call out offers to buy and sell in an area called "the pit." The pit consists of ascending levels of floor space, each level corresponding to a future date of the commodity. If a broker wants to make contracts to buy or sell 2011 March wheat, he stands on that level. Each commodity has its own pit.[4]

The basic idea of commodities trading is this: Suppose the current price in January of March wheat is $3.00 a bushel. If Mary thinks the price in March will be higher than $3.00, she can contract now with John to receive 5000 bushels of wheat in March for $15,000 (wheat trades in 5000-bushel units). Then in March, if the price is $3.20, she can sell the wheat delivered to her for $16,000 and make a profit of $1000.

On the other hand, if Mary thinks the price will fall, she can contract with John in January to deliver March wheat for $3.00 a bushel ($15,000), and in March when wheat is selling for $2.80 a bushel, she can buy 5000 bushels for $14,000, deliver 5000 bushels to John for $15,000, and make a profit of $1000.

There are two concepts of supply and demand involved in understanding the operation of commodity markets. First, there is the market supply and market demand for the commodity *in the economy* at some future date—for example, wheat in March 2014. The market supply of March 2014 wheat is the quantity that will be supplied to the market in March 2014 by businesses that grow and/or store wheat for sale. The market demand for March 2014 wheat is the quantity that will be demanded in March 2014 by businesses that buy wheat to store and/or consume in production. The price of wheat in March 2014 will equate the market demand for wheat in March 2014 to the market supply in March 2014. Speculators make estimates of the future supply and future demand for a commodity as the basis for estimating the future price. This is not the only basis on which speculators trade (a great deal of trading is based on technical analysis), but this is the economic base, the ultimate grounding in reality.

Second, there is the supply and demand *of speculators* today for the commodity on some future date, for example, the supply and demand of speculators in January 2014 for wheat in March 2014. The supply and demand of speculators *today* determines the price one can contract for *today* (in January 2014) to deliver or receive wheat in March 2014.

Many thousands of speculators invest in commodity markets, and the information on which they base their estimates of future supply and demand includes things like weather forecasts, prospective crop yields, political changes, the timing of recessions and economic expansions—and not just for the United States, but for the world. Most of the relevant information is inexact, and consequently speculators' estimates of futures prices vary over a range. As a result, there is the same basis for the law of demand and the rule of supply for commodity futures as for stocks.

For example, in January, as the price of March wheat rises, it rises above the estimated March price of more and more speculators. Consequently, they will expect the March price to fall, and fewer and fewer of them will want to contract at the current price to receive wheat in March. Thus, as the price of March wheat rises, the demand for March wheat falls. On the other hand, if the price of March wheat falls, it falls below the estimated March price of more and more speculators, and they will expect the price to rise. Consequently, more and more of them will want to contract to receive the commodity in March. Thus, as the price of March wheat falls, the demand for March wheat rises.

The same reasoning can be used to derive a rule of supply for commodity markets. As the price of March wheat rises, it rises above the price of March wheat expected by more and more speculators and more and more of them will want to sell wheat for delivery in March. Alternatively, as the price of March wheat falls, it falls below the expected price of more and more speculators, and fewer and fewer of them will want to contract to deliver wheat in March.

Today's price of March wheat reflects the supply and demand today by speculators for March wheat. Just as with stocks, an excess supply of March wheat today causes the price to fall, and an excess demand for March wheat today causes the price to rise. For example, if there is an excess demand, brokers in the pit with orders to buy March wheat have to offer higher prices. As the price rises, brokers with limit orders to sell at higher prices are able to execute those orders, additional speculators enter the market to sell, and some speculators withdraw their orders to buy. The price stops rising when the excess demand has disappeared.

If there is an excess supply of March wheat, brokers in the pit with orders to sell March wheat have to offer to sell at lower prices. As the price falls, some speculators withdraw their orders to sell, brokers execute limit orders to buy at lower prices, and additional speculators enter the market to buy. The price stops falling when there are no more unfilled orders to sell.[5]

Big changes in the supply and demand of commodity futures originate with changes in the facts that speculators expect to affect the market demand and the market supply of the commodity in the future. As an example, suppose news reaches the wheat pit of the Chicago Board of Trade on September 20, 2014 at 2:15:00 PM that there is going to be a crop failure in the Ukraine. Immediately, at 2:15:01, the demand for March 2015 wheat rises, the supply of March 2015 wheat falls, and the price of March 2015 wheat rises—that is, the price of wheat to be delivered and received six months from today rises today. At the same time, for the same reason, demand exceeds supply in all the other futures markets for wheat, and speculators bid up the price—of wheat to be delivered five months from today, three months from today, one month from today, and tomorrow. The result is that the users and consumers of wheat start economizing on wheat today, six months before the shortfall hits the market—so that when the shortfall does hit the market, it has no effect on any current or future prices. It is not even noticed—here, or in the Ukraine.

On the other hand, suppose the news reaches speculators at 10:26:30 AM on October 14, 2014, that a bumper crop of wheat is expected in the American northwest. Immediately, at 10:26:31 AM, the demand for March 2015 wheat falls, the supply of March 2015 wheat rises, and the price of March 2015 wheat falls. At the same time, wheat contracted to be delivered tomorrow, the day after tomorrow, one month from today, two months from today, six months from today, and so forth, all fall in price today. The motive to economize on wheat is reduced today, six months before the bumper crop appears for sale, and uses for wheat which previously were too expensive are now taken up (chapter 10).[6] When the bumper crop appears for sale, it slides without a ripple into the wheat markets of the country at the going price.

An increase in the expected supply of a commodity relative to its expected demand lowers futures prices. A decrease in a commodity's expected supply relative to its expected demand raises futures prices. Futures prices are a measure of expected relative scarcity—expected by the

men for whom making these estimates is a full-time occupation, and
whose income varies with the accuracy of their judgment.

V. Conclusion

In preparation for chapter 12, let us sum up chapter 11 by looking at the
simultaneous effects of changes in supply and demand on both price and
relative scarcity.

For products with negotiated prices, price changes are based on the
grasp of the relevant economic facts by the negotiators, and prices
change by their choices alone. If demand increases or decreases, the effect on price depends on whether or not businessmen can increase or decrease supply to meet the change in demand. If they can, the relative
scarcity of the product is unaffected and the price does not change. If
demand increases and producers cannot increase supply, then the quantity demanded exceeds the quantity supplied, and sellers negotiate higher
prices. The higher prices reflect the increase in relative scarcity. If demand decreases and the sellers cannot reduce their supply, they negotiate
lower prices. The lower prices reflect the decrease in relative scarcity.

In the case of sealed bid prices, contractors bid higher total prices in
response to an industry-wide increase in construction costs and bid lower
total prices if construction costs decrease. The equivalent of a market
price in the construction industry is the percentage markup over cost.
Given an unchanged total capacity, contractors raise their markup over
cost if the demand for construction projects increases and reduce that
markup if demand decreases. The price in the construction industry is a
measure of the relative scarcity of the capacity to carry out construction
projects.

Auction prices of unique items (collectibles and works of art) increase with increases in demand, where demand is understood as the
maximum price someone is willing to pay for the individual item. Likewise, auction prices for unique items fall with decreases in demand—
which is a fall in the maximum price. An increase in demand for a quantity constant at one represents an increase in the relative scarcity of that
item and simultaneously an increase in its price. Changes in the relative
scarcity of unique items move in lockstep with changes in price.

Stocks, bonds, and commodity futures increase in price when the
quantity demanded exceeds the quantity supplied. Their prices fall when
the quantity supplied exceeds the quantity demanded. This means that
the prices of stocks and bonds increase with increases in their relative

scarcity and decrease with decreases in their relative scarcity. At any point in time, the price of a stock (or bond) measures its scarcity relative to other stocks (or bonds). The prices of commodity futures are measures of each commodity's scarcity expected in the future by the speculators who buy and sell them.

CHAPTER TWELVE

SCARCITY AND PROFIT

I. Absolute Scarcity

What facts of reality give rise to the concept of scarcity? Consider these concrete instances: (1) Soldiers have a scarcity of bullets on the battle-field; (2) A hunter encounters a scarcity of game; (3) Firemen have a scarcity of water to fight a fire; (4) Rescuers have a scarcity of medicine following an earthquake; (5) A young lady has a scarcity of suitors; (6) A weekend sailor faces a scarcity of wind.

Each of the above scarcities depends on the same fundamental facts. First, there are values at stake that men must act to gain and/or keep. Second, the means these people possess are insufficient to reach their ends. Third, the insufficiency is hard or impossible to rectify. Scarcity is the concept of an insufficiency of means that cannot easily be fixed. We measure the means' insufficiency by reference to the goal or end which the means is required to reach. We measure a scarcity of bullets on the battlefield by what is necessary for the soldiers to defend themselves. We measure a scarcity of game by a hunter's ability to shoot what he needs to feed his family. We judge a scarcity of water in a fire by the amount of water that is necessary to contain or control the fire. And so forth.

This is a concept of *absolute scarcity*. Scarcities of this kind stand alone. None of the instances of scarcity listed above requires reference to any other scarcity in order to be understood. In each case, (1) there is a clear end that a means is insufficient to reach, (2) the end is the standard for identifying the insufficiency, and (3) the insufficiency is not easy to fix. This concept of absolute scarcity is the concept that rules modern economics and, as far as I can tell, has always ruled economics. Typically, economists do not bother to define scarcity, but when they use the term, they mean absolute scarcity as defined here.

Modern economists hold that scarcity is the fundamental fact of the economy. All economic phenomena, they say, depend on the existence of scarcity; if nothing were scarce, there would be no need to economize and an economic system would be superfluous. Consequently, economists say, scarcity is the fundamental cause of economics as a science and every economy as such is an economy of scarcity.[1]

In opposition to this view, let us observe that modern industrial economies are economies of abundance, not scarcity. It is absurd on its face, in light of the unprecedented explosion of goods and services created by the semi-capitalist countries of the modern world, to hold that scarcity is their fundamental characteristic. Nobody dies of malnutrition in these countries—unless they are anorexic. Nobody goes hungry—unless they are on a diet. Nobody goes without shelter—unless they choose to live on the street. Nobody goes without clothes—unless they are nudists.

The existence of a scarcity depends on the fact that one cannot easily eliminate it. It would be ridiculous for someone to complain that there is a scarcity of salt to season his dinner—because he can go out and buy more salt. The same reasoning is valid for more expensive items. Whatever the goods and services that a man has become accustomed to consuming, he does not complain that any of them are scarce. If he does not have as much as he needs, he buys more. A woman may cry, "I have nothing to wear," when she is unexpectedly invited to a party. But then she finds something to wear. She does not have a scarcity of clothes.

In an advanced industrial economy, there is no goal by which the supply of any economic good or service can be identified as insufficient.[2] Neither diamonds nor rhinestones can be said to be scarce without reference to some goal or end. But what would be the end? Is there a scarcity of yachts? Of Gulfstream jets? Of spaces aboard cruise ships? Of trips on the space shuttle? Of salt? Of pepper? Of Stilton cheese? At the going price, the demand equals the supply and everyone is able to buy all they want to buy. For the purpose of understanding how the economy works, that is all we need to know.

Absolute scarcity is a deficiency; it implies that there is something wrong. Something certainly *is* wrong in third world countries where people die of famine, malnutrition, exhaustion, and disease. On the standard of man's life on earth, those *are* economies of scarcity; the goods and services they produce are insufficient to sustain the lives of their citizens. The conditions of life in the economies of the advanced Western world are "living conditions." The equivalent in third world countries are dying conditions. That is the difference between economies of abundance and economies of scarcity.

Absolute economic scarcity is useful as a concept to identify conditions of extreme deprivation. But absolute scarcity is not relevant to understanding anything about a capitalist economy.

II. Relative Scarcity

Relative scarcity is the concept of scarcity that is relevant to economics.

A. The Meaning of Relative Scarcity

The concept of relative scarcity is like the concept of price. Chapter 3 showed that all prices are relative. The meaning of every individual price to human beings depends on its relation to the network of other prices. There are no absolute prices (prices that stand alone) in an economic system. Alternatively, every price is an absolute, but its absolutism consists of its relation to other prices.

Scarcity is relative. There is no such thing as an absolute scarcity of any individual good in an industrial economy. All goods are scarce, but only relative to the scarcity of other goods. If a good is very, very scarce, we can make that assessment only by comparison to the scarcity of most other goods. Similarly, a good can be abundant, but only relative to the abundance of other goods. Abundant means much less scarce than most goods.

Relative scarcity is the demand relative to the supply of one good compared to the demand relative to the supply of another good. Thus, there are two relationships involved in every case of relative scarcity. First, there is the demand relative to the supply of good A. The relative scarcity of cars, for example, is measured by their price, and that price reflects, not just the supply (the number of cars offered for sale), but that supply relative to the demand (the number of cars customers want to buy).

Second, there is the scarcity of good A relative to the scarcity of good B—for example, the scarcity of cars relative to the scarcity of dishwashers. No scarcity stands alone in exactly the same way and for the same reason that no price stands alone. Every good's relative scarcity is grasped by comparing its price to the price of some other good or goods.

The network of relative prices is also a network of relative scarcities. Relative prices tell us the scarcity of every good and service relative to the scarcity of every other good and service. The evaluation of a good as abundant or scarce or very scarce or extremely scarce depends on the scarcity of the goods to which one is comparing it—and it is only by comparison that a good's scarcity can be estimated. Thus, the high price of diamonds compared to rhinestones means that diamonds are much more scarce than rhinestones. The high price of houses compared to bicycles tells us that houses are many times more scarce than bicycles, but relative to the scarcity of Gulfstream jets or super yachts, houses are abundant.[3]

B. The Subject Matter of Relative Scarcity

The subject matter subsumed by *objective prices* is every market price of every good and service in the economy. By contrast, the subject covered by the concept of relative scarcity is *industry-wide prices* or at least prices across a wide range of items. An industry-wide price is the average price charged by all the firms in an industry *as grasped by human beings.* Thus, in order to measure relative scarcity, the average price usually does not have to be calculated. Anybody can compare the average price of compact cars to the average price of mid-sized cars to the average price of full-sized cars, and grasp that full-sized cars are more scarce than mid-sized cars, and mid-sized cars are more scarce than compact cars. On a wider scale, anyone can compare the average price of cars to the average price of trucks to the average price of helicopters and conclude that cars are less scarce than trucks which are less scarce than helicopters.

The theory of objective prices is that every market price of a good or service is the objective economic value of that product because it reflects the economic facts. In this book, we have focused on the facts of demand, cost, and competition. Supply is not among these facts—yet relative scarcity is the demand for a good relative to its supply.

Businessmen produce the supply that their customers demand at the price they charge. Supply is something the businessman creates, not a fact he responds to. And further, businessmen know and care nothing about relative scarcity. They certainly do not change their prices because of changes in demand relative to supply. Then how is it that the prices set by businessmen reflect demand relative to supply? Sections C and D following answer this question, while elaborating the meaning of relative scarcity.

C. Increases in Relative Scarcity

1. Demand increases relative to supply

Relative scarcity increases when demand increases relative to supply[4]— for example, at the current price, the quantity demanded increases while the quantity supplied is unchanged. An unchanged supply may occur because businessmen are unable to increase their supply. Suppose the lumber industry sells 1,000,000 board feet of lumber a day @ 25¢ a board foot, and lumber customers want to buy 1,500,000 board feet a day. If environmental restrictions prevent the lumber industry from cutting down trees, the industry is unable to increase its output. Consequently, speculators in the commodity markets bid up the price of lumber to, let us say, 32¢ a board foot, and the quantity demanded drops back to 1,000,000 board feet a day. Lumber companies supply the same quantity as before the increase in demand, and the higher price reflects the increase in relative scarcity.

As this case illustrates, when demand increases for a product fixed in supply, usually the price rises. Speculators bid up the price in commodity markets or business owners raise their prices (pp. 189–90). Each businessman raises his price in response to the increase in demand for his product, but across the whole industry, demand increases relative to supply, the relative scarcity of the industry's product increases, and the increase in average price reflects that fact.

Often the businesses in an industry can increase their supply to equal an increased demand. Their costs have not changed, they are satisfied with their profit margins, and they can add to their profits by selling additional output. There is no increase in relative scarcity. A greater quantity demanded equals a greater quantity supplied at the same price.[5]

2. Supply decreases relative to demand

Relative scarcity also increases when supply decreases relative to demand, for example, supply decreases while demand is unchanged. This happens during the long-run process of economic adjustment (though not only then) when the businesses in an industry are losing money (pp. 199–

201 above). If the industry is cattle-ranching, the least efficient cattlemen go bankrupt, others withdraw their capital, and the quantity of cattle supplied falls. Let us suppose that initially the cattle ranchers had been selling 1,000,000 pounds of beef a day at $2 a pound. Now the market supply has fallen to 700,000 pounds a day. In response, speculators bid up the price of beef in commodity markets—let us say to $2.75 a pound—and at that price, 700,000 pounds a day is the quantity demanded.

This is how changes in supply relative to demand affect prices. In a loss-making industry, as the least efficient businesses go bankrupt, their customers have to buy their goods from the businesses that remain. For those businesses, these new customers represent an increase in demand and, since they are losing money at their current prices, they are eager to raise them. This process continues until the industry's losses disappear and its profits are restored at a level that permits the surviving firms to maintain their capital.

D. Decreases in Relative Scarcity

1. Demand decreases relative to supply

Relative scarcity decreases when the quantity demanded decreases and the quantity supplied is unchanged.[6] A fall in the demand for cars from ten million a year to six million a year means there is a big decline in the relative scarcity of cars. Normally, car companies reduce the price when the demand for cars falls by offering discounts, rebates, give-backs, and low-interest loans. The decrease in price raises the quantity demanded back toward ten million, while the car companies reduce their output. At the end, the quantity of cars supplied and demanded is, let us say, eight million, and a lower price reflects the decline in relative scarcity.

If businesses do not reduce the price when there is an industry-wide decrease in demand, then their supply declines one for one with the decrease in demand and relative scarcity is unchanged. For example, if the car companies keep their prices unchanged when demand falls from ten million to six million cars a year, they have to reduce their output to six million because that is all they can sell. Both the demand and supply of cars declines by four million, leaving the relative scarcity of cars, and the price, unchanged.

If the decrease in demand ends up focused on a basic commodity such as wheat, speculators bid down the price. If the supply is fixed over the short run (hotel rooms, for example, p. 197 above) and demand decreases, businessmen reduce their prices. Their motive is to minimize the reduction in their profits; the decrease in price reflects the decrease in relative scarcity.

2. Supply increases relative to demand

Relative scarcity also decreases when the quantity supplied increases while the quantity demanded is unchanged. This happens during the long-run adjustment process when an industry is making above-normal profits (though not only then). If the companies manufacturing personal computers (PCs) are making unusually high profits, capital flows into the industry, capacity expands, and eventually businessmen produce additional PCs. In order to sell the additional PCs, they have to lower their prices and all other PC companies have to follow. The decreases in price cause the quantity demanded to increase to equal the rising quantities supplied. At the end, PC companies supply a greater quantity of PCs; the lower price reflects the decrease in the relative scarcity of PCs.

This is how increases in supply reduce price. An increase in an industry's supply can only be sold at lower prices and competing businessmen have to follow the price reductions initiated by others. Their motive is to remain competitive and to sell their output; the falling price measures the decrease in relative scarcity.

In conclusion, when an industry's demand changes relative to its supply or its supply changes relative to its demand, there is a change in price that reflects the change in relative scarcity. *Relative scarcity is measured by the average price in an industry necessary to equate the quantity demanded to the quantity supplied.*[7] A higher price for a product indicates greater relative scarcity; a lower price indicates less relative scarcity or greater relative abundance.

E. Relative Scarcity and the Cost of Production

Chapter 10 (pp. 197–201) showed that businessmen change their prices when the average cost of production changes, and that over the long run, increases in cost cause decreases in supply and decreases in cost cause increases in supply. Now we can observe that changes in cost usually reflect changes in the relative scarcity of the factors of production. Consequently, over the long run, the changes in price that result from changes in cost reflect a dual change in relative scarcity: first a change in the relative scarcity of the factors and second a change in the relative scarcity of the product the factors produce.

Costs in general are reducible to goods and services whose prices reflect their relative scarcity—prices that increase with increases in demand relative to supply and that decrease with increases in supply relative to demand. By far the most important of these costs are the wages and salaries of employees (chapter 9), which increase and decrease for each kind of worker with changes in the workers' relative scarcity. The other costs that reflect relative scarcity are the prices of basic commodities whose brokered prices constantly rise and fall with changes in supply and demand (chapter 11, part IV). Traced back through the chain of production, the price of every good and service can be broken up into these two components: (1) basic commodities and (2) workers, that is, human beings. The material components of every good originally came from the earth and most of these components are basic commodities (for example, crude oil, natural gas, copper, lumber, and wheat)—and every good and service, including the basic commodities, is produced by human beings.

The cost of production of a product is the consequence of two elements: (1) the relative scarcity of the factors employed and (2) the quantity of the factors employed. High costs of production reflect either more scarce factors or a greater quantity of less scarce factors, or both.

III. Relative Scarcity and the Theory of Objective Prices

What is the point of the concept of relative scarcity? What does it add to the theory of objective prices?

Relative scarcity adds a new dimension to our understanding of the role of prices in the economy. Viewed as objective economic value, the price of every product tells us the ranking in men's hierarchies of values and what they are willing to pay, based on their grasp of the economic facts; in other words, the price tells us how *valuable* the product is to people. Viewed as relative scarcity, the price of every product reflects a different set of facts: the demand for the product relative to the supply—the price tells us how *scarce* the product is.

Consider the nonhuman factors of production: The producers of those factors set or negotiate the price based on the facts. A high price signals a high objective value to the businessmen who buy and sell it, and the reverse for a low price. Alternatively, a high price measures high relative scarcity; it tells us that across an industry, the demand for the factor is high relative to the supply—that relative to the demand by businessmen, there is not much of this factor.

factor is high relative to the supply—that relative to the demand by businessmen, there is not much of this factor.

Chapter 9 showed that the wage rate for each type of worker reflects the demand for that type of worker relative to the supply. A high salary tells us that the businessmen who hire that type of worker put a high value on him, that he is important to their businesses. High relative scarcity tells us that relative to the demand by businessmen, there are not many workers of this type.

The price of each consumer good and service tells us the objective economic value of the item to the people who buy and sell it. High prices tell us that the buyers and the sellers put a high value on the item. High relative scarcity tells us that relative to the demand by consumers, there are not many units of this good available.

IV. Derived Demand

Derived demand is the demand for a good or service that is caused by the demand for another good or service. For example, the demand for computer chips by a computer manufacturer is derived from the demand for computers by the company's customers. The more computers the company sells per month, the more computer chips per month it demands from its suppliers. Most economists believe that the demand for most employees and for all producer goods and services are derived demands—derived from the demand by consumers for consumer goods and services. There is an important sense in which this is true.

In Aristotle's terminology, *the final cause* of all economic action is man's life on earth. That is the end toward which men direct their economic actions (putting aside nonobjective goods). The goods which directly support man's life are consumer goods and services. A business whose product did not contribute at least indirectly to the production of a consumer good or service could not exist. There would be no place for the product to enter the chain of production. Whatever it was, no other business would have any use for it.

Again in Aristotle's terminology, *the efficient cause* of economic activity is production. Economic production is the creation of goods and services for sale. The output of each business in the economy functions as a link in a chain of cause and effect, the final link being a consumer good or service. The end of economic activity is to support man's life on earth; the means to that end is production. This is the principle underly-

Most economists also interpret derived demand in a sense which is *not* valid: that consumers control the economy and that the economy is for the sake of the consumers. Chapter 10 (pp. 204–5) demonstrated that capitalism is a system of producer sovereignty. Usually changes in the structure of production do not originate with changes in consumers' demand, but with changes in producers' ideas.

The subject of derived demand also bears directly on an important theoretical error. Chapter 5 (pp. 87–88) observed that the subjectivists hold that the bedrock of the economic system is consumer preferences, that consumer preferences determine the prices of the factors of production, which in turn determine the prices of the factors' products. (For an example of their reasoning, see Böhm-Bawerk 1959, 248–56). The root of this idea is the notion that the higher the price consumers are willing to pay for a product, the higher the price businessmen will pay for the factors (primarily workers) which produce that product. This offshoot of derived demand is an error.

The most simple example of derived demand comes from Böhm-Bawerk (1959, 176; 1892, 70, 72). He pointed to the case of land that is used to grow grapes from which wine is produced. Is the wine high-priced because a high price must be paid to rent the land, or is the rent high because consumers are willing to pay a high price for the wine? Since the demand for the land is derived from the demand for the wine, Böhm-Bawerk thought that it was self-evident that the land is high-priced because the wine is high-priced.

However, high prices indicate greater relative scarcity. From that perspective, we can rephrase the question: Is the wine unusually scarce because the land is unusually scarce, or is the land unusually scarce because the wine is unusually scarce? And we reach a different conclusion. The scarcity of the wine reflects the scarcity of the land. If the land were less scarce, the wine would be less scarce.

The demand for the land *is* derived from the demand for the wine, but consumer demand for the wine does not create the price of either the wine or the land. If the demand for his wine decreased, the vintner would have to reduce the price of his wine and, to stay in business, he would have to negotiate a lower rent with his landlord. Alternatively, if more acres of land able to produce this wine became available, the landlord would have to lower his rent. A few years later (after the grapes had changed into wine), more wine of this type would appear and the vintner would have to lower his price. The rent of the land does not fall because the price of the wine falls (obviously not, since it falls *before* the price of the wine falls). The rent falls because the relative scarcity of this kind of land decreases and in order to rent his land, the landlord has to accept a lower price. Nor does the vintner charge a lower price for his wine because his rent has fallen. He charges a lower price because the relative scarcity of his wine has decreased and a lower price is necessary to sell his wine. There is a connection between the two prices. The vintner is able to charge a competitive price and remain in business only because his rent falls. We will return to this point in the last paragraph of this section.

The theory that derived demand determines the prices of the factors of production survives, at least in part, because its advocates have failed to grasp the complexity of the causal connections that tie the demand for consumer goods to the demand for producer goods and services. Consequently, let us consider a case where the causal chain is less direct.

Suppose Mr. Edwards' business produces copy paper which he sells to Mr. Santiago to stock his copy machines. Mr. Santiago produces electric motors which he sells to Mr. Baird to operate his loading belts. Mr. Baird uses the loading belts to load computers onto his trucks. The trucks deliver computers to retail stores that sell them to consumers. Note that none of these goods (copy paper, electric motors, loading belts, trucks) has any direct use in producing computers. "Direct use" means a use that can be directly observed (Fog's concept, p. 77 above). Derived demand means that the demand ultimately can be traced back to the demand for a consumer good, but the causal connection between producer goods and consumer goods can be quite remote and indirect—and often is.

The primary form of derived demand is a causal chain—a chain of cause and effect that results in the creation of a consumer good. Derived demand also can be thought of as a value chain, a chain whereby one item is a value because it is the means to another value that is a means to another value, and so forth. The chain ends when we reach the consumer good which is the final economic value.[8] For example, land has value because it is the means to grapes which have value because they are the means to wine which the consumer values as a means to his enjoyment of life. Copy paper has value because it is a means to operating a copy machine, which is a means to producing electric motors, which are the means to moving loading belts, which are the means to loading computers onto trucks, which are the means of transporting computers to computer stores.

But, contrary to the subjectivists, derived demand does not create a chain of *prices*. Certainly businessmen produce goods or services in anticipation of demand, but that anticipation does not create a causal relation between the price of the product and the prices of the factors used to produce it. The reason is that the cause and effect connection of factors to consumer goods usually is (I do not know of any other way to say it) *all mixed up*. The price of every factor (steel, for example) reflects its relative scarcity, and that is determined by the demand (relative to the supply) of many different producers, some of which produce products that consumers value highly (like automobiles) and some of which produce products that consumers do not value so highly (like can openers), and many of which produce products that consumers do not value at all (producer goods like steam shovels, machine lathes, and office buildings). All those demands together, relative to the supply, constitute steel's relative scarcity and are reflected in its price. The connection of the price of steel to consumer demand is one step removed up the causal chain for automobiles, many more steps removed for can openers, and virtually nonexistent for office buildings. (There has to be some connection of an office building to consumer demand, but if the office building has one thousand tenants, the connection could be to a thousand different items, not all of which are consumer items.)

If an entrepreneur is planning to produce a product that has not been produced before, then he is concerned about the demand in the future. *But the new product need not be a consumer good.* A businessman may produce something consumers have never heard of and never will hear of, for example, an improved piece of equipment for business customers that lowers costs or raises quality or increases the rate of production. This equipment may be used in the production of things whose impact on consumer goods is very distant and indirect and impossible to measure.

The subjectivists, and explicitly Jevons (chapter 5) and the Austrians,[9] held that consumers' demand for products determines the wages of the employees who produce those products. If we are talking about employees with generalized skills (which is most employees), like middle managers, secretaries, computer programmers, engineers, new MBAs, accountants, clerks, truck drivers, and so forth, the demand for those employees comes from hundreds of different businesses producing hundreds of different products at hundreds of different prices reflecting hundreds of different quantities demanded by consumers—and also by producers. In addition, most businesses hire many different employees with many different skills. The idea that consumer demand somehow determines the wage rates for all these workers, and that their wage rates somehow reflect the value to consumers of all the products they help to produce, is absurd.

Normally, different units of the same factor will participate directly and indirectly in the production of many different consumer goods, each with a different selling price. For example, oil is used (1) to produce gasoline and heating oil, (2) to power generators to produce electricity, (3) to manufacture many artificial fibers which are used to produce countless items of clothing. Consequently, a definite relation between the price of oil and the prices of all the different products it helps to produce is impossible. It is not even clear what such a relation would mean. Most factors are not "direct" in Fog's sense; that is, they do not help to produce a businessman's product in any hands-on way. Consequently, the subjectivists have to claim that there is a necessary relation between the price of the factor and the prices of all the products produced by all the companies which employ that factor in any capacity whatever. That claim is unintelligible.

Sometimes, infrequently, a business asks its customers what features they would like a product to have (a motel room, for example) and what they would consider a fair price for a product with those features. Then the businessman tries to build a product that has those features and which he can sell for that price. Marriott Courtyards was developed in this way. In such cases, it is possible that the average price the customers said they would pay may affect the prices of some of the factors. If a price is negotiable, the businessman may feel pressure to negotiate a price at which he can provide the product his customers want and still make a profit selling at the price they consider fair. But not all prices are negotiable, nor is there any guarantee that the businessman will be able to negotiate the prices he needs—particularly because his customers have no basis for their notion of a fair price apart from what they are accustomed to paying.

There is only one relationship that economics can identify as necessary between the value of a product and the value of the factors used to produce it—the former must exceed the latter; that is, the businessman's total revenue must exceed his total cost; that is, over the long run, the business must make a profit sufficient to maintain its capital. We can add nothing to this requirement.

V. The Distribution of
the Factors of Production

A typical modern economy has millions of workers with perhaps hundreds of thousands of different specialized skills. At the same time, all the businesses that are not producing consumer goods and services are producing nonhuman factors of production, consisting of hundreds of thousands of different goods and services. Somehow, all those human and nonhuman factors are divided up among the millions of different businesses in the economy. How does that happen?[10]

The underlying principle is economizing. Economizing means to reduce one's use of a good or service by using it more carefully or by substituting an alternative (pp. 31 and 38 above). The identity between higher prices and greater relative scarcity means that in production, businessmen are motivated to economize on the scarcest factors—that is, to economize more on the factors that are more scarce. In doing so, they minimize their costs and make the factors of greater relative scarcity available to those businessmen who can make the best (most profitable) use of them.

When a businessman weighs the price of a factor in deciding upon its purchase, he is simultaneously weighing the relative scarcity of that product. His decision of whether or not to buy is motivated by the end to which this factor is a means. Whatever the price, a given factor is purchased by those producers who, in their judgment, have the most important ends for the factor. Those with less important ends, also in their judgment, buy less expensive factors.

Thus, producers give the maximum amount of thought and care to those goods with the highest relative scarcity, that is, those goods with the greatest demand relative to the supply—which means those goods which are most highly valued by other producers for their own productive ends. In thinking carefully about expensive purchases, it is as if producers were thinking, "The high price of this factor means that it is important to other producers, so I am not going to pay that price, and remove it from another man's use, unless I am going to get a greater benefit than he would get." If he buys the factor, he does get a greater benefit, because the man thereby excluded from the factor excludes himself by refusing to pay the price. The value in production that businessmen receive from the factors they buy exceeds the value that would have been received by the businessmen who do not buy, both in the judgment of the individuals involved. *This is the principle by which capitalism distributes the factors of production among all the economy's businesses.*

For example, suppose that the price of steel per ton exceeds the price of aluminum per ton. This means that steel is relatively more scarce than aluminum. Businessmen do not care about relative scarcity, but the relative prices they face motivate them to act as if they cared. If steel per ton is more expensive than aluminum per ton, then other things equal, producers will prefer aluminum over steel in production. Those who choose to use steel in spite of the higher price will be the businessmen who value steel more highly for their productive purposes.

Relative wages for human factors have the same effect as relative prices for nonhuman factors. Those workers who are relatively more scarce are also more expensive, and businessmen are motivated to economize on them. Chapter 9 showed that higher prices eliminate some firms from the market for both human and nonhuman factors, restricting the market to the businessmen who place the highest value on a particular factor. Now we can see that this means that the effect of high prices is to reserve the scarcest factors for those businessmen that can make the best use of them.

The principle of economizing on the use of scarce factors also influences the method of production that businessmen choose. They choose the method that uses the least scarce or the most abundant factors, which means that, other things equal, they choose the low-cost method.

Another implication of minimizing the use of scarce factors is that goods which are relatively more scarce are treated with more care because such goods and services have higher prices. The purchase of multimillion dollar machine tools gets a lot of attention and consideration by business managers, whereas copy paper is purchased routinely. This means that the more expensive items get more thought than the less expensive items, which is a requirement for a rationally functioning *business*. At the same time, it means that the relatively more scarce items get more thought than the less scarce items, which is a requirement of a rationally functioning *economy*.

All this is duplicated by consumers in their purchase of consumer goods and services. First, the most scarce consumer goods flow disproportionately to those whose labor is the most scarce, that is, to those who receive the highest incomes. Then, given their incomes, consumers evaluate goods and services as means to the enjoyment of their lives. Each man who chooses to pay the current price has a use for the good that he ranks higher than the price he has to pay. Those who choose not to pay the price rank the good below the price they have to pay. Within the context of his income and hierarchy of values, each consumer satisfies his most highly ranked ends and leaves the more expensive and more scarce goods for those who rank them higher than he does.

Relative wages have the same effect on consumers as they do on businessmen to the extent that consumers employ people like housekeepers and nannies. Their demand is motivated by the use they have for the worker. Whatever the wage rate, the quantity of every kind of worker is distributed to those consumers who, in their judgment, have the most important uses for workers of that kind. Those with less important uses, also in their judgment, employ less expensive workers, or none.

VI. The Economic Significance of Profit

The ultimate standard by which businessmen decide what to do is their long-run expected rate of profit.[11] This is the standard that lies behind the decisions in the preceding section of whether or not to buy or hire a particular factor. We saw in chapter 6 that this is the standard by which businessmen decide what price to charge. Chapter 10 argued that a capitalist economy is characterized by producer sovereignty. Long-run expected profits ultimately determine everything about the economy: what is produced, in what quantities, at what prices, in what time period, by what method, in what structures, employing what workers, in what numbers, for what wages, and so forth. It follows that in order to confirm the objectivity of a capitalist economy, we have to identify the objective basis of profits. If profits were not tied to reality, if profits were somehow arbitrary or arbitrarily distributed among businesses, then everything about the economy would be arbitrary as well. There would be no reason to expect such an economy to provide the material support for man's life on earth.

Chapter 9 introduced and explained *the rate of profit*. The rate of profit governs what businessmen do in directing the operation of the economy. In a capitalist economy, the scarcest goods and the greatest quantities of goods flow to those who value them the most and who have the most money (actual or prospective) to pay for them. This means that the scarcest factors of production flow in the greatest quantities to businesses with the highest rates of profit and away from those businesses with the lowest rates of profit or losses. What does that mean for the working of a capitalist economy? What is the significance of a high rate of profit versus a low rate of profit?

Since price measures the objective economic value of the business-man's product, and since this is true of every separate item the business-man sells at every separate price for which he sells it, his total revenue measures the objective economic value of his total output over a year. Let us distinguish the total output of a business from the total output of the economy by calling the latter *aggregate* output, as is the custom in modern economics. Then an economy's aggregate output for a year is approximately measured by summing up the total revenue of every busi-ness in the economy.[12] That total is the aggregate objective value of all the goods and services produced and sold.

A businessman's total cost is the total value of all the human and nonhuman factors he uses in the production of his product. Each of those factors has a price that is its objective economic value. The summation of each price times the number of units bought, hired, or leased at that price is the total objective economic value of each factor a businessman uses in production. The sum of those totals for every factor a business hires, plus depreciation, is the business's total cost.

Profit is total revenue minus total cost. It is the difference between the objective economic value of the businessman's output and the objec-tive economic value of the factors he uses to produce that output. His rate of profit measures what the businessman gets out of his factors. The greater the difference between total revenue and total cost, the greater the output per dollar input.

Let us return to Excel Menswear and New World Furniture from chapter 9 (pp. 156–57). Excel's rate of profit is 10%. That means the value of Excel's output is 10% greater than its costs. Excel produces $110 worth of output for each $100 invested in production. The rate of profit of New World Furniture is 100%. The value of New World's out-put is 100% greater than the value of its costs. New World produces $200 worth of output for each $100 invested in production.

When a firm makes an above-average rate of profit, its total revenue exceeds its total cost by more than the average percentage. If the busi-nessman's rate of profit exceeds the average rate, then he is getting more from his factors than other businessmen using factors of the same value. For example, suppose the average rate of profit is 10% across the econ-omy[13]. Return again to Excel Menswear (with a 10% rate of profit) and New World Furniture (with a 100% rate of profit). Suppose both busi-nesses have costs of $100 million. Then Excel Menswear contributes $110 million to the value of the economy's output and New World Furni-ture contributes $200 million. Given the magnitude of its costs, the higher the rate of profit, the greater the value of the output a business produces. Businesses with the highest rates of profit produce the most.

Usually a loss-making business will have some total revenue. That revenue measures the value of the output the loss-making business contributes to aggregate economic output, and it need not be negligible. But, when a businessman makes a loss, his factors are employed in producing a product of less value than they could produce—in the united judgment of the other businessmen who hire these factors—because they make a profit while paying the same price for the factors as the loss-making business pays. Suppose the loss-making business has been paying a specialized worker $100 an hour. When this business goes bankrupt, that specialized worker will be hired at $100 an hour by other businessmen who can make a profit while paying that wage and *the aggregate output of the economy will increase.*[14]

In general, when those human and nonhuman factors employed by a loss-making business move to a profit-making business, aggregate output increases. The same kind of increase arises from factors moving to businesses making a higher rate of profit from businesses making a lower rate of profit. Aggregate output increases because with the same costs, a profit-making businessman produces more output than a loss-making businessman—and a businessman with a higher rate of profit produces more output than a businessman with a lower rate of profit.

The advocates of self-sacrifice frequently have attacked capitalism for its heartlessness because businessmen making losses cannot survive. But this is an integral part of capitalism's virtue as an engine of production. A businessman making losses is wasting his factors relative to a businessman making profits. Businessmen with the highest rates of profit are making the most out of the factors they hire. It is to everyone's interest that their greater profits enable them to claim a disproportionate share of the economy's factors. In a free economy, factors flow to businesses with the highest rates of profit and away from businesses making the lowest rates of profit or losses. This means that the economy is continually moving in the direction of producing the maximum aggregate output that can be produced with the economy's current supply of human and nonhuman factors of production.

The Theory of Economic Growth

An economy's rate of economic growth is governed by the allocation of its total productive capacity between producing more capacity and producing consumer goods.

For example, suppose two countries, Athens and Sparta, have economies of roughly the same size and population. Suppose ninety percent of Sparta's capacity is devoted to adding capacity and ten percent to producing consumer goods, while ten percent of Athens' capacity is used to add capacity and ninety percent is used to produce consumer goods. Then, compared to Athens, the people in Sparta are poor and compared to Sparta, the people in Athens are rich. However, Sparta is growing much faster than Athens, which means that the standard of living in Sparta is growing much faster than in Athens. Over the long run (for this subject, about fifty years), Sparta will leave Athens in its dust.

Economic growth reflects the choice of a country's citizens between (1) a higher current standard of living and lower economic growth, and (2) a lower current standard of living and higher economic growth— resulting in a higher future standard of living. Each individual makes exactly that choice when he chooses what to save and to consume. The more he saves, the less money he has to spend on his current consumption. But over time his savings earn interest and as a result, he will have more money to spend on his future consumption. This choice made by all the citizens of an economy determines an economy's rate of growth. Every dollar saved is a dollar less spent on consumer goods and a dollar less demand for consumer goods. At the same time, it is a dollar more made available for businessmen to invest in adding capacity.

There is no basis for saying what proportion of their income people *should* save or consume. But we can observe that the savings rate is highest in societies which are more rational, which make private property secure, and which give their citizens reason to believe that the future will be better than today.

The economic significance of profit is that in their pursuit of profit, men maximize the objective economic value of the output produced with the existing productive capacity of the economy. As a direct consequence, given men's decisions of what portions of their income to save and consume, the pursuit of profit also maximizes the long-term rate of economic growth. These two outcomes explain the rise in the standard of living that capitalism has brought to every country on the globe that has dared to try it. A rising standard of living depends on increasing the output of consumer goods relative to the number of workers. This is precisely the effect of the ever-increasing flood of consumer goods and services that pours forth from a capitalist economy. When we consider how hampered every semi-capitalist economy has been, it is clear that that flood could have been, and can be yet, a deluge. The rise in living standards in the West in the last 200 years is just a hint of what is possible to men on earth if they will give up the initiation of force and leave the producers free to produce and profit.

VII. The Moral Justification of Wages and Profits

When people denounce the free market as "cruel," the fact they are decrying is that the market is ruled by a single moral principle: *justice*. And *that* is the root of their hatred for capitalism (Rand 1966, 69).

This brief section is an excursion into ethics. As such, it is not part of economics' subject matter. Nevertheless, this comment is necessary.

The justification for the different wages that workers receive is that each worker's wage measures his employer's evaluation of his productive contribution. Employees who contribute the most receive the greatest rewards, and they receive those rewards in direct proportion to what they contribute. This is the principle of justice inherent in a capitalist economy. By justice, I mean giving men what they deserve. In this, I take man's life on earth as the standard of value, so what men deserve is what they produce, as gauged by the businessmen who hire them.

The economic significance of profits described in part VI above is not the justification for profits. Profit is the reward to the owner(s) of the business for investing the money necessary to set up and run the business. Profits do not measure any value that is *to* any human being, except to the owners of the business, as their reward for production. The justification of profits is that they are earned in free exchange with other men. If men want goods to be produced, the producers have to be paid for their work, on whatever terms they care to set.

Firms making the highest rate of profit are producing goods for which the percentage difference between total revenue and total cost is the greatest. This means the output of the economy is greater and its economic growth is faster than if businessmen making lower profits or losses employed the same factors. Is this good for the people who participate in the economy? If they buy the product the businessman sells, they gain. If they do not buy it, they do not gain. Only the owners of the business benefit directly from the profits earned by the business, which is the additional income they receive. If the business is a corporation, the stockholders are the owners and they receive dividends. If the corporation reinvests its profits, the price of the stock rises to reflect the higher value of the corporation and the owners' wealth increases. From either dividends or retained earnings, the owners, and only the owners, bene-fit.[15]

Profits and wages are not to be justified on the grounds of their effect on the general welfare. The "general welfare" is a collectivist standard, which has dominated and degraded economic thought from its inception. Collectivism is evil in theory and practice. Its opposite is the idea that every man is an end in himself and has a *right* to whatever he can earn in free exchange with his fellow men. The justification of capitalism is not that the economy grows faster than it grows under any other system—under which it does not grow at all. The justification of capitalism is not that the goods pour forth. The justification of capitalism is that it is the only economic system consistent with the requirements of man's rational nature, that it protects man's rights and leaves each individual free to act in his own private, individual self-interest, based on nothing but his own uncoerced, rational judgment. That is the human mode of survival; that is what man's nature requires of him if he is to live on earth. The abun-dance of a capitalist economy is a consequence of its coherence with man's rational nature. That is its fundamental justification—not its con-sequence as an engine of production. The correct moral argument for capitalism is not that capitalism is good for man because it leads to mate-rial abundance. The correct moral argument is that capitalism leads to material abundance because it is good for man.

CHAPTER THIRTEEN

TOTAL SPENDING AND PRODUCTION

I. The National Income and Product Accounts

The national income and product accounts (NIPA) are the accounting data for the total economy. Government agencies collect and tabulate the data; in the United States, the Commerce Department reports the latest results each quarter on an annual basis. Modern economists think that these accounts measure a country's total economic *output*. The standard method for calculating these figures is an error.

I will focus on the United States' national income accounts. The largest number commonly reported is the Gross Domestic Product (GDP). This is supposed to measure the total value of all the goods and services produced by a country's citizens over a year. The GDP is reached in two ways: (1) by adding up the total spending by consumers, businesses, and government on all the final goods and services produced (to simplify, I ignore foreign trade), and (2) by adding up the total income (primarily profit and wages) received by businesses and individuals in the process of producing the GDP. I will call this total the "income received for production" to distinguish it from other sources of income like government welfare payments. For reasons we will see, the total numbers reached by these two methods vary from each other only by a "statistical discrepancy."

Calculated by method (1), by far the largest percentage of spending consists of consumption spending. In 2009, consumers purchased 69% of GDP, government spending accounted for 20%, and businesses purchased 11%.[1] This is the basis on which economists consider consumption spending as the most important cause of aggregate output, and changes in consumption spending as the most important cause of economic expansions, recessions, depressions, price inflation, and economic growth or decline.

From this point forward, I will delete government on the premise that in a laissez-faire economy government spending on output would be negligible. Thus, taking GDP as the summation of consumer and business spending only, in 2009 consumers purchased 86% of national output and businesses purchased 14%.[2] *The relative importance of consumer and business spending in the economy is the exact opposite of that indicated by these numbers.*

The error in the standard calculation of GDP is that this measure counts spending on only *final* goods and services. The basis of that error is an implicit concept of intrinsic value. The demonstration of that error, its consequences, and its correction are the subjects of this chapter.

First, let us make clear what final products are. A final product is a new product that someone purchases for use, in production or consumption, not to resell at a profit. (Used goods are not included in current GDP because they were produced, and counted, in the GDP of prior years.) Final goods include all consumer goods and services and all business fixed investment, which includes producers' durable equipment (machines and tools), structures (factories, plants, and buildings), and all business construction, including residential construction. When a consumer buys a new car, he buys it to use, consume, and enjoy. He may resell his car some day, but that is not why he buys it. Similarly, some day a business may resell a machine tool, but it buys the machine tool to use in production.

In contrast to final products, businesses buy intermediate goods and services in order to resell at a profit. Intermediate goods are the materials (including raw materials), parts, and ingredients that businesses turn into their products. Materials like wheat, iron, steel, copper, oil, wood, and so on, are the intermediate goods out of which producers make everything else. Producers incorporate intermediate goods into their products and sell them to the next business in the chain of production. For example, millers manufacture flour out of wheat and then bakers manufacture bread out of flour.

Intermediate services are services that businesses produce and sell to each other, like insurance, accounting, finance, legal advice, advertising, transportation, and electricity. Intermediate services do not become physical components of goods, but they are essential components of the *business* that buys them. They make it possible for the business to continue to function as a business.[3]

Why do the national income accounts add up the value of only final goods and services to calculate GDP? There are three steps in the argument: (A) The value businesses produce is measured by the income businesses and individuals receive for production; (B) The income received is equal to the value added; (C) The total value added equals the value of the final products.

A. Income Received for Production Equals the Value Produced

Consider Table A:

TABLE A

product	selling price
wheat	20¢
flour	50¢
bread	$1.10
bread in store	$1.49

This is an essentialized chain of production for a single loaf of bread. Wheat, flour, and bread are intermediate goods. Let us assume that the miller needs a bushel of wheat to make a pound of flour and the baker needs a pound of flour to make a loaf of bread. The wheat farmer charges the miller 20¢ for a bushel of wheat, the miller charges the baker 50¢ for a pound of flour, the baker charges the grocer $1.10 for a loaf of bread, and the grocer charges his customers $1.49 for the loaf in his store. To simplify the story, let us assume that the farmer grows wheat without intermediate goods like fertilizer and pesticide (which in modern parlance makes the wheat "organic"). In addition, we assume that wheat is the only ingredient in flour and flour is the only ingredient in bread. These assumptions strip this concretization down to its essentials.

Out of this chain of products, the standard calculation of GDP would count only the value of the bread in the grocery. The argument goes as follows: The farmer produces the full value of the wheat because (by assumption) he does not use any intermediate goods. But the miller needs wheat to produce his flour. Consequently, he does not produce the full value of the flour. The miller's contribution to production, economists hold, is what he adds to the value of the wheat, that is, 30¢. On the same reasoning, the flour is required to produce the bread, so the baker does not produce the full value of the bread, but only the difference between the value of the flour and the value of the bread (60¢). And similarly, the grocer does not produce the full value of the bread in his store, but only the difference between the price he paid the baker and the price he charges (39¢).

The value businesses produce, as described in the preceding paragraph, is equal to the income received in the process of producing each business's product. This is the income received for production, defined as income payments by businesses to their employees[4] plus profits or minus losses. From this perspective, the costs of businesses have only two components: (1) payments to other businesses (for intermediate goods and services),[5] and (2) the income payments the business makes to its employees. As a consequence, the income received for production necessarily equals the value of the business's output.[6]

For example, the baker pays the miller 50¢ for a pound of flour and sells his loaf of bread to the grocer for $1.10; the value of his production is 60¢. If he pays his employees 55¢ to bake the bread, then he makes 5¢ on each loaf and the income received is 60¢ (55¢ + 5¢). If he pays his employees 65¢, then he has a loss of 5¢ on each loaf and the income received again is 60¢ (65¢ - 5¢).

In general, for any product at any stage of production, if total revenue exceeds total cost, the difference is profit that is added to income payments to equal the income received for production. If total cost exceeds total revenue, the difference is a loss, which is subtracted from income payments to equal income received for production. Whatever the value a baker, for example, adds to the value produced by other businesses, that additional value is equal to the income he and his employees receive for producing bread.

Thus, we can add a second column, income received, to Table A to get Table B. Each amount at each stage is the difference between the price charged and the price paid for the output of the previous stage.

TABLE B

product	selling price	income received
wheat	20¢	20¢
flour	50¢	30¢
bread	$1.10	60¢
bread in store	$1.49	39¢

B. Income Received for Production Equals the Value Added

Economists call the value that businesses add to their products *value added*. Value added is defined as the selling price of the businessman's product minus the value of his purchases of intermediate goods and services from other businesses. By definition, value added equals the income received for production, Thus, we can add a third column, value added, identical to the second column, to derive Table C.

TABLE C

product	selling price	income received	value added
wheat	20¢	20¢	20¢
flour	50¢	30¢	30¢
bread	$1.10	60¢	60¢
bread in store	$1.49	39¢	39¢
TOTAL		$1.49	$1.49

C. Total Value Added Equals Value of the Final Product

Note that the totals for income received and value added are both equal to the price the grocer charges for a loaf of bread. This equality is the basis on which economists measure national output by summing up the value of only the final products. To see why, let us trace the components of price back up the chain of production.

The price of the bread in the store is the price of the bread to the grocer plus 39¢ of value added by the grocer. The price of the bread is the price of the flour plus 60¢ of value added by the baker. The price of the flour is the price of the wheat plus 30¢ of value added by the miller. By assumption, wheat does not require any other product for its production so the price of the wheat is the 20¢ of value added by the farmer.

The relation we see here is universal across the economy. As we move further and further up the productive chain, every price resolves into the value added by this business plus the cost of purchases from other businesses. Ultimately, there is no mathematical difference between the sum of all the values added and the price of the final product. The price of each final product equals the sum of the values added by intermediate goods and services throughout the chain of production, plus the value added by the producer of the final product.

Table C is highly simplified. In reality, the products of many other businesses are required to produce wheat or flour or bread. Then each of those businesses in turn requires the output of other firms in order to produce their output. Instead of a simple chain, there is a branching of businesses supplying this business and then a branching of businesses supplying each of the branches. But the simple chain in Table C represents the essence of the relationship.

D. The Double-Counting Argument

The double-counting argument is the formal justification for the principle of measuring GDP by adding up the value of the final products. The double-counting argument says that *to measure production by adding the value of the output of two successive stages of production would be counting the same value twice.* For example, the value of the bread ($1.10) is the value of the flour (50¢) plus the 60¢ of value added by the baker. Consequently, to measure production by adding the value of the bread to the value of the flour ($1.10 + 50¢ = $1.60) would count the value of the flour twice—once in the flour and again in the bread. Modern economists believe that to measure the total value of production (GDP) by adding up the price of every product produced would grossly overstate the economy's output.

E. Total Spending Equals Spending on Final Products

The national income and product accounts are based on the three-way equality identified in Table C: the value of the final product equals the income received for producing that product and that equals the value added in producing that product. Or, alternatively:

| the value of a final product | equals | the income received for producing the final product | equals | the value added in producing the final product |

Since this is true of every individual final product, it is true of all final products put together. Thus, GDP = Aggregate Income Received = Aggregate Value Added. It follows that the total value of an economy's production can be calculated three ways: (1) by adding up total spending on final goods and services; (2) by adding up the total income received in exchange for productive work; and (3) by adding up the total value added in production. The accountants of national income cannot follow this third alternative in practice, but a separate calculation is made of income received for production, which differs from the calculation of spending on final goods and services by the statistical discrepancy mentioned at the beginning of this chapter (p. 258).

As the final inevitable consequence, modern economists hold that total spending or aggregate demand equals total spending on final products. This last step is where modern economics goes completely off the tracks, but the preceding accounting relationships are what make the wreck unavoidable. Abstractly, it seems that it would be possible to accept these accounting relationships (and I do accept them), and still get aggregate spending right. But as a practical matter, it is not possible and it did not happen. Let me explain.

II. Intrinsic Value in the National Income and Product Accounts

Intrinsic value is the idea that value is in things, prior to and independent of the values and evaluations of men. The naïve view of intrinsic value (chapter 2) is that value resides in things as a kind of substance, essence, or stuff and an item's value is determined by how much value substance it contains. This is the concept of intrinsic value at the base of the national income accounts.

That premise, that value is a kind of substance, underlies every step and every argument I presented above. We can most easily see the value stuff premise in the double-counting argument. "The same value" in that argument is intrinsic value. We cannot measure production, the argument says, by adding the value of the flour to the value of the bread because the value of the flour is in the bread. The key word in that sentence is "in." The implicit premise is that the value of the flour exists as a substance IN the flour and bakers incorporate that substance with the flour IN the bread, so the value of the bread contains the value of the flour.

Another consequence of intrinsic value is the idea that producers do not produce products. Rather they produce additions of value (intrinsic value) to the products produced by others, who in turn do not produce products but produce additions of value to the products produced by still others, and so on indefinitely. This conception of production would be impossible without intrinsic value. It depends on taking value as an independently existing thing that businesses create in production, adding to the value substance created by others.[7]

Another signpost of intrinsic value is the idea that businessmen produce the *difference* between the value of the products they produce and the value of the products they buy from other businessmen. Businessmen produce *a difference*. What is that? This conception of production also would be impossible without intrinsic value. If we assume the existence of intrinsic value, then the difference is the value stuff produced by the businessman, which is the difference between the value stuff he buys from other businesses and the value stuff he sells.

The services that businesses buy from each other, like insurance, accounting, finance, legal advice, transportation, advertising, and electricity, are not physically incorporated in the final good. Nevertheless, the national income accounts treat them as if they were. All the payments a firm makes to other businesses are taken as measuring the contribution of those businesses to the value of the firm's output. The cases where intermediate materials are physically incorporated in subsequent products are the paradigm cases; they establish the mind set for treating all intermediate products as if they were physically incorporated. The underlying essential here is that throughout, economists conceive of value as intrinsic value, as an independently existing thing that businesses produce and sell to other businesses.

What is wrong with this incarnation of intrinsic value? What harm does it do? What error does it cause?

First and foremost, it results in a complete misapprehension of the nature of production. Firms do not produce value or additions of value to what others have produced. Firms produce products, goods and services, which *have* value.[8] The value-added can be calculated, but that does not turn it into a thing.

To get a national income and product accounts that reflects reality, we have to start over.

III. National Income Based on Objective Value

Gross Domestic Product (GDP) should measure the total value of the goods and services *produced* by a country's citizens over a year—which the current measure does not do. To remedy the deficit in the current approach, we need to go back to fundamentals. The key term in the conception of GDP is "produced." Production in its widest conception is the creation of a value. Economic production is the creation of a value for sale (chapter 3, part I). Values created in order to be sold are goods and services. The value of a good or service is its price, which measures its objective economic value and its relative scarcity. The good itself may be objective or nonobjective, but the price of the good is objective if the purpose of the seller is to make a profit. Proof of that was the subject of chapters 5 through 8. As the sum of the prices of all the goods and services produced, GDP is also objective—the objective value of the economy's output. But it cannot be measured by adding the value of only final goods and services.

Return to Table A:

TABLE A

product	selling price
wheat	20¢
flour	50¢
bread	$1.10
bread in store	$1.49

Let us consider the production of bread, and describe objectively what is going on. An objective description requires that, at a minimum, we answer the questions "to whom?" and "for what?" (p. 32 above).

The miller produces a pound of flour which he sells to the baker for 50¢. To whom is the value of the flour 50¢? First to the miller; it is his reward for producing the flour. Second to the baker; 50¢ is the value that he places on the flour, and the value at which his accountant carries the flour on his books. For what purpose is the flour's value 50¢? For the miller, the flour contributes 50¢ to the continued operation of his business. With that 50¢, he can buy more wheat and materials, pay his workers, and keep his business going. For the baker, 50¢ worth of flour is the means to produce a loaf of bread that he can sell at a profit for $1.10.

The value added by the miller and the baker can be calculated. The miller adds 30¢ to the value of the wheat and the baker adds 60¢ to the value of the flour. But there is nobody *to whom* that is the value of anything. There is no *purpose* for which the value added is produced. The value added is not *for* anything. There is nothing anybody can do with 30¢ of value-added or with 60¢ of value-added. Value added does not exist as anything other than a calculation.

To sum up: The farmer produces wheat that has a value of 20¢. The miller produces flour that has a value of 50¢. The baker produces bread with a value of $1.10. All of them produce goods that have value. They do not produce additions of value. They do not produce the difference between one value and another. They produce products that *have* value.

Things are different with the grocer. The grocer does not produce bread; he performs a service. A service is an action a man is paid to perform because it creates an economic value (p. 45 above). The value the grocer creates is bread on a shelf in his store ready to pick up and take home.

Retailers and wholesalers do not produce the goods they provide; they produce (perform) services. The wholesaler's service is essentially transportation; he brings the product to the retailer. The retailer's service is to make the product available to his customers. In the stylized chain of production represented in Table A, the value of the services of retailers and wholesalers is the difference between the prices they pay for the goods and the prices at which they sell them. The value of the grocer's service is the price for which he sells the bread minus the price he pays the baker. This is what we have been calling value-added, but the grocer does not produce a value added. He performs a service whose product (the convenient availability of the bread) has value to his customers.

GDP should be measured by adding up, not just the prices of final goods and services, but also the prices of intermediate goods and services. Each intermediate good or service is a real product that has value to someone for some purpose.

The facts just named are represented by a new column added to Table A in order to create Table D.

TABLE D

product	selling price	value of output
wheat	20¢	20¢
flour	50¢	50¢
bread	$1.10	$1.10
bread in store	$1.49	39¢
TOTAL		$2.19

The total value of the economy's output is much greater than is indicated in the national income and product accounts. Including all intermediate goods and services in that measure could easily double it. However, this is not the most important consequence of getting rid of intrinsic value. *The total value of GDP is inconsequential.* There are many inaccuracies, rough estimates, and fudging involved in the underlying calculations and nobody thinks GDP is an exact measure, nor is it important that it should be. The significance of the GDP figure is more like that of an index number. The important numbers that are derived from it are the rate of growth or decline in the economy and the general rate of price inflation.[9] Expanding GDP to include intermediate goods and services would probably have very little impact on those numbers.

A. Total Spending

The critical importance of basing GDP on objective value is that it changes the concept of total spending (which economists call aggregate demand). Based on the national income and product accounts, modern economics takes total spending as spending on final goods and services. That is wrong. First, there is all the business production spending on intermediate goods and services, of which no account whatever is taken. We can illustrate this with another column added to Table D, and call it Table E.

TABLE E

product	selling price	value of output	spending on output
wheat	20¢	20¢	20¢
flour	50¢	50¢	50¢
bread	$1.10	$1.10	$1.10
bread in store	$1.49	39¢	$1.49
TOTAL		$2.19	$3.29

The orthodox interpretation here is that total spending is measured by the purchase of the final good only—the bread in the store by consumers. In fact, however, this viewpoint leaves out 20¢ spent by the miller for wheat, 50¢ spent by the baker for flour, and $1.10 spent by the grocer for bread. Total spending represented in this table is $3.29, not $1.49.

In addition, the traditional viewpoint leaves out of total spending all business production spending on the wages and salaries of workers. To represent this spending, let us bring back the column measuring the income received for production, rename it business spending for employees and add it to Table F.

TABLE F

product	selling price	value of output	spending on output	business spending for employees
wheat	20¢	20¢	20¢	20¢
flour	50¢	50¢	50¢	30¢
bread	$1.10	$1.10	$1.10	60¢
bread in store	$1.49	39¢	$1.49	39¢
TOTAL		$2.19	$3.29	$1.49

As the fourth column shows there is another $1.49 of total spending that goes unrecognized in modern economics, for a total of $4.78. (The total of $1.49 overstates business spending for employees to the extent that businesses earn net profits.)

How is it that in their theory of total spending, economists have been able to overlook these obvious and transparent expenditures? Certainly there is nothing hidden about them. The fact that businesses make payments to their suppliers and employees is well-known. The fact that this *production spending* by businesses is separate and distinct from the purchase of final goods by consumers is also well-known. What blinded economists to these facts? Intrinsic value. On the premise of intrinsic value, the value of the intermediate goods and services is contained in the final good, along with the value of income payments. The key to the modern theory of national income is that it takes spending on final goods and services as *identical* to spending on intermediate goods and services and, simultaneously, as *identical* to spending on employees. The consequence has been to nullify—simply to wipe out of awareness—spending on intermediate goods and services and spending on workers. In their theory, economists treat all such spending as if it is accounted for in spending on final goods and services.

The purchase of a good at any stage of production does not pay for the intermediate goods and services required to produce that good. If I buy a new house from a builder, that is not the same thing as buying the lumber, bricks, pipes, and shingles. The builder bought and paid for those things in order to build the house. Nor is my purchase of the new house the same thing as paying the wages of the carpenters, plumbers, roofers, and masons. The builder paid their wages as they worked on the house. The NIPA treat the final good as if somehow, all the intermediate goods and labor are packed into that final good so everything is purchased at the same time in that one single purchase of the final good.

Nor does my purchase of the house pay for the factors required to *replace* the house. The builder must purchase those factors in the future, *if* he decides to replace that particular house. My purchase of the house pays for my house and for nothing else.

If the price covers the cost of production, that is, if the businessman is making a profit, the purchase of his product places in his hands enough money to hire the labor and buy the intermediate goods that are necessary to replace the good sold, *if he chooses to do so*. But if and when he makes those expenditures, they are acts of *production* spending, separate and distinct from the spending by his customer who purchased the original product.

Finally, modern macroeconomics treats total business *profits* as accounted for in the spending on final goods and services—that is, in macroeconomic theory, economists suppose that some portion of that spending is received by businesses as profit. But, as we have seen, profit is the difference between total revenue and total cost (p. 98 above). It is piling error upon error to treat profit as an income receipt included in the spending on final products—which is the standard practice in macroeconomics.

B. Objective Value in the National Income and Product Accounts

The beginning of this chapter said that the standard accounting of national income attributed 81% of the national output to consumer spending and 19% to business spending. Now let us see the relative importance of consumer and business spending when the national income and product accounts are based on objective value. We will base this comparison on data from the 2009 national income and product accounts. All numbers are in billions of dollars.

Proprietors' income = $1,041.0$[10]
Corporate profits before tax = $1,308.9$[11]

These are the two forms of business profit measured in the national income accounts. Their total is $2,349.9.

The estimate I want to reach is total business spending for productive purposes—business production spending. Nothing in the national income accounts approaches this number, but the average rate of profit on sales often has been estimated at about 5%. Consequently, multiplying total business profits by twenty gives us a rough estimate of the value of total business sales (and aggregate total revenue) in 2009. That estimate is $46,998.

However, this number includes the value of output that businesses sold to parties other than business firms. To get to business spending on output, I need to deduct (1) consumer purchases of final goods and services, and (2) all government purchases from businesses of final goods and services.

(1) Personal consumption expenditures = $10,089.1$[12]

(2) Government consumption expenditure and gross investment = $2,930.7$[13]

These two amounts deducted from $46,998 leaves $33,978.2 billion as the measure of business purchases from other businesses. Of this total, $1,749.7 is fixed investment[14], that is, business purchases of final goods such as structures and equipment from other businesses. The rest is an estimate of business purchases of intermediate goods and services from other businesses, which economists do not view as final purchases, and which therefore they do not count on principle. In that uncounted spending inheres most of the economy's aggregate spending.

To complete this calculation of business production spending, we need to add the value of the wage and salary payments businesses make to their employees.

Compensation of Employees	$7,791.6[15]
Government	$1,182.4[16]

Government wage and salary payments subtracted from total compensation of employees leaves $6,609.2 of wage and salary payments by businessmen. Added to $33,978.2 gives $40,587.4 as the measure of total production spending by businesses in 2009. Total consumption spending was $10,089.1, which added to total production spending gives an estimate of total spending on new produced output of $50,676.5. Of this total, 20% is consumption spending and 80% is production spending.[17] Furthermore, most of consumption spending originates in business wage and salary payments. Rationally considered, in the generation of aggregate economic production, business production spending is the first cause.

APPENDIX A

THE THEORY OF PRICE IN MODERN ECONOMICS: A CRITIQUE

I. Market Structure

"Market structure" is the concept at the root of modern economics' theory of price. There are two aspects to market structure, as modern economists understand it: (1) The number and relative size of the firms producing a product. There can be millions of firms, or just a few firms, or only one firm. The firms can all be the same size or all different sizes or one big firm and many small firms, and so on. (2) The difference in the products produced by the firms in the industry. They may produce identical products, slightly different products, or very different products.

On this basis, modern economics identifies the following four types of market or industry:

1. Pure competition or perfect competition

Pure competition consists of many, many firms, all of them producing an identical product. In the standard interpretation, the distinguishing feature of pure competition is *powerlessness*. This powerlessness consists of the inability of any individual firm to control the price for its product. No firm sets its price. Instead, the price is given to the firm by the impersonal market forces of supply and demand. Agricultural markets are the closest to a real world counterpart. Farmers do not set the price for their crops. Rather, they receive the current price for whatever quantity they bring to the market.

2. Monopolistic competition

Monopolistic competition consists of many, many firms producing slightly different products. Monopolistic competition has as many firms as pure competition, but the product of each firm is a little different from the product of every other firm and each firm sets its own price. Retail markets, such as those for dry cleaning, shoes, and groceries, are standard examples of monopolistically competitive markets.

3. Oligopoly

An oligopoly has just a few firms. These few firms can produce the same product or they can produce different products. The defining characteristic of oligopoly is a small enough number of firms so that what one firm does (for example, change its price) can change the sales and profits of the other firms. Economists call this characteristic "interdependence." Its consequence is a condition of rivalry among the firms in an oligopoly. The automobile industry is a common example.

4. Monopoly

Modern economics defines a monopoly as a single producer of a product. Standard examples are public utilities, such as water, gas, and electric companies.

Now let us consider modern economics' theory of price for each of these four market structures.

II. Pure Competition

Modern economists hold that the law of supply and demand determines price only in purely competitive markets. Let us see why.

Because the price is given to the purely competitive firm by the law of supply and demand, a schedule can be drawn up of the individual firm's profit-maximizing quantities at each of the prices that might be given to it. This is the firm's supply schedule; a graph of this schedule represents the firm's supply curve. Such schedules and their corresponding curves are the exclusive meaning of *supply* in modern economics.

Only in pure competition do the concepts of a supply curve and a supply schedule have any meaning. When the price is *not* given to the firm, when the producer sets his own price, it is senseless to ask what quantity he would want to sell at a higher price because the only way the price could be higher is if the producer raised it. Outside of pure competition, there is no supply as modern economists understand it. If there is no supply, there is no law of supply and demand.

In pure competition, nobody on the demand side has any control over the price either. Each buyer is like a consumer in a retail store; the store sets the price and his choice is only whether or not to pay it.

Modern economists call the price determined by the law of supply and demand the equilibrium price. They define it as the price at which the quantity demanded equals the quantity supplied. The equilibrium price is alleged to appear only in pure competition, but pure competition has the unfortunate feature that there is no way to explain the origin of the price. If neither the buyer nor the seller has any control over the price, if neither of them can set a price or name a price or select a price or make a price, there is no way to explain how the price comes into existence. If there is no way to explain how the equilibrium price comes to be, there is no basis for believing that the price that does come to be will be the equilibrium price.

How are economics' professors able to teach the law of supply and demand to their students in the face of this contradiction? The standard argument appears in all principles of economics texts: Suppose the price happens to be above the equilibrium price (either an increase in supply or a decrease in demand will bring this about). Then the quantity supplied exceeds the quantity demanded, firms produce more goods than they can sell, inventories accumulate, and every firm is motivated to cut its price in order to sell its excess output. Consequently, firms will bid down the price to the equilibrium price where they are able to sell all they want to sell. A similar argument applies to below equilibrium prices, though in such cases, the texts often say that consumers will bid up the price in the face of a shortage.

This argument ignores the defining condition of pure competition— that neither the firm has, nor do its customers have, any control over price. If a firm bids down its price, it does so by setting a lower price, which requires that the firm has the *power* to set a lower price, which means that the price is *not* given to the firm. Similarly, consumers can bid up a price by offering a higher price, but this requires that consumers have the power to offer a higher price, that they do not take the price as given and outside their control.

If we adhere to the actual meaning of pure competition, the meaning that makes it possible to define a supply curve, then in principle, there is no way to explain how or where the price is set because no one sets it. This difficulty has been recognized by a number of economists, some of them prominent: for example, Arrow 1959, 41-43; Fisher 1983, 12, 21, 47, 49; Fisher 1987, 26-7; Guerrien 2002; Hahn 1987, 137; High 2001, xxxviii; Janssen 1993, 111; Mas-Colell 1980, 121; Scitovsky 1971, 15. Of these, only Fisher and Guerrien see this problem as fundamental. *"[I]t is not too strong to say that the entire theory of value is at stake,"* Fisher says (1987, 27, my emphasis).

Economists say that at the market price, the quantity demanded will equal the quantity supplied, but they cannot say how or why such a price will come to be the market price. Nor can they say how or why the price will change when either demand or supply changes. In modern economics, the law of supply and demand is the basis for holding that there will be neither shortages nor surpluses at market prices, but the law gives no *theoretical* basis for holding that market prices have that attribute, or any other attribute.

It is absurd, but the law of supply and demand is the closest thing modern economics has to a general theory of price. It is absurd because the law is restricted to pure competition which, if we could say it exists at all, would be limited to agricultural markets, which account for about one percent of aggregate output.[1] A general theory of price that explains (actually, that does *not* explain) the prices of one percent of the economy's output is not a general theory.

III. Monopolistic Competition and Oligopoly

By tradition, economists ascribe the oligopoly market structure to national markets dominated by a few large firms, like the automobile, steel and aluminum industries. In contrast, markets with many small firms, like retailers, frequently are designated as monopolistically competitive.

According to the theory of oligopoly, each firm sets its own price, and that price may affect the profits of the other firms in the market. According to the theory of monopolistic competition, each firm sets its own price, but that price *cannot* affect the profits of the other firms. The reason for this, it is alleged, is that there are so many firms in monopolistic competition (for example, hundreds of thousands of dry cleaners), that a change in price by any one of them will not have any noticeable effect on the quantity sold by any of the others.

Modern economics' conception of market structure, as reflected in the two preceding paragraphs, is invalid. It is not true that retail firms are independent of one another. The relevant market for such firms is local, not national, and within their local markets, dry cleaners, drugstores, groceries, and shoe stores are interdependent.[2] Each dry-cleaner knows approximately what prices his competitors are charging and the quality of their work. Each firm may respond when his competitors change their price or quality. Each firm is likely to give some thought to how his competitors will respond if he changes his price. Nor do the market conditions described by monopolistic competition exist anywhere else in the economy. No price-setting firms choose their prices independently of the prices charged by their competitors. Nothing in reality corresponds to the economic model of monopolistic competition.[3]

The markets that economists traditionally call monopolistically competitive are actually oligopolistic. Local retail stores are just as interdependent as the giant firms that are designated oligopolies. Most firms in the economy are oligopolies in the sense that a change in price by one firm can affect the sales receipts of other firms and cause them to change their prices too. Logically, monopolistic competition and oligopoly must have the same theory of price. What is that theory?

IV. Modern Economics' Theory of Price for Oligopoly

Modern economists generally acknowledge that they have no theory of price for oligopoly. The cause, it is alleged, is the interdependence of oligopolistic firms. Because oligopolies set their prices, economics cannot define a supply curve, and interdependence makes it impossible to define a demand curve.

A firm's demand curve gives the schedule of quantities the firm can sell at each of a series of prices. It tells us what quantity the firm's customers will buy (demand) at each price the firm might charge. This is the counterpart of the firm's supply curve described above (p. 274). The intersection of these two curves on a graph constitutes modern economics' law of supply and demand.

The problem of defining a demand curve is that in an oligopoly, the quantity a firm can sell at a price depends on what prices its competitors are charging at the same time. For example, if Ford Motors lowers the price of its cars, General Motors, Chrysler, Toyota, Nissan, and so forth, may match its reduced price, or they may ignore it, or they may undercut the lowered price, or they may raise price instead. (In a research paper, a student described a dry cleaner who raised his price in response to a price reduction by a competitor.) Since there are many competitors, they may all do something different. Consequently, at any particular price, Ford Motors could sell an unlimited number of alternative quantities, depending on the prices its competitors charge at the same time. Since economists believe that in principle there is no way to know in advance how competitors will respond to a change in price, there is no way to predict what quantity the firm will be able to sell at any price other than the current price. This means that oligopolistic firms do not have demand curves. Since they do not have supply curves either, neither demand nor supply apply to oligopolistic firms and *the law of supply and demand is moot.*

Economists widely ignore this unavoidable conclusion. They apply supply and demand to monopolies, to oligopolies, to taxes, to price controls, to price floors, to shortages, to surpluses, and so forth. In an economics profession that takes seriously its own definitions, these applications are invalid.

This is the issue on which the theory of oligopoly has foundered. For the foregoing reasons, modern economists believe that we are helpless to derive a price theory for oligopoly. All we can do, and all that has been done, is to derive specific, narrow theories on the basis of either (1) restrictive assumptions about the response of competitors,[4] or (2) assumptions that are true only in narrowly defined submarkets and time periods.

A. Game Theory

As a consequence of the failure of supply and demand to explain oligopolistic prices, economists embraced game theory, which has dominated graduate economics for the last thirty years. Following path (2) above, game theory has led to some interesting results, but not to anything resembling a general theory of price. Colander describes modern applied microeconomics as "a grab bag of models with a model for every purpose" (2000, 139). In contrast, Myerson views game theory (specifically, Nash's theory of noncooperative games) as "one of the outstanding intellectual advances of the twentieth century" with "a fundamental and pervasive impact in economics and the social sciences which is comparable to that of the discovery of the DNA double helix in the biological sciences" (1999, 1067). Myerson holds that the goal of game theory is "to build a canon of some *dozens* of game models" (1999, 1080, my emphasis)—which is what Colander calls "a grab bag of models," and about as far as one can get from a general theory.

How would dozens of game models for firms in various concrete circumstances advance our knowledge of the economy? When one understood all of them, what would one *know*? The precedent for this kind of misunderstanding is the Ptolemaic system of the heavens. Ptolemy held that all the stars, including the sun, are embedded in heavenly spheres that revolve in circles around the earth. His problem was to account for the motion of the seven planets across the sky as seen from earth. (These seven include the sun and the moon. We can see only five planets without a telescope.) The paths of some of the planets describe loops in the sky, turning back on their path, while others, like the sun and moon, describe simple circles. Ptolemy's solution was to imagine spheres within spheres for each planet. Bronowski describes seven mechanical models, constructed about 1350, consisting of systems of wheels within wheels, a different system for each planet, so that when the wheels are turned, the planet on the rim of a wheel follows the path that we observe from earth (Bronowski 1973, 194-5).

These constructions are acts of great ingenuity. There was just one thing wrong with them. Each planet required different machinery to generate its path. But, as Bronowski says, "the heavens must have one machinery, not seven" (p. 196). What did the astronomers prior to Copernicus actually understand about the motion of the heavenly spheres? Nothing. They had mechanical models. They had no knowledge.

The fundamental problem was not that their conception of the universe was wrong. The fundamental problem was that their epistemology was wrong. They believed that they had reached knowledge with seven different mechanical explanations for the motion of entities in the same realm. Exactly the same thing is wrong with an ideal of dozens of game models for firms in various concrete circumstances. Like the movement of the planets in the heavens, we have to explain prices by one principle, not dozens.

B. Modern Economics' Conception of Price Theory

At the root of modern economists' inability to think of a theory of price for oligopoly is a basic premise concerning what "a theory of price" should be. The premise is that a theory of price has to take the form of mathematical formulas, formulas that will allow us to solve for numerically determinant prices, given the values of the variables in the formulas.[5] This premise is by now many decades old and today has an iconic status, the more impervious because it is implicit. In fact, in the history of economic thought, economists have never debated this premise. They have never explicitly adopted it. They never mention it to this day (Montgomery 1994, 47). It has simply grown topsy-turvy.

The premise that a theory of price must be a mathematical equation is arbitrary. There is nothing in the nature of the theory of price that requires such a formula, and the modern insistence on it has precluded a theory of price for most of the economy. A theory of price must have the characteristics identified in chapter 8. It should answer one basic question: what are the essential factors that cause the price. A mathematical formula that would allow us to calculate the price would have to incorporate the causal factors in their correct relationships. However, such a formula is not a necessary feature of a price theory and in the case of oligopoly, a mathematical formula for the price is impossible.

Since I am not burdened by the requirement that price theories take the form of mathematical formulas, I am able to say some things about price setting in the real economy which that requirement would not allow me to say (in chapters 10 and 11).

V. Pure Monopoly

Modern economics defines pure monopoly as a single producer of a product. "Mono" means one, which makes this conception of monopoly unavoidable. However, "a single producer of a product" is worthless as a standard for identifying anything of economic significance about businesses. If we define "product" narrowly enough, everyone is a monopolist. If we define the product widely enough, then there are no *free-market* monopolists in the United States—nor have there ever been, with the single exception of Alcoa before WWII.

A free-market monopoly is a monopoly achieved and held in free and open competition, with no government protection or support. It is unusual for a firm to sell even fifty percent of an industry's output over a significant period (several years). To sell one hundred percent, on the rare occasions that it occurs, represents an extraordinary productive achievement. It is possible only if the monopolist produces a better product than any other firm can match, and/or charges a price at which other firms would make unacceptably low profits or losses. (Alcoa did the latter.) Such a monopoly is in the interest of the firm's customers, as well as its stockholders.

A free-market monopoly is distinguished from a government-created monopoly in that a free-market monopolist must plan and act long range. If he does not, if he sets high prices based on his current position of dominance, he invites competitors into his market. In contrast, when government creates and protects a firm's monopoly, no short-range policies by the monopolist can attract other firms because the government will close them down.

Modern economics' theory of pure monopoly holds that the monopolist maximizes profits by changing his price up and down, depending on the momentary state of the market (Rand 1966, 98). This is because every small change in demand or cost causes a change in the profit-maximizing price. This theory represents the limit in short-run profit maximization, but it is not completely inappropriate in the context of a government-protected monopoly.[6]

It is typical of modern economics that the theory that prices change with every change in demand or cost has been taken not just as a theory of what businessmen do, but also of what businessmen *should* do. The fact that this is *not* what businessmen do did not lead economists to question their theory. Instead, they launched a search for another theory to explain why prices are "sticky"—that is, to explain why prices do not constantly change up and down. This search is now many decades old and embodied in a vast literature encompassing at least twenty different theories (Blinder and others 1998).

Prices are not sticky. The theory that implies they are sticky implicitly depends on the assumption of a government-protected monopoly. Firms that have competitors or potential competitors avoid constantly changing prices as a competitive measure, that is, in order to accommodate their business customers (Hall and Hitch 1939, 22), who naturally want to be able to plan on the cost of their factors for more than a day.

Monopoly, in the sense of an economic entity that violates the rights of its customers, should be defined as *a business with an exclusive right, created by the state, to produce and/or sell a product.*

Patents and Copyrights

This definition does not apply to exclusive rights achieved through patents or copyrights because, strictly speaking, the state does not *create* such rights; it *recognizes* and *secures* them (Rand 1966, 126). "Patents and copyrights are the legal implementation of the base of all property rights: a man's right to the product of his mind" (Rand 1966, 125). Since free markets presuppose the existence of property rights, when the government secures patents and copyrights, it is securing one of the foundations of a free economy. Consequently, monopolies reached through patents are a means to their customers' welfare, and on two counts. (1) Most importantly, patents that protect the creator's rights also protect the customers' rights, on the principle of "that which violates the rights of one violates the rights of all," and (2) Patents make it possible for businessmen to profit from the innovations which benefit their customers.

Setting aside patents and copyrights, the modern economic theory of pure monopoly could be correct; that is, a completely uncontrolled, government-guaranteed monopoly might maximize profits the way economic theory says it would. But such a case of pure monopoly is a fantasy. All government-guaranteed monopolies are also government-controlled. The pure monopoly of modern economic theory does not exist.

VI. Overview of Modern Economics' Theory of Price

Of the four theories of price for the four market structures, the price theory of pure monopoly is the only one that has some connection to reality. Pure competition rules out any causal explanation of price and there is no theory of price for oligopoly or monopolistic competition.

The fundamental flaw in modern economics' theory of price is the concept of market structure at its base. Market structure is a rationally unusable and invalid concept. Nothing of any economic significance necessarily varies with the market structure in which firms operate. For example, an industry may have a single firm producing its entire output, and that firm can be dynamically progressive, as Alcoa was in the aluminum industry. A single firm may completely dominate an industry, with many small firms struggling to compete, and still move the whole industry forward, as Standard Oil did in the oil-refining industry. An industry may consist of three large firms in which one of them stops competing, as Ford Motors did in the late 1920s. One industry may have hundreds of businesses who pay little attention to each other while in another industry with a similar number of firms, the competition is intense.

Modern economics has no theory of price. By definition, a theory of price limited to narrowly defined submarkets and time periods is not a theory. Without an integrated, general conception of how prices are created, any "theory" of a specific price cannot rise above the level of a concrete description. Cut off from reference to any general theory, there is no way in principle to know whether the factors identified as causing a price are the fundamental causal factors and, consequently, no way to know whether those factors will continue to be causes in the future.

Modern economists do not know how prices are set or what principles determine prices. They do not know what attributes a market price can be expected to have, or why it can be expected to have those attributes. They are in a state of virtually perfect ignorance regarding prices.

To my noneconomist readers, the preceding observations undoubtedly sound like a damning indictment of modern economics. However, most economists would be undisturbed. The reason for their complacency is the method of modern economics (appendix B).

VII. Conclusion

Expressions of dissatisfaction with the method and content of modern economics have been growing louder and more frequent over the years. Although no economist completely shares my view of modern economics, in professional journals and meetings, other economists have raised some of the objections that I have raised here. Their effect on the practitioners of modern economics has been zero.

Most modern economists think that their subject is soundly grounded and progressing well (Baumol 2000). The superficial impression of intellectual vigor is created by the extraordinary inscrutability of the work being done at the so-called "cutting edge" of modern economics. In particular, the mathematical knowledge required to publish in modern economics' journals is very advanced. A prominent economist tells the story of being advised to get a Ph.D. in mathematics rather than economics (which he did) in order to avoid having "a hang-up about math" (Colander, Holt, and Rosser, 2004, 158). It has been said that there are perhaps only six or seven economists in the country who know enough mathematics to understand some of the articles published in major journals.

Muddy waters are rarely deep, and in the modern case, there is very little water involved. Modern economics is mostly a mudslide of arbitrary concepts that originate with pure competition, concepts completely dependent upon taking pure competition as the standard for evaluating markets and economic activity. These concepts include market power, economic power, monopoly power, market control, monopoly returns, restricted production, administered prices, monopoly prices, administered profits, planned profits, workable competition, barriers to entry, industrial concentration, and by far the most important, market failure. Apart from the purely competitive model, these concepts have no meaning whatever.

The concept of "oligopoly" also springs from pure competition. Taking the purely competitive structure as the standard, economists define oligopoly by contrast, as a deviation from pure competition (that is, so few firms that they are interdependent). However, far from being a deviation, oligopoly is the norm of a market economy. Oligopoly is the competitive case, where businessmen have other businessmen with which they compete. Apart from farmers and public utilities, the economy is composed of such businesses. Consequently, the terms "oligopoly" and "interdependent" should disappear from economics and the terms "competition" and/or "competing businesses" should take their place. Further, economic thought should take the existence of competition as the norm—unless otherwise qualified, economists should assume that any business under discussion has competitors. That has been my practice throughout this book.

APPENDIX B

THE METHOD OF
MODERN ECONOMICS:
A CRITIQUE

Appendix A shows that modern economics has no theory of price. This appendix explains why modern economics is impervious to this charge. What makes it impervious is the method of model building that dominates modern economics. Exclusive reliance on mathematical models is what distinguishes the economics of the last forty years from the economics of all preceding eras.

There is such a thing as a valid model. A valid model is a concrete, physical representation of another concrete thing that is not directly perceivable. Common examples are models of the atom, the solar system, and the construction model of a building. The purpose of such models is to make it possible for men to grasp entities and relationships among entities that are not open to direct observation. Such models permit an increase in understanding that we cannot achieve in any other way.

The following critique also does not apply to the models economists use to forecast things such as the rate of economic growth and the inflation rate. Since economists want these forecasts to be as accurate as possible, these models are as realistic as their practitioners (primarily business economists) can make them. The models that are the stock in trade of modern academic economists are something else altogether. The purpose of these models is not to forecast, but to analyze, to criticize, to identify new theories, to reach new knowledge about the economy. Unreality is their key feature.

Academic economists resist specifying exactly what a model is (Krugman 1995, 70), so let us specify it. In modern economics, a model is a set of imaginary conditions that represent an imaginary economy or an imaginary industry or an imaginary business. The model defines these imaginary conditions in terms of mathematical symbols and equations, and then, using the procedures of mathematical deduction, the economist deduces conclusions about the nature of the imaginary entity represented in the model. Almost without exception, the imaginary conditions include features that do not exist and that are actually impossible. The most

popular of these impossible features are perfect knowledge (omnis-
cience) and perfect mobility (the instantaneous transfer of factors from
one use to another).

Thus, the most obvious thing wrong with economic models is that
they deliberately and self-consciously incorporate falsehoods into their
pictures of the economy. This objection does not disturb modern economists. They regard it as irrelevant to object to a model that it is untrue or
unrealistic. "The world is not like that," the critic says. "Of course not,"
the model makers respond. "That is what makes it a model."

How does the economist decide what to put in his model? The first,
primary criterion of modern economics is that the model must be mathematically tractable. A theory that is not capable of mathematical mod-
eling cannot be published and if it is published, it will be ignored (Krugman 1995, 5, 25–6, 64, 68). Consequently, relatively simple economic
facts are twisted out of any recognizable relation to reality so that those
facts can be represented in a mathematical equation.

The second criterion for judging models is prediction. Prediction is
the alleged goal of all economic theory. In this view, it is irrelevant
whether anything in reality corresponds to the theory. It is important only
that the theory make predictions that economists can compare with reality. This position originated in a famous essay by Milton Friedman
(1953), though Friedman was more subtle than his modern followers are
(Montgomery 1994, 54–61).

In economics, predictions take the form of statistics, so a valid economic theory must be capable of predicting statistics that economists can
compare with statistics collected from the economy. If the statistics predicted by the model appear in the data, then the model is *not* falsified. If
the predicted statistics do not appear, then the model *is* falsified. This is
the falsifiability standard for evaluating theories created by Karl Popper.
It is still the most popular justification for the method followed by modern economists, though it has been long since rejected by philosophers.

Modern philosophy has largely abandoned the field of method under
the heading of "anything goes"—thus embracing explicitly the position
implicit in the original subjectivist reaction to intrinsicism (chapter 2).
This viewpoint has been filtering into economics, as it must, because qua
economists, economists have to take whatever the philosophers give
them. As a consequence, under the heading of method, some economists
are studying what economists do (Coats 2000, 148). Other approaches
are possible (see Hand 2001) including, for example, studying the social
relations among scholars that influence the acceptance or rejection of a

particular method. These are nothing but alternative forms in which the subject of method is given up. Method is nothing if it is not prescriptive.

The method one follows is the only way to distinguish knowledge from wishful thinking or any other arbitrary idea one may happen to have (chapter 1). Thus, the attack by modern philosophy on method is an attack on knowledge as such—the most recent attack of a movement going back to Hume and Kant. Its ultimate consequence will be to make it impossible for men to live on earth. Modern economists do not see the long-range consequences of their method. Their failure is narrower. A method is valuable only if it yields knowledge, and the method of model building does not.

The method of model building explains why modern economists take for granted, as entirely unremarkable, the unreality of the theories that dominate their discipline. As Clower (1998, 404) says, "the concern of neoWalrasians is with a model world, not any real-world economy." The outstanding example is pure competition. In reality, there is no market with millions of firms producing identical products on the supply side, selling to millions of consumers on the demand side, with a price at which the quantity demanded equals the quantity supplied somehow established by no one.

In the face of this fact, pure competition (and all model building) is defended on the grounds that any theory must abstract from reality. A theory cannot incorporate every detail of the real world. If it did, it would not add to our knowledge. It would just confront us all over again with the concrete facts that the theory is supposed to explain. I agree. The issue is: what does it mean to abstract from reality?

To abstract means to separate (Rand 1967, 10). When we abstract from reality, we mentally separate out specific facts of reality from all the other facts. We do this for essentially two, interrelated reasons: (1) to identify those facts as causes of the general phenomenon we are trying to understand, and therefore, (2) to isolate those facts for special focus, attention, and study. To abstract does not mean to ignore some facts or to make up new facts. Imaginary features cannot be causes because they do not exist. They cannot be the object of study for the same reason. To mentally separate out facts that *do* exist is one of the foundations of human cognition. It is an opposite method—and not of cognition—to make up facts that do not exist.

Thus, when Prescott says, "The models constructed with this theoretical framework are necessarily highly abstract. Consequently they are necessarily false . . ." (1986, 10), he has it exactly wrong (though he deserves credit for his frankness). His models *are* necessarily false, not because they are abstract, but because they are *not* abstract. The models of modern economists do not abstract from reality; they make up an alternative reality.

Thus, my initial objection to model building that it incorporates features that do not exist does not quite name what is wrong with this method. As represented by pure competition, the problem is not primarily that a model incorporates unreal and impossible features. The problem is that, as a theoretical construct, pure competition is a fantasy. In addition to the features named earlier, pure competition assumes that both producers and consumers have

> complete knowledge of a complete set of prices over the entire space and time span, including future prices... Producers have full knowledge of all technically possible production possibilities. Both consumers and producers have perfect ability to solve instantaneously problems of choice involving large numbers of variables in complex relationship with each other. (Fusfeld 2000, 175)

Finally, as we saw in appendix A—the most bizarre assumption for a theory of price—the price is given to both producers and consumers somehow by anonymous market forces. The method of model building requires the construction of complete alternative realities and its advocates insist that this is the only valid method to knowledge in economics. But knowledge of what? Of models.

From a different perspective, the purely competitive model is still worse. Not only does it fail to abstract anything essential from competition in the real world, but pure competition also obliterates every aspect of competitive rivalry.[1] It rules out the basis of competition in reality, which is interdependence. The only thing that purely competitive firms have in common with real firms is that they produce and sell goods, and even *production* often is deleted in general equilibrium models. There is nothing in reality that corresponds to the model of pure competition. The model models nothing.

Nevertheless, some of the theorists of pure competition think that their work in general equilibrium models has significance for our understanding of a market economy. Those who care about understanding the real economy (and many do not) would respond that the *results* of pure competition resemble the *results* of a market economy. On the prediction standard, this is the main line of defense of model building—the "as if" conception of theory.

The "as if" conception is that a theory may be false, but the theory is valid if the real economy functions "as if" the theory were true. For example, firms do not set price by equating marginal revenue and marginal cost, but the prices they set are the same "as if" they equated marginal revenue to marginal cost. Consumers do not have budget lines and indifference maps in their heads, but they make choices "as if" they did. There are no purely competitive industries in reality, but the economy functions "as if" all industries were purely competitive. Intersecting supply and demand curves do not set prices, but prices are set "as if" they equated the quantity demanded to the quantity supplied.

In answer to this defense, a colleague remarked that there is no "invisible hand," but the economy functions "as if" there were. If the "as if" conception of theories were valid, we could assume the existence of a real invisible hand and jettison all the paraphernalia of pure competition and most of the rest of economic theory as well. The "as if" conception of theory permits any assumptions whatever and thus negates the value of every theory.

Some of the results of pure competition that are supposed to mimic the results of the real economy include an optimum allocation of resources, with the marginal units all allocated to their most valuable outputs, with all goods produced in exactly the proportions that consumers want to buy them, and sold for prices that just cover the costs of bringing them to market. These alleged results raise an obvious question: what reason is there to think that those are actually the results in the real economy, or even that the real economy tends toward those results, if we cannot explain how real firms generate those results?

The method of model building confuses fantasy with cognition. Creating imaginary worlds in the mind does not yield knowledge. To reach knowledge, one must grasp the facts, and to grasp the facts, one must look at reality. The fatal flaw in the method of modern economics is that there is nothing in that method that requires economists to look at reality.

The use of statistics to falsify theories does not constitute such a requirement. Economic statistics are complex human products, the result of deliberate human processing, involving many different steps including: collection, selection, calculation, adjustment, guessing, tweaking, fudging—and then many other mathematical manipulations of the data too complex to describe here. As such, statistics are many levels removed from the reality of what they are intended to measure. In addition,

[a]lmost every economic datum is the result of thousands of complexly interacting, direct and indirect causes, ultimately involving the entire economy. This means that a failure of prediction is always attributable to an extraneous cause, and that makes it virtually impossible ever to prove a theory false by means of statistics. Thus the final meaning in practice, the "cash value," the "bottom line" (and the hidden purpose) of the modern methodology is the perpetration of a fraud: preserving the appearance of concern with reality while sanctioning theories that are patently false and impervious to the facts. (Buechner 1982)

The pure prediction standard of theories is the view that a theory can be *anything* as long as it predicts correctly. I have four objections to this standard:

1. The pure prediction standard does not satisfy its own standard. It does not make any predictions. No data could conceivably falsify it.

2. One can have no confidence in the predictions of a theory that has no connection to the facts it is predicting. Even if the predicted statistics gave an exact correlation, one would have to assume that the correlation was a coincidence. A famous illustration of this point is an exact correlation between the number of semicolons on the front page of *The New York Times*, and the number of deaths from famine in a remote province of India.

In pure competition, no one has any control over price, no one sets the price, there is no way in principle to say how a price is established, and the intersection of supply and demand curves does not reflect any human action. Consequently, when the quantity supplied equals the quantity demanded in any particular market, the model of pure competition does not give us any *theoretical* basis for believing that that equality is anything other than fortuitous.

3. A false theory eventually will yield false predictions. A false theory is one that abstracts nonessential facts from reality and identifies them as the cause, or, more obviously, one that identifies nonexistent facts as the cause, or still more obviously, one that is simply a fantasy. Not every prediction of a false theory need be false, but even true predictions of a false theory do not constitute knowledge, and eventually false predictions will appear.[2]

For example, the purely competitive model often has been interpreted to imply that an increase in the number of firms in a market will increase competition. This prediction has been taken seriously and applied repeatedly in antitrust cases. It is not true, but its falsehood can be grasped only from the perspective of a valid conception of competition, that is, a conception that incorporates rivalry (chapter 3). A theory of competition that excludes rivalry can tell us nothing about what will increase competition. Rivalry *is* competition.

4. Correct prediction depends on correct understanding. This is the most important point. To treat understanding and prediction as opposing, alternative standards for evaluating theories is an epistemological error.

Understanding precedes prediction and is the means to it. "Understanding" a phenomenon means grasping the cause and effect relationship that brings it about. "Prediction" is based on our understanding that a particular effect follows from a particular cause. If one pulls the epistemological cause (understanding) out from under its effect (prediction), one ends up with neither understanding nor prediction—and the irrationality that characterizes modern economic theory.

In order to use a theory to make predictions that one can rely on and that are useful for human life on earth, one must understand the causal relation in reality specified by the theory. Only then can one apply the theory to reality where that causal relation exists. One cannot know how or where or when to apply a theory that is asserted arbitrarily, independently of the facts. For example, since there are no purely competitive markets, we cannot rationally apply pure competition to *any* markets. Therefore, as a theory, it offers us nothing—neither understanding nor prediction.

APPENDIX C

MARGINALISM IN MODERN ECONOMICS: A CRITIQUE

Marginalism and subjectivism entered economics together in the early 1870s with the solution to the diamond/water paradox.[1] Economists usually have discussed this paradox in terms of nonessentials. The following exposition presents it in terms of essentials, so the terminology used here differs somewhat from what is traditional.

Adam Smith pointed out in *The Wealth of Nations* (1776, 28) that goods of the greatest importance for supporting human life often have very low prices (for example, water) while goods which are relatively unimportant in supporting human life often have very high prices (for example, diamonds). He concluded that the prices of goods are independent of men's evaluations of goods, because if they were not, water would be expensive and diamonds would be cheap. The cause of prices, he decided, must be looked for elsewhere, and chapter 2 showed that Adam Smith's answer, along with the rest of the British classical school, was something intrinsic in reality.

The paradox was solved in books published in three different languages at almost the same time: Jevons in English (1871), Walras in French (1874) and Menger in German (1871). Each of these authors reached the same solution independently. Smith's error, they said, was that when he compared water to diamonds, he thought of both goods as classes, whereas men do not value goods as classes; they value them the same way they acquire them, that is, one by one.

The law of diminishing marginal utility (which we will call the law of utility) says that the greater the quantity of any specific good a man has, the less he values one more. Marginalism is the idea that the additional unit[2] is the basis for human evaluation, decision-making, and action.

The solution to the diamond/water paradox follows directly: since in modern industrial civilization there is a great abundance of water, we value an additional gallon very low (perhaps to spray the leaves off the sidewalk) and we are willing to pay a correspondingly low price. By comparison, there are very few diamonds in the world, so one diamond has great value to the man who acquires it and he is willing to pay a high price.[3]

The consequence of the discovery of marginalism was a revolution in economic thought. The British classical school, following Adam Smith, had explained price by the cost of production. Menger, Jevons, and Walras said that was wrong. Instead of the cost of production, they argued that the prices of goods reflect men's subjective valuations of goods, which vary according to the quantity they have available. The next generation of economists entrenched these linked conclusions: the foundation of human evaluation is marginalism and prices reflect men's subjective valuations. Marginalism and subjectivism have been the watchwords for economic thought ever since.

The idea that men's values determine prices is a variation of philosophical subjectivism—the idea that what men think determines reality. In this original form, though wrong, economic subjectivism was relatively benign. But in the realm of ideas, you cannot get away with just a little poison. The implications of an idea eventually will out. The rise of philosophical subjectivism throughout all fields of study in the twentieth century was duplicated in economics, resulting in the completely subjectivist economics documented in chapter 2.

A. The Law of Utility

There was some truth in the discovery of Jevons, Walras, and Menger. Certainly, the explanation for the relative prices of water and diamonds has something to do with the value men place on them, and that in turn has something to do with their relative scarcity. As a broad generalization, it is true that men put greater value on things that are scarce than on things that are abundant. But there is no specific relationship of the kind projected by the law of utility that applies to everything.

For the law of utility to hold, all the units in one's possession must be identical. This point is well recognized. If every pair of shoes one owns is the same, then any pair is interchangeable with any other pair, and any individual pair selected at random has the same value in one's hierarchy. It is not well recognized, however, that men rarely buy identical items. As chapter 4 noted (p. 70), the purchase of identical items is limited to things such as heating oil, water, gasoline, and electricity. Almost everything else we buy, including most food items, is not identical to other units. If the additional units are not identical, the second unit may have more value than the first, and the law of utility is irrelevant.

The law is also irrelevant if we can easily replace items at the same price. In that case, the value one places on the good is its price, regardless of how many identical units one may have or how highly one might rank the good if it were not easily replaceable.[4] Consider, for example, a standard 26 ounce container of table salt or a five-pound bag of sugar. Both are very inexpensive and no one has reason to think much about them or to consider their objective value. But if salt and sugar were rare and hard to get and each container cost $500, men would view both as precious commodities like caviar.

Alternatively, suppose you have one roll of paper towels left in your kitchen, so you buy a package of fifteen identical rolls on your next shopping trip. If storage is not a problem, this does not change the value to you of an individual roll. The proof is introspection—that is, each of us can imagine ourselves in these circumstances and grasp that our ranking of a roll would not change. The reason is that since we can buy more paper towels whenever we need them, we have no reason to value them at anything other than their price.

Apart from the items named above, it is hard to think of any economic good for which the law of utility is valid. It is valid for the five identical sacks of grain imagined by Böhm-Bawerk (1959, 143–48). It is valid for the farmer Menger imagines with two hundred identical bushels of wheat (1871, 129). It would be valid for other crops that are largely uniform, like corn and rice. But consumers evaluate agricultural crops only in the products they are used to produce—and then they value those products at their price whether they have a single unit or many.

Nevertheless, this necessity of uniformity leads us to the one economic value in a money economy for which the law of utility is valid. That is money itself. Money is uniform. Each dollar or $100 is identical to every other dollar or $100. Consequently, money is subject to the law of utility, as chapter 4 (pp. 67–69) showed.

Apart from money, the context in which the law of utility would be relevant is a barter economy, which is the context universally assumed by its advocates. In a barter economy, a farmer would rank an individual bushel of wheat less when he had a good harvest than when he had a poor harvest. After a good harvest, he could take extra bushels to town on market day and trade them for something he valued more. After a poor harvest, one bushel might be the difference between going hungry or not in the weeks before the next harvest. But this is all a fantasy.

Properly, economics has no interest in a barter economy or in the principles that govern it, because barter economies do not exist (p. 19 above).

In addition to the law of utility, marginalism dominates modern economics in two basic doctrines: (1) Businesses maximize profits by equating marginal revenue to marginal cost; (2) Businesses maximize profits by hiring factors of production up to the point where the factor's price equals its marginal revenue product. This second theory is the alleged basis for the law of demand for factors. Both of these doctrines are false.

B. The Fallacy of Marginal Cost Pricing

The end of chapter 4 (part IV) and chapter 6 (p. 101 above) explained that businessmen generally use average cost (average fixed cost plus average variable cost) as the basis for setting their prices because total revenue must exceed total cost if the business is to remain in existence. In opposition to this business practice, the advocates of marginal cost pricing, which include all modern economists, hold that price should be based on variable costs alone—and not just on variable costs, but on a particularly narrow and obscure version of variable costs, that is, marginal cost. Economists define marginal cost as the change in total cost for a one-unit change in output. Marginal revenue is the change in total revenue for a one-unit change in output. Economists hold that profits are maximized when marginal revenue equals marginal cost.[5]

Marginal cost pricing would be possible only in the pure monopoly model (appendix A)—if it existed; nevertheless, marginal cost pricing is modern economics' theory of price. Economists acknowledge that businessmen do not use marginal cost pricing, but they hold that because marginal cost pricing maximizes profits, there is survival value in this method. Their argument is that the businessmen who come closest to the price where marginal revenue equals marginal cost will make the most profits and will tend to replace those businessmen setting a different price (Browning and Zupan 2009, 244).

The objections to marginal cost pricing as a theory of price are overwhelming.

(1) The whole idea of marginal cost pricing is senseless for all those businessmen who produce and/or sell many different variations of many different products. In those cases, the businessman allocates his variable costs to each unit of each variation of each product, just as he does his fixed costs (pp. 77–78 above). The unit cost or average cost the busi-

nessman calculates at any level of output is a conglomeration of both variable and fixed costs.[6] Neither exists as a separate amount.

(2) Marginal cost pricing is the extreme version of short-run pricing.[7] Marginal cost pricing requires that the businessman change his price with every small change in demand or cost because every such change will change marginal revenue or marginal cost. Ayn Rand often contrasted the principled action of her heroes with action on "the range-of-the-moment." Range-of-the-moment action could not have a better representative than this theory. It is particularly inappropriate for the business world where business decisions look to the indefinite future and businessmen sign 99-year leases. A focus on the long run is one of the leading virtues of the business community relative to the rest of the population. Marginal cost pricing obliterates that virtue.

In principle, there is no survival value in range-of-the-moment action. The reverse is true. Short-run profit maximization is suicidal, as chapter 6 shows. Attributing the rule of marginal revenue equals marginal cost to actual business firms and then trying to figure out why their prices are "sticky" is the absurd consequence of an *idée fixe* completely out of touch with reality (appendix A). Short-run action is antihuman and antisurvival. The human is the rational and rational action is principled and long range and hence life supporting.

(3) Businessmen do not know what their marginal costs are, and Blinder and others (1998, 216–17) found it impossible to communicate the concept to them. It is a certainty, therefore, that businessmen do not set prices by reference to the relation between marginal revenue and marginal cost.[8] If they did, if something as momentous for the firm's success as its *price* was determined by marginal cost, businessmen certainly would know what it is without any prompting from economists.

Firms plan to produce a particular quantity of output, and they build plants or lease space that can produce that quantity. Then they set a price that yields an acceptable rate of profit on costs, if the quantity demanded falls within the range for which they planned. Then, if all their estimates were correct, they produce the quantity demanded at their price and make a profit. Marginal revenue and marginal cost do not enter these decisions at any point.

(4) Marginal cost pricing is impossible for the 95 percent of businessmen in the economy who have no demand curve (see appendix A on oligopoly). Marginal revenue is deduced from a demand curve; without a demand curve, there can be no marginal revenue and no relation of marginal revenue to marginal cost. This means that marginal cost pricing is

impossible to any businessman who is not a government-protected monopolist.

(5) Viewed from the principle that all knowledge begins with induction, it is absurd to think that the proper concept of cost for economic theory could be anything other than the concept of cost that businessmen actually use.

C. Marginal Revenue Product and the Law of Demand for Factors

Modern economics bases the law of demand for the factors of production (land, labor, and capital) on the factors' marginal revenue products.[9] Economists define marginal revenue product as the addition to a firm's total revenue from employing one more unit of a factor. Thus, marginal revenue product is the quantity the factor adds to the firm's output times the price for which that output is sold. The law of diminishing returns says that as additional units of a factor are added to a fixed plant and equipment, each additional unit adds less and less to total output. Consequently, modern economists hold that the marginal revenue product of every factor declines as a business employs more units of that factor.

We will not take time to explain this theory. It faces the insuperable problem that businessmen do not know the marginal revenue product of their workers and have no way to find it out. Consequently, marginal revenue product is invalid as a general theory of factor demand. Specific objections include:

(1) A worker's wage is what his employer is willing to pay to reach the end to which the worker is a means. *That end need not be, and frequently is not, more output.*

Businessmen hire workers to increase output, but they also hire workers to improve product quality and customer service, to increase efficiency and lower unit costs, to sell or market the product, to improve the processing of records, to improve communications between the firm and its suppliers and customers, to improve accounting procedures, to speed the communication of information to upper management, to facilitate overall management control, and many, many other things. If a worker does not produce output, and most of them do not, marginal revenue product is meaningless.

(2) Marginal revenue product is equally meaningless when a worker *does* produce output. Chapter 7 (p. 124) pointed out that a business has no way to distinguish the contribution to revenue of one factor from the

contributions of the other factors which are also required to produce the business's product. In an effort to deal with this problem, Marshall "defined the net product of a factor as the increase in value yielded by an increment of the factor less the value of other inputs purchased in conjunction with that increment" (Mandler 1999, 24).[10] To see the unreality of this approach, suppose a custom shirt manufacturer is considering adding another tailor to his staff. To do so, he has to supply the tailor with a sewing machine and cloth. Suppose the going wage for tailors is $30 a day, a tailor can make one shirt each day, the cloth per shirt costs $20, depreciation on the sewing machine is $1 a day, and each shirt can be sold for $75.

Marshall's idea is that one should subtract the sum of the cost of the cloth plus depreciation from the price of the shirt, and get $54 as the tailor's "net product." But one could just as well subtract the sum of the tailor's wage plus depreciation to get a net product for the cloth of $44, or subtract the sum of the tailor's wage plus the cost of the cloth to get a net product for the sewing machine of $25. These three net products add up to $123, which implies that the total contribution of the factors is $48 more than the price of the shirt—which is absurd. From the businessman's point of view, each of these calculations is equally irrelevant. He has no reason to care about these imaginary net products. All he needs to know is that he can sell additional shirts for $24 more than they cost.

D. The Origins of a Business

A business begins with an idea in an entrepreneur's mind. He has something he wants to produce and/or sell and he buys, hires, leases, rents, and builds the factors that he needs in order to produce and/or sell it. The standard governing his choices of what he buys, hires, leases, rents, and builds is what he needs in order to bring into existence the enterprise he envisions. Depending on that vision, his rationality, his ambition, his confidence, his ability, and the capital he has available, he may buy new equipment or used, hire top quality labor or ordinary, build a new facility or rent an old one. Whatever his specific choices in this regard, his standard is the business as a whole and what is necessary for it to function. He does not estimate, and he cannot estimate, the contribution that any individual item will make to his total revenue.

Once the business is set up and running, the entrepreneur faces decisions about changes in operations. These decisions are properly designated marginal decisions because they involve changes in how the business functions. The normal business context for marginal analysis is the effect on profits of a change in policy or a change in operations, not the effect on profits of an isolated action or choice, such as adding one more worker. Marginal decisions in the valid sense confront business decision-makers continuously. They also are not at all subtle. Businessmen do not need economists to tell them that an advertising campaign should be expected to increase revenues more than costs over the long run.

Nevertheless, marginal decisions may involve individual factors. Consider again the custom shirt manufacturer. He sets up his facilities to employ a certain number of tailors and to produce a certain number of shirts. If he is doing well, he may consider making an addition to his facilities. If demand decreases, he may lay off some tailors to reduce output to meet the decreased demand, and hire them back if demand increases again. It is possible that an increase in demand is so small that one additional tailor can produce the number of shirts required to meet the increased demand. The manufacturer does not hire the additional tailor because the tailor's marginal revenue product exceeds his wage rate. He hires the additional tailor because the shirts he produces can be sold for more than they cost.

The standard for marginal decisions is whether the change will augment long-run profits. Modern economic theory views marginalism virtually exclusively as the means to short-run profit maximization (in the doctrine that marginal revenue should equal marginal cost). Thus, the fact that in reality businessmen use marginalism as a means to long-run profits is worth emphasizing. When a shuttle airline adds a plane for one additional passenger because the first plane is full, the addition to cost greatly exceeds the addition to revenue. By the standard of short-run profits, it makes no sense. But the airline's commitment to add a plane if necessary to accommodate additional passengers is the foundation for its passenger traffic over the long run. Adding a plane for one passenger makes complete sense from the perspective of long-run profits.

To the best of my knowledge, the argument from marginal revenue product is the only argument extant that the law of demand applies to factors of production, with the following exception:

Reisman argues (1998, 206–9) that the law of demand for factors is derived from the law of demand for consumer goods, which in turn depends on the law of diminishing marginal utility. When the price of a factor falls, the quantity demanded goes up, he says, because the firms producing consumer goods with that factor will be able to sell more at the lower price necessary to cover the lower price of the factor. This argument fails immediately for all those factors that do not produce more output. In addition, to produce more output, a firm needs more of all the complementary factors that are necessary to increase output—factors whose prices have not fallen. To make such an increase in production profitable, the fall in the factor's price would have to be extraordinary, or the factor would have to be a major portion of the firm's costs, and probably both. In reality, often a factor's price is such a small portion of a consumer good's total cost that changes in the factor's price have no effect on the consumer good's price. For example, changes in the price of wheat usually do not change the price of bread.

E. Conclusion

Modern economists do not recognize any distinction between (1) marginalism as a basis for evaluating changes in business operations (chapter 6) and (2) marginal cost pricing as the means of profit maximization and (3) marginal revenue product as the basis of the demand for factors. They frequently point to businessmen's use of marginalism in (1) as evidence for the validity of marginalism in (2) and (3). I dispute the validity of marginal cost pricing and the idea that factors are hired according to their marginal revenue products, not the principle of marginalism as such.

APPENDIX D

THE MEANING OF SCARCITY IN MODERN ECONOMICS: A CRITIQUE

Chapter 12 denies the relevance of absolute scarcity for economic thought because there is no end by which one can evaluate the supply of any economic good or service as insufficient. Nevertheless, modern economists hold that there is such an end. They call it *the satisfaction of men's subjective wants*. Since everyone cannot have all they want of everything they want, economists argue, the supply of everything is insufficient and therefore every good and service is scarce. By scarce, they mean scarce in the absolute sense.

The standard proof of this alleged universal scarcity is to imagine the price of any good reduced to zero. Suppose that hamburgers were free to everyone who wanted them. Then many more people would want hamburgers than want them now when people have to pay a price. The quantity demanded of hamburgers would greatly exceed the quantity supplied. If the price of *every* good and service were reduced to zero, the quantity demanded of each and every one of them would exceed the quantity supplied. Consequently, economists conclude that everything that has a price is scarce.

There are three fallacies in this reasoning. First, looking at scarcity in terms of the relation of the quantity demanded to the quantity supplied confuses scarcity with shortage. Modern economists define a shortage as an excess of the quantity demanded over the quantity supplied at the current price (p. 43 above). Suppose a legal price ceiling holds the price of gasoline below the market price. Then people may want to buy ten million gallons of gasoline while the gas stations have only nine million gallons to sell. The one million gallon excess of the demand over the supply constitutes a shortage. But here is the point: even if the price is zero, the excess of the demand over the supply is by definition a shortage—not a scarcity.

Second, economists are not entitled to ignore the fact that if the price of everything were zero, nothing would be produced, we would all die, and nothing would be scarce.

Third, this argument implies that everything is equally scarce. There is no way to compare the quantity of cars that people would want if cars were free with the quantity of computers or candy bars that they would want if they were free. On this premise, candy bars and cars are equally scarce. Since that is absurd, something is wrong with this thinking.

What is wrong with it is the implicit premise at its base. That premise is *wishing should make it so.* Modern economists hold that the supply of everything is insufficient because wishing does *not* make it so. Their underlying conception is the Garden of Eden. If the supply of everything were sufficient, they hold, we could pick whatever we wanted off a tree or a shelf. There would be no work, no production, no exchange, no economizing, and no necessity for choice. It was the expulsion of Adam and Eve from the Garden of Eden, the Bible says, that made it necessary for man to earn his bread by the sweat of his brow, and modern economists agree. Scarcity, they hold, is the cause of all economic phenomena.

We have seen this method of modern economics before. It consists of imagining some unreal, impossible, out-of-this-world condition of existence, and then using that condition as the base from which to explain or evaluate or criticize the world that exists. (The purely competitive model is the outstanding example.) In this case, that base is a world in which anyone can have any economic value at the price of a wish. The essence of their argument is that, since wishing does not make it so, we have this problem of scarcity to deal with. If everything we want is not available to us for free, without effort, then scarcity rules and the quantity of everything is insufficient. But scarcity rules only on the premise that wants are primary, that somehow people should have whatever they want—that wishing should make it so.

It hardly seems necessary to explain this error. To understand the world, one must look at the world. The cause of production in this world is not scarcity; it is the fact that everything that men need in order to survive has to be produced. The cause of exchange in this world is not scarcity; it is the enormous advantages of the division of labor. The cause of economizing is not scarcity; it is the increase in their standard of living that men achieve by the careful use of their resources. (The cause of choice is not scarcity either. Even if wishing made it so, men would have to choose what to wish for.) The fact is that if one looks at this world, things are not scarce. The concept of absolute scarcity has no meaning in relation to goods and services because there is no standard based in this world by which we could identify any good or service as insufficient in supply.

Many modern economists also hold the view that to be scarce is the equivalent of being limited. The quantity of productive resources is limited, they say, and this fact combined with the allegedly unlimited wants of human beings is what makes it necessary to choose what to produce and in what quantities. If resources were unlimited, everything could be produced in whatever quantities people wanted for free. Again, they invoke the unreal as a base from which to explain the real.

In reality, everything is limited, including the stars in the heavens and the number of atoms in the universe. The proper designation for the opposite of limited is infinite, and if infinity can be said to exist at all, it is only as a potential (one more can always be added), not a fact (Rand 1990, 18, 148). An infinite *thing*, an infinite *resource*, is impossible. It cannot even be imagined.

In their understanding of scarcity, as in their understanding of everything else in economics, modern economists are true to their subjectivist premise—they treat emotions as primaries (wants, wishes, desires, yearnings). As a consequence, the whole issue of man's nature and the requirements of his survival drops out of sight. If we take men's desires as the root of economic activity, we cut loose from reality the entire realm of economics. What people feel about something cannot be a standard of anything—except of what they feel. For the economist, the issue must be: what are the relevant economic facts? The fact at the base of economic activity is man's nature as a rational animal. Because of his faculty of reason, man is able to produce the things he needs to survive, to trade the product of his work for the product of the work of others, and to manage his economic means to reach his most important ends.

Consider the modern concept of scarcity in objective terms. Taking the totality of a modern industrial economy, it is true that there are not enough human and nonhuman factors to produce more of every consumer good, and there are not enough consumer goods to satisfy every pro-life use. What name should we give to this condition? It is not a shortage because the quantity demanded equals the quantity supplied. It is not scarcity because there are no insufficiencies that cannot be met. What is it? It is an irrelevant economic fact.

Wishing does not make it so. The fact that we could wish for more goods and we could do something useful with them is irrelevant in this world. We could wish that dragons existed and flew to the rescue of people in trouble. We could wish for angels to give us comfort and support when life is hard. Scarcity is no more the cause of production and exchange than the absence of dragons and angels is the cause of human suffering.

The Consequences

What in modern economics depends on the concept of absolute scarcity and its place at the foundation of modern economic thought? The worst consequence is the universal viewpoint that the price system of a free market is a system of rationing. The function of prices, economists hold, is to limit the demand of buyers to the quantity made available by sellers. This view makes the price system indistinguishable from the rationing engaged in by governments when price controls have crippled the economy and there is a shortage of everything. Modern economists confound the operation of the price system and its origin in the free choices of businessmen with the decrees of government bureaucrats enforced by threats of physical force and violence. Nothing in modern economics damns it more than this.

Rationing is like censorship. Properly understood, it is something only governments can do. The price system of a free economy is not a system of rationing. It is a system of rewarding the producers and sellers for making their goods available and of distributing those goods to those willing to offer the highest rewards. It has nothing in common with the threats of fines and prison and death that are the motivating elements of any system of rationing.

The fundamental cause of this error is the method of imaginary worlds—worlds such as those where wishing makes it so or where resources are infinite. We have seen that this method is the foundation for modern economists' view of scarcity. It is also the foundation for practically everything else in modern economics. Economists call it model building. Appendix B discusses this method at length. Virtually everything that is wrong in modern economics has model building at its base.

APPENDIX E

THE EFFECT OF CHANGES IN COST ON SET PRICES: EXPANSION OF THE ARGUMENT IN CHAPTER TEN

There is no ambiguity about the effect of changes in price on profits if demand is inelastic. Increases in price increase profits and decreases in price decrease profits. The ambiguities occur when demand is elastic.

If demand is elastic, an increase in price will cause a greater percentage decrease in quantity and reduce total revenue. Whether or not profits increase depends on what happens to total cost. To measure that, Appendix E introduces a new concept, *the quantity elasticity of average cost* (E_{AC}). E_{AC} is the percentage change in average cost divided by the percentage change in quantity (%ΔAC $\div$ %ΔQ). The quotient is the percentage change in average cost for a 1% change in quantity. If average cost changes by 2% when the quantity increases by 10%, E_{AC} is 0.2. This means that a 1% change in quantity causes a 0.2% change in average cost. If average cost changes with changes in output, E_{AC} tells us how much it changes. In what follows, I will ignore the sign of E_{AC} as I ignored the sign of E_D in chapter 10.

The context for the following discussion is an industry. An increase in the price of a factor causes the initial increase in average cost. The origin of the tables that follow are the values for price, quantity, and average cost from the Acme Enterprises example of chapter 10 (pp. 181–85). We assume that the values for the price elasticity of demand (E_D) and the quantity elasticity of average cost (E_{AC}) in those tables are the same for each firm in the industry.

A. Increases in Average Cost

Let us consider first the case of an increase in average cost (from $80 to $90) that reduces Acme's profits to $10,000 per week. Our purpose is to see under what conditions Acme can raise its profits above $10,000 by raising its price, when all the other firms in the industry follow that increase.

There are four tables in this section. In each one, the first row of each column across the top gives alternative values for the quantity elasticity of average cost (E_{AC}) starting with zero, and rising to 0.5. The first column of each row represents alternative price elasticities of demand (E_D) increasing in half point increments from 0.5 to 5.0. I assume that Acme raises the price by 5% (in Tables I and III) or 10% (in Tables II and IV). Every cell in each table gives the amount by which Acme's profit exceeds $10,000 for the corresponding values of E_{AC} and E_D. Thus, Table 1 (below) shows us, for example, that if $E_{AC} = 0.20$ and the $E_D = 1.5$, a 5% increase in price raises Acme's profits by $5,124 above $10,000, or a total profit of $15,124.[1]

The tables differ by the assumed increase in price and by whether the industry is increasing cost or decreasing cost. Thus:

Table I: A 5% increase in price in an increasing cost industry.

Table II: A 10% increase in price in an increasing cost industry.

Table III: A 5% increase in price in a decreasing cost industry.

Table IV: A 10% increase in price in a decreasing cost industry.

In each of the tables, the constant cost industry is represented by the first column, the one for which $E_{AC} = 0$. The percentage change in average cost is zero for any change in quantity in a constant cost industry, so $\%\Delta AC \div \%\Delta Q = 0$.

1. A constant cost industry

TABLE I
(Price increases 5%)

$E_D\backslash E_{AC}$	0.00	0.01	0.03	0.05	0.07	0.10	0.20	0.50
0.50	$4,625	$4,647	$4,691	$4,735	$4,779	$4,844	$5,064	$5,722
1.00	$4,250	$4,293	$4,378	$4,464	$4,549	$4,678	$5,105	$6,388
1.50	$3,875	$3,937	$4,062	$4,187	$4,312	$4,499	$5,124	$6,997
2.00	$3,500	$3,581	$3,743	$3,905	$4,067	$4,310	$5,120	$7,550
2.50	$3,125	$3,223	$3,420	$3,617	$3,814	$4,109	$5,094	$8,047
3.00	$2,750	$2,865	$3,094	$3,324	$3,553	$3,897	$5,045	$8,488
3.50	$2,375	$2,505	$2,765	$3,025	$3,285	$3,674	$4,974	$8,872
4.00	$2,000	$2,144	$2,432	$2,720	$3,008	$3,440	$4,880	$9,200
4.50	$1,625	$1,782	$2,096	$2,410	$2,724	$3,194	$4,764	$9,472
5.00	$1,250	$1,419	$1,756	$2,094	$2,431	$2,938	$4,625	$9,688

Table I, Column 1 shows that in a constant cost industry, a 5% increase in price raises profits for all elasticities of demand up to and including 5.0.

TABLE II
(Price increases 10%)

$E_D\backslash E_{AC}$	0.00	0.01	0.03	0.05	0.07	0.10	0.20	0.50
0.50	$9,000	$9,043	$9,128	$9,214	$9,299	$9,428	$9,855	$11,138
1.00	$8,000	$8,081	$8,243	$8,405	$8,567	$8,810	$9,620	$12,050
1.50	$7,000	$7,115	$7,344	$7,574	$7,803	$8,148	$9,295	$12,738
2.00	$6,000	$6,144	$6,432	$6,720	$7,008	$7,440	$8,880	$13,200
2.50	$5,000	$5,169	$5,506	$5,844	$6,181	$6,688	$8,375	$13,438
3.00	$4,000	$4,189	$4,567	$4,945	$5,323	$5,890	$7,780	$13,450
3.50	$3,000	$3,205	$3,614	$4,024	$4,433	$5,048	$7,095	$13,238
4.00	$2,000	$2,216	$2,648	$3,080	$3,512	$4,160	$6,320	$12,800
4.50	$1,000	$1,223	$1,668	$2,114	$2,559	$3,228	$5,455	$12,138
5.00	$0	$225	$675	$1,125	$1,575	$2,250	$4,500	$11,250

Table II, Column 1, shows that a 10% increase in price in a constant cost industry raises profits for all elasticities of demand up through 4.50.

Since product elasticities higher than 3.0 are unusual, Tables I and II indicate it is highly probable that an industry with constant AC can increase its profits by raising price. The business that raises its price first can expect to be followed.

2. An increasing cost industry

With the exception of column one, both Tables I and II give the results when the price increases in an increasing cost industry.

Graph G

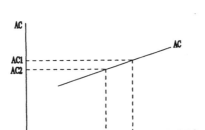

Since the price rises, the quantity falls (from Q1 to Q2) and average cost also falls (from AC1 to AC2) as in the above graph.

Table I shows that a price increase of 5% adds to industry profits in an increasing cost industry for all the possible combinations of E_D and E_{AC} in Table I. Table II shows the same thing for a price increase of 10%.

3. A decreasing cost industry

Tables III and IV give the effect of increases in price on profits in a decreasing cost industry.

Graph H

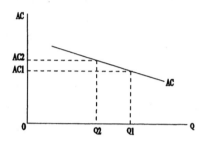

Since the price rises, the quantity falls (from Q1 to Q2), and the average cost rises (from AC1 to AC2).

TABLE III
(Price increases 5%)

$E_D\backslash E_{AC}$	0.00	0.01	0.03	0.05	0.07	0.10	0.20	0.50
0.50	$4,625	$4,603	$4,559	$4,515	$4,471	$4,406	$4,186	$3,528
1.00	$4,250	$4,207	$4,122	$4,036	$3,951	$3,823	$3,395	$2,113
1.50	$3,875	$3,813	$3,688	$3,563	$3,438	$3,251	$2,626	$753
2.00	$3,500	$3,419	$3,257	$3,095	$2,933	$2,690	$1,880	($550)
2.50	$3,125	$3,027	$2,830	$2,633	$2,436	$2,141	$1,156	($1,797)
3.00	$2,750	$2,635	$2,406	$2,176	$1,947	$1,603	$455	($2,988)
3.50	$2,375	$2,245	$1,985	$1,725	$1,465	$1,076	($224)	($4,122)
4.00	$2,000	$1,856	$1,568	$1,280	$992	$560	($880)	($5,200)
4.50	$1,625	$1,468	$1,154	$840	$526	$56	($1,514)	($6,222)
5.00	$1,250	$1,081	$744	$406	$69	($437)	($2,125)	($7,188)

Table III shows that a 5% increase in price raises profits in a decreasing cost industry for almost all values of E_{AC}. The exceptions are $E_{AC} = 0.20$ when losses are made for E_D above 3.0; $E_{AC} = 0.50$ when losses are made for E_D above 1.5; and the single case where $E_{AC} = 0.10$ and $E_D = 5.0$.

TABLE IV
(Price increases 10%)

$E_D \backslash E_{AC}$	0.00	0.01	0.03	0.05	0.07	0.10	0.20	0.50
0.50	$9,000	$8,957	$8,872	$8,786	$8,701	$8,573	$8,145	$6,863
1.00	$8,000	$7,919	$7,757	$7,595	$7,433	$7,190	$6,380	$3,950
1.50	$7,000	$6,885	$6,656	$6,426	$6,197	$5,853	$4,705	$1,263
2.00	$6,000	$5,856	$5,568	$5,280	$4,992	$4,560	$3,120	($1,200)
2.50	$5,000	$4,831	$4,494	$4,156	$3,819	$3,313	$1,625	($3,438)
3.00	$4,000	$3,811	$3,433	$3,055	$2,677	$2,110	$220	($5,450)
3.50	$3,000	$2,795	$2,386	$1,976	$1,567	$953	($1,095)	($7,238)
4.00	$2,000	$1,784	$1,352	$920	$488	($160)	($2,320)	($8,800)
4.50	$1,000	$777	$332	($114)	($559)	($1,228)	($3,455)	($10,138)
5.00	$0	($225)	($675)	($1,125)	($1,575)	($2,250)	($4,500)	($11,250)

Strangely, Table IV shows that a 10% increase in price reduces profits for the same E_D as a 5% increase when $E_{AC} = 0.20$ and 0.50. However, there are eight more cells with losses when the price rises 10% than when the price rises 5%. In both cases, we have to allow for the possibility that a price increase will reduce profits in a decreasing cost industry.

Summing up, if industry demand is elastic and the industry is constant cost or increasing cost, an increase in price is almost certain to raise the profits of the businesses in the industry. If it is a decreasing cost industry, probably an increase in price will raise profits—but it is only probable—becoming less probable the higher the E_D and the E_{AC}.

B. Decreases in Average Cost

Continuing with the Acme Enterprises example of chapter 10, suppose Acme's average cost per can opener falls from $80 to $70, profit per can opener rises from $20 to $30 and total profits on Acme's can opener business increase from $20,000 to $30,000 per week. Can Acme raise its profits above $30,000 by cutting its price if all the other can opener producers follow? I showed in chapter 10 that if demand is inelastic, a price reduction will reduce profits. Consequently, the following cases assume an elastic demand.

When demand is elastic, a decrease in price causes a greater percentage increase in quantity sold, raising total revenue. But the total cost of producing a greater quantity is higher. What happens to profits depends on how average cost changes with increases in quantity—that is, it depends on the quantity elasticity of average cost (E_{AC}).

There are four more tables in this section, each with the same rows and columns as the first four. The difference here is that we are calculating the effect on profits of a decrease in price. Consequently, quantity increases, and one can see the effect on average cost in graphs G and H (pp. 310 and 311 above) by tracing the increase from Q2 to Q1. Each table is based on an average cost of $70. The other assumptions for the four tables are:

Table V: A 5% decrease in price in an increasing cost industry.
Table VI: A 10% decrease in price in an increasing cost industry.
Table VII: A 5% decrease in price in a decreasing cost industry.
Table VIII: A 10% decrease in price in a decreasing cost industry.
Again, the constant cost industry is represented by the first column in each table.

TABLE V
(Price decreases by 5%)

$E_D\backslash E_{AC}$	0.00	0.01	0.03	0.05	0.07	0.10	0.20	0.50
0.50	($4,375)	($4,393)	($4,429)	($4,465)	($4,501)	($4,554)	($4,734)	($5,272)
1.00	($3,750)	($3,787)	($3,860)	($3,934)	($4,007)	($4,117)	($4,485)	($5,588)
1.50	($3,125)	($3,181)	($3,294)	($3,407)	($3,520)	($3,689)	($4,254)	($5,947)
2.00	($2,500)	($2,577)	($2,731)	($2,885)	($3,039)	($3,270)	($4,040)	($6,350)
2.50	($1,875)	($1,973)	($2,170)	($2,367)	($2,564)	($2,859)	($3,844)	($6,797)
3.00	($1,250)	($1,371)	($1,612)	($1,854)	($2,095)	($2,458)	($3,665)	($7,288)
3.50	($625)	($769)	($1,057)	($1,345)	($1,633)	($2,064)	($3,504)	($7,822)
4.00	$0	($168)	($504)	($840)	($1,176)	($1,680)	($3,360)	($8,400)
4.50	$625	$432	$46	($340)	($726)	($1,304)	($3,234)	($9,022)
5.00	$1,250	$1,031	$594	$156	($281)	($938)	($3,125)	($9,688)

TABLE VI
(Price decreases by 10%)

E_D\E_{AC}	0.00	0.01	0.03	0.05	0.07	0.10	0.20	0.50
0.50	($9,000)	($9,037)	($9,110)	($9,184)	($9,257)	($9,367)	($9,735)	($10,838)
1.00	($8,000)	($8,077)	($8,231)	($8,385)	($8,539)	($8,770)	($9,540)	($11,850)
1.50	($7,000)	($7,121)	($7,362)	($7,604)	($7,845)	($8,208)	($9,415)	($13,038)
2.00	($6,000)	($6,168)	($6,504)	($6,840)	($7,176)	($7,680)	($9,360)	($14,400)
2.50	($5,000)	($5,219)	($5,656)	($6,094)	($6,531)	($7,188)	($9,375)	($15,938)
3.00	($4,000)	($4,273)	($4,819)	($5,365)	($5,911)	($6,730)	($9,460)	($17,650)
3.50	($3,000)	($3,331)	($3,992)	($4,654)	($5,315)	($6,307)	($9,615)	($19,538)
4.00	($2,000)	($2,392)	($3,176)	($3,960)	($4,744)	($5,920)	($9,840)	($21,600)
4.50	($1,000)	($1,457)	($2,370)	($3,284)	($4,197)	($5,567)	($10,135)	($23,838)
5.00	$0	($525)	($1,575)	($2,625)	($3,675)	($5,250)	($10,500)	($26,250)

1. A constant cost industry

If average cost does not change with increases in quantity, a price reduction of 5% reduces profits up to a price elasticity of 4.0 (Table V). A 10% price reduction reduces profits up to a price elasticity of 5.0 (Table VI).

2. An increasing cost industry

If average cost increases with increases in output, a 5% reduction in price reduces profits for every elasticity of demand up to 4.5, and profits decline more as the E_{AC} increases from 0.01 (Table V). The same pattern exists for a 10% reduction in price, only the decrease in profits is greater (Table VI).

3. A decreasing cost industry

Only if average cost falls with increases in output is there some ambiguity in these results.

TABLE VII
(Price decreases 5%)

$E_D\backslash E_{AC}$	0.00	0.01	0.03	0.05	0.07	0.10	0.20	0.50
0.50	($4,375)	($4,357)	($4,321)	($4,285)	($4,249)	($4,196)	($4,016)	($3,478)
1.00	($3,750)	($3,713)	($3,640)	($3,566)	($3,493)	($3,383)	($3,015)	($1,913)
1.50	($3,125)	($3,069)	($2,956)	($2,843)	($2,730)	($2,561)	($1,996)	($303)
2.00	($2,500)	($2,423)	($2,269)	($2,115)	($1,961)	($1,730)	($960)	$1,350
2.50	($1,875)	($1,777)	($1,580)	($1,383)	($1,186)	($891)	$94	$3,047
3.00	($1,250)	($1,129)	($888)	($646)	($405)	($43)	$1,165	$4,788
3.50	($625)	($481)	($193)	$95	$383	$814	$2,254	$6,572
4.00	$0	$168	$504	$840	$1,176	$1,680	$3,360	$8,400
4.50	$625	$818	$1,204	$1,590	$1,976	$2,554	$4,484	$10,272
5.00	$1,250	$1,469	$1,906	$2,344	$2,781	$3,438	$5,625	$12,188

In Table VII, we see that if the price decreases 5% and the E_{AC} = 0.01 or 0.03, profits increase if the E_D is 4.0 or higher; if E_{AC} = 0.05, 0.07, or 0.10, profits increase if E_D is 3.5 or higher; if E_{AC} = 0.20, profits increase if E_D is 2.5 or higher; and if E_{AC} = 0.50, profits increase if E_D = 2.00 or higher.

Appendix E

TABLE VIII
(Price decreases by 10%)

$E_D \backslash E_{AC}$	0.00	0.01	0.03	0.05	0.07	0.10	0.20	0.50
0.50	($9,000)	($8,963)	($8,890)	($8,816)	($8,743)	($8,633)	($8,265)	($7,163)
1.00	($8,000)	($7,923)	($7,769)	($7,615)	($7,461)	($7,230)	($6,460)	($4,150)
1.50	($7,000)	($6,879)	($6,638)	($6,396)	($6,155)	($5,793)	($4,585)	($963)
2.00	($6,000)	($5,832)	($5,496)	($5,160)	($4,824)	($4,320)	($2,640)	$2,400
2.50	($5,000)	($4,781)	($4,344)	($3,906)	($3,469)	($2,813)	($625)	$5,938
3.00	($4,000)	($3,727)	($3,181)	($2,635)	($2,089)	($1,270)	$1,460	$9,650
3.50	($3,000)	($2,669)	($2,008)	($1,346)	($685)	$308	$3,615	$13,538
4.00	($2,000)	($1,608)	($824)	($40)	$744	$1,920	$5,840	$17,600
4.50	($1,000)	($543)	$370	$1,284	$2,197	$3,568	$8,135	$21,838
5.00	$0	$525	$1,575	$2,625	$3,675	$5,250	$10,500	$26,250

Surprisingly, if the price decreases 10%, the outlook for profits is mixed compared to a 5% decrease. Thirty-three cells show an increase in profit when the price is reduced 5% (Table VII), compared to twenty-four cells when the price is reduced 10% (Table VIII). But for E_{AC} of 0.20 and 0.50, the increases in profit are greater for a 10% decrease in price. Indeed, the increases in profit for a 10% decrease in price are approximately double the increases in profit for a 5% decrease in price. I conclude that in a decreasing cost industry, we have to allow for the possibility that the businessmen in the industry can raise their profits by cutting their prices. If that is the case, a fall in average cost is likely to cause a fall in the industry price,[2] regardless of the competitive context (p. 186).

ENDNOTES

INTRODUCTION

1. Wealth is defined on pages 48–49 below.
2. Half of chapter 2 consists of an elaboration of this paragraph.
3. In the history of economic thought, the concept of value that I am calling intrinsic value also has been called objective value. In this book, I reserve the term "objective" for a different concept of value.
4. Chapter 2 expands on the nature of that relationship.

CHAPTER ONE

1. For the application of Ayn Rand's epistemology to induction for physics, see Harriman 2010, pp. 5–35.
2. 15-hour lecture course, "Objectivism Through Induction," given by Leonard Peikoff in 1997. Also see Aristotle's *Posterior Analytics*, Bk. II, Ch. 19.
3. I will define narrower conditions as necessary for specific economic theories.
4. In a modern industrial economy, people sometimes make exchanges by barter, often to escape taxes (Jain and Tomic 1995, 7–9). These are barter exchanges within a money economy and they are entirely dependent on established money prices. It is only by looking at existing money prices that a dentist and a house painter can agree to trade a painted house for a capped tooth.

Under certain emergency-type conditions, barter may be more widespread: for example, after a war or natural disaster, when the means of production have been destroyed and people are struggling to survive. Barter also has been widespread in prisoner-of-war camps (in WWII camps, cigarettes took on the functions of money). Since there is no production under these conditions, they cannot last. Exchange by barter is possible as an interim economic condition, not as the base of an economic system.

5. There was a brief flurry of interest in this subject in the 1980s. Some examples are Cowin and Kroszner 1987, Glasner 1989, Sargent and Wallace 1982, Selgin 1988, and White 1984.
6. That it would work means that anything resembling the financial crisis of 2008 would be impossible. The best exposition I have seen of the causes of the 2008 catastrophe is Woods 2009. Woods bases his analysis on the Austrian theory of the business cycle, with which I disagree, but that theory is not essential to his case.

CHAPTER TWO

1. An equivalent meaning of economic value is the market price or market value, that is, the terms on which each good and service in an economy is available for purchase or sale. The theory of market price is what most of this book is about.

2. Chapter 3 defines market and price and shows that the meaning of price depends on whether one's conception of value is intrinsic, subjective, or objective.

3. The subjectivist premise that economic activity is inherently unintelligible is a contributing cause of the prevalence of model building in modern economics. It is not the only cause (see appendices A and B).

4. Ayn Rand defined reason as "the faculty that identifies and integrates the material provided by man's senses" (1964, 20). Since reason functions by means of concepts, I treat "conceptual consciousness", "rational consciousness", "reason," and "man's mind" as designating the same thing—man's reasoning mind. The exact relation among these aspects of a conceptual consciousness can be found in Peikoff 1991.

5. This is the view underlying Frank Knight's articles on capital theory in the 1930s and 1940s. It is also the view at the base of modern national income accounting, as chapter 13 shows.

6. Cantillon 1959, also includes land, pp. 27–31.

7. Some less philosophical economists take this expression to mean that the cause of preferences is the subject matter of some other discipline, such as psychology (e.g., Stigler and Becker 1977, 76). That interpretation contradicts the meaning of subjectivism.

8. The idea that value depends on a type of relationship is not new in economics. Menger had this idea (1871, 52, note and 120), and it appears occasionally in some of the other early marginalists/subjectivists (for example, Jevons 1871, xxxiv; also see Kohler 1990, 33).

The introduction noted that Menger based his economic theory on an (implicit) concept of objective value. In perhaps his best statement, Menger identifies value as "a judgment economizing men make about the importance of the goods at their disposal for the maintenance of their lives and well being" (1871, 121). In this and other statements (pp. 75, 77, 116), Menger treats "man's life" as the standard of value for economic values. In addition, Menger holds that human knowledge of the facts is a prerequisite for economic value (1871, 52, 120) and his theory is permeated with the view that value depends on facts, a view with which I emphatically agree (see part C below).

9. This statement touches on an issue discussed briefly in the preface—the fact that any objective economic analysis of capitalism must presuppose an ethics of rational self-interest in which it is proper for a man to want what benefits him. If that is an evil motive, a system that satisfies it is also evil. The morality of altruism would wipe out everything I have to say, plus economics as a science

and, existentially, anything resembling an economic system. The Dark Ages show the effect of altruism on economic systems.

10. This point, but only this point, is made explicitly in Stigler and Becker (1977, p. 84).

11. A complex conception, a hierarchy of values, is necessary to grasp fully what is involved in the ranking of values in one's mind. Part I of chapter 4 explains the meaning of a hierarchy of values.

12. Many economists do not hold this view in conscious, explicit detail, but it is the dominant implicit view, and the only view that is consistent with subjectivism.

CHAPTER THREE

1. The relationship between property rights and the law of supply and demand described in the text also runs in the other direction, that is, enforcement of property rights makes the law of supply and demand possible. Without property rights, businessmen would not exist so there would be no supply and nothing for consumers to demand (for example, the former Soviet Union).

2. This is in part a consequence of the modern interpretation of the law, which confines it to a very small sector of the economy (appendix A). But more important, it is a consequence of the modern definitions of supply and demand. See note 4 following.

3. In this context, a time period has to be at least implicit for a quantity to have a clear meaning. For example, if a man eats five slices of pizza, that is a lot per week and hardly any per year. Unless otherwise indicated, our time period will be a month.

4. This end note is for those who know something about supply and demand in modern economics. Appendix A presents my reasons for rejecting demand curves and supply curves. Briefly, the supply curve is meaningless outside of perfect competition and demand curves cannot be defined for competing firms. Thinking of supply and demand as curves has nullified the law of supply and demand.

5. Contractors and auction houses are exceptions. Chapter 10 explains the different meanings of supply and demand in the context of sealed bid prices and auction prices.

6. I take up worker markets at the end of chapter 7 and in chapter 9. I cover hotel rooms, housing, and so forth in chapters 9 and 11. My comments on retail stores are scattered throughout (see the index).

7. Economists have taken the archetype of a service-provider to be the musician, whose value (the sound he creates) vanishes in the moment of his performance. This characterization of service, if it were accurate, would apply to the entire realm of art and entertainment. When the concert is over, it is gone, and unlike the janitor, the musician does not leave even a clean floor behind.

There is a streak of philistinism in economics that goes back to Veblen, and this view of services is an example. What is left behind by a work of art or entertainment is in the minds of the audience which, hopefully, have been elevated by the experience and given emotional fuel to go on with their lives. In the best cases, works of art change men's lives, as Ayn Rand's novels changed mine.

8. It has been common in economics to think that goods "yield" services, that goods are valued for the services they yield, and that the present value of a good is equal to the discounted value of its future services. I reject this view. The so-called services of goods are their attributes or consequences that make them a means to an end (p. 35 above); for example, a teacup does not yield services; it holds tea. Thinking of the attributes of goods as services leads to hopeless contradictions, for example, see Frank Knight (1935, 39-48, 1936, 438-40); for an indication of the contradictions, see Buechner (1971, 84-101). It is impossible to integrate the idea that goods yield services with the conception of services as actions of human beings.

9. John Ridpath suggested the exception of a farmer hiring a man to pile up pieces of wood. A man can do this without tools, but that is all he can do, and even that presupposes the tool used to split the log.

10. In today's markets, the place now includes cyberspace.

11. Market often is used more restrictively to mean just the buyers, that is, the market *for* a product.

12. One of the evils of a runaway, or even a moderate, price inflation is that prices rise so fast that people's knowledge of the current value of money fades away.

13. If one is also familiar with a range of prices for a given category of goods like shoes, then one knows that a $200 pair is a good pair of shoes. But that is a separate issue. A price of $200 for an Eisen socket tells one nothing about the Eisen socket, but the price is perfectly clear nonetheless.

14. Chapter 4, part I, shows that people usually make purchases by weighing the value of one good at a price versus the value of another good at a price, and ultimately they weigh the value of a good versus the value of the money they must give up to get it.

15. This is completely misinterpreted by Ricardo 1951, 13-14.

16. The actions I have described as competitive are the same actions a *free-market* monopolist (appendix A) must take to keep his monopoly. The actions of the monopolist, however, cannot be called competitive because he is not competing *with* anybody. I suggest *economic value creation* as the name for a monopolist's productive activity.

CHAPTER FOUR

1. But the second highest value in a high building need not be higher than the second highest value in a lower building.

2. Chapter 7 takes up the meaning of afford.

3. The pattern I have described makes absolute sense to me, but it certainly has exceptions. There could be and should be research on the extent to which people follow this pattern.

4. In economics, marginal usually means one more or one less (appendix C).

5. Item/price combinations are not part of modern economics and hence do not figure in this argument.

6. I am indebted to Harry Binswanger for this point. ("Philosophic Issues in Economics" [two lectures], OCON, June 2008.)

7. The principle of gains from trade does not say that you cannot lose money on an investment. People who buy stocks or bonds understand that there is the possibility that the price of the stock or bond will fall. Neither does the principle apply when businesses invest in plant and equipment in order to produce new products.

8. On the principle of opportunity cost, economists include an average profit as a fixed cost. I do not. See chapter 3, pp. 53–54.

9. These concepts are not part of modern economic thought, at least not in the United States.

10. However, the practice of recalculating average cost in order to justify the price does appear to be senseless.

CHAPTER FIVE

1. For what is wrong with the cost-of-production theory, see part IV of chapter 4.

2. At this point, one might want to ask, what is modern economics' theory of price? Appendix A shows that economics does not have a theory of price. The theory it does not have is a conglomeration of intrinsic, subjective, and objective elements.

CHAPTER SIX

1. This is not to say that the amount of total costs is always obvious. In the early years of the 21st century, there was a major controversy over whether or not the stock options that businesses gave to their executives should be treated as a current expense (see Greenspan 2007, 432–35).

2. Thanks to Ted Gray for this point.

3. For an overview of many pricing methods and policies that are important to marketing professionals, see Kurtz (2008, 605–55).

4. This point depends on the assumption that demand is elastic, which it is for individual firms. For in indication of why, see p. 181 above.

5. See appendix A (p. 283) for a list of these. Everything has been seen and interpreted through the distorting lens of pure competition, an error Weston largely avoids, but which Lanzillotti 1958 embraces. Many of Lanzillotti's errors are answered by Weston 1972.

6. In some companies, a goal may ossify into an end in itself, in which case, the goal will cease to serve the end of long-run profit maximization. As Weston (1972) says, "These rigidities represent a pathological condition, not characteristic of companies with good performance results" (p. 9).

7. To avoid the clutter of parenthetical references on this page, I am placing all the references in this paragraph in this endnote with numbers corresponding to the numbers in the paragraph: (1) Jobber and Hooley 1987, 169 & 171; Lanzillotti 1958, 932–43; Lanzillotti 1964, 13–14; Weston 1972, 8, (2) Lanzillotti 1964, 13–14, (3) Hall and Hitch 1939; Lanzillotti 1958, 932, (4) Jobber and Hooley 1987, 169; Lanzillotti 1958, 923 & 928–31; Lanzillotti 1964, 13–14; Weston 1972, 4 & 8, (5) Lanzillotti 1958, 934–36, Lanzillotti 1964, 14, (6) Jobber and Hooley 1987, 169; Weston 1972, 8, (7) Baumol 1959; Jobber and Hooley 1987, 169; Weston 1972, 8, note 12.

8. If one can see through the distortion caused by pure competition, which Lanzillotti could not.

9. For example, Haynes 1962, 47–9; Jobber and Hooley 1987, 169, 171; Weston 1972, 4, 8; all commenting on (2) a target rate of profit on sales or costs.

10. They attribute this observation to Kotler et al 1985.

11. See West 1972 for an alternative analysis of the goal of market share with the same conclusion (p. 8).

CHAPTER SEVEN

1. This subsection considers the thinking of businessmen as buyers for the first time.

2. See appendix C for an elaboration of this point.

3. I am grateful to the president of Monarch Construction Company, Ronald A. Koetters, who sent me written comments on this section (February 6, 2009).

4. Koetters 2009 (see note 3).

5. People with average incomes are able to grasp sums of money much greater than they could ever spend, like a million dollars, but the meaning in purchasing power is vague in their minds compared to the meaning of a thousand dollars. By contrast, the meaning of a million dollars to a billionaire is not vague because he knows many things he could buy with it.

6. In opposition to the opportunity cost doctrine, I hold that the interest he does not earn is not a cost. It is an alternative that he should consider, just as he should consider all the alternatives open to him.

7. Chapter 11 has much more to say about fair market value.

8. Since the CEO is responsible for the whole operation, if the business paid him what he added to revenue, he would add nothing to profit. Similarly, if each

lower-level executive were paid what his division added to revenue, there would be no addition to profit. If the CEO were then also paid what all the divisions together added to revenue, the addition to total cost would be twice as large as the addition to total revenue.

9. This is a variation on Böhm-Bawerk's principle (1959, 182; 1892, 54, 57) that goods that are easily replaced are valued at the price it costs to replace them. This is an important principle and the rest of this book makes considerable use of it. Appendix C defends it at length.

10. See appendix C for my critique of this doctrine.

CHAPTER EIGHT

1. In fact, though the article did not include the value of the doctor's patients, normally the net worth method does include that value.

2. Chapter 4, p. 83.

3. This point is elaborated in chapter 12 (pp. 248–49).

4. This includes brokered prices, even though many such prices change from moment to moment. The constant fluctuation of brokered prices reflects people's constantly changing grasp of the constantly changing market conditions. See chapter 11.

5. Chapter 3 (p. 44) said that this is where the law of supply and demand fails. Appendix A proves this.

6. This is the answer to the question at the end of the first paragraph in part F above.

CHAPTER NINE

1. The term employee is misleading because many workers are self-employed. Nevertheless, their wages are subject to the same principles as those who are employed by others.

2. If this is so, one might ask, why have I waited until now to say it? Because this is not a textbook.

3. Market prices, as distinct from objective prices, require both a buyer and a seller. A price which no buyer will pay or which no seller will accept is not a market price, though it could be an objective price.

4. See appendix C for elaboration of this point.

5. This concept is close to what is called the rate of return on investment (ROI). My concept differs by including all costs, not just fixed plant and equipment.

6. This is another variation on Böhm-Bawerk's principle (1959, 182; 1892, 54, 57) that goods that are easily replaced are valued at the price it costs to replace them (p. 135 above).

7. This is another reason that businessmen change prices less frequently than economists think is reasonable.

8. The exact time period is not important as long as it is relatively short (less than a year), and the same for both demand and supply.

9. This is the market demand defined at the beginning of part A above.

10. This is certainly a widespread phenomenon of the welfare state, but probably not of laissez-faire capitalism, where "preferring not to work" would be the equivalent of "preferring to starve."

11. Supply also decreases when men start looking for work or training for work in a different worker pool because jobs in their original occupations are disappearing and/or wage rates for those jobs are stagnant or declining, or wages are higher elsewhere.

12. Independently of recessions, supply increases in particular fields as workers train for relatively higher paying occupations, and move from lower-wage pools to higher-wage pools.

13. See Friedman and Schwartz 1963, 41–2; for concrete instances, see Hessen 1975, 75–77.

14. There may be men who have recently resigned because they lost out to someone else in their career path.

15. Sometimes, this may seem absurdly high because it must include the discounted present value of all retirement and other benefits he has earned over his years of employment with the other business. If he has been there many years, his initial salary may be many times his future annual salary. (Thanks to Kathryn Eickhoff for this point.)

16. Chapter 11 elaborates this point.

CHAPTER TEN

1. For elaboration, see appendix A (p. 277 below).

2. There are cases that fall between the two I have distinguished, cases where, for example, a change in costs affects many of the competitors but not all, or that affects all of them to different extents. Then the outcome of a change in price depends on the specific facts of the case.

3. The Woolworth's retail chain followed this policy early in the twentieth century (Winkler 1940, 209).

4. Usually, economists interpret cost classification as a long-run phenomenon, representing how costs change when there is enough time to change plant and equipment. I also use this interpretation when it is relevant.

5. The labels on the lines (curves) have no significance other than to distinguish the original cost curves (AC1, AC2, AC3) from the increased cost curves (AC11, AC22, AC33). By definition, the constant cost curves must be parallel straight lines. The increasing and decreasing cost curves need not be straight lines and the higher cost curves (AC22 and AC33) need not be parallel to the lower cost curves (AC2 and AC3).

6. When only Acme changes price, the elasticity of demand for Acme can openers is the $\%\Delta Q \div \%\Delta P$.

7. When every firm in the industry changes price by the same percentage, Acme's E_D is equal to the E_D of the industry ($\%\Delta Q_{industry} \div \%\Delta P_{average}$ = the percentage change in quantity of the whole industry divided by the percentage change in the average price of all the producers in the industry).

8. We can look at this relation in terms of the equation for total cost [TC = Q(AC) (p. 98 above). In a decreasing cost industry, AC rises as Q falls. If the percentage increase in AC exceeds the percentage decrease in Q, total cost rises. This would mean that the total cost of producing a smaller quantity was greater than the total cost of producing a larger quantity. If such a case is possible, it must certainly be rare.

9. This is the total cost of the whole industry, that is, the total cost of each business in the industry all added together. The analysis in the text implicitly assumes that a change in total cost for the industry is divided among the individual firms in proportion to their total cost before the change in price—both here and in part B following.

10. There is a way to make this analysis more precise, which is also more difficult. Appendix E presents this approach.

11. Or when demand falls. See part III, B below.

12. Economists are not entirely ignorant of this. For example, see Baumol 1959, pp. 75–76.

13. In this part, I repeatedly use as examples chains of production involving three industries (for example, wheat, flour, and bread). If I took into account that each industry might be constant cost or increasing cost or decreasing cost, I would have to analyze (and the reader would have to follow) 27 different possibilities. For example, (1) all three are constant cost; (2) wheat is constant cost and the other two are increasing cost; (3) wheat is increasing cost, flour is constant, and bread is decreasing cost; and so forth.

14. See the Federal Reserve's table "Capacity Utilization Rates."

15. There is a parallel adjustment in the hamburger case quoted above (p. 189). The primary effect of the increase in demand for hamburger is to increase the price of beef all along the chain of production. Butchers will respond to the increased price of hamburger by using some cuts of meat for hamburger which they ordinarily would not use for that purpose. This increase in the supply of hamburger mitigates the increase in hamburger's price, while raising the price of the cuts of meat diverted to hamburger. Since the total supply of beef is unchanged, prices adjust along the chain of production so that total demand remains at its original level. The profits of the cattle ranchers increase; the profits of the meat packers and butchers do not. (The meat packers and butchers may profit a little on the inventory they are holding when the price rises.)

16. The price elasticity of demand implied in the preceding example is about 3.0; the price elasticity of the demand for cars commonly is reported as 1.5.

17. This is an instance of the case described in chapter 8 (p. 146 above): if the asking price turns out to be too high and the house does not sell, the price was objective, but it was not a market price.

18. Part IV of chapter 11 explains how prices rise and fall in commodity markets.

19. The demand for flour is quite inelastic (as is the demand for bread), so a decrease in price reduces total revenue (pp. 177–78 above).

20. The market for beef is a little different: A decrease in the demand for beef by consumers is passed back to the meat packers and then to the cattle markets. The quantity of cattle supplied cannot be reduced very much over the short run, so the price of cattle falls, reducing the average cost of the meat packers and the butchers, who compete down prices all along the chain of production, with no corresponding decrease in supply. The profits of the cattlemen fall while the meat packers and butchers maintain their profit margins at lower prices and sell the same quantity. Only the cattlemen have a motive to lay off workers.

21. An increase in average cost equal to the rate of price inflation is not a real increase in average cost, and an increase in selling price at the same rate is not a real increase in price (pp. 49–51 above).

22. The other major form of income is profit. Chapter 12 shows the relation of profit to production.

23. On information technology, see Greenspan 2007, pp. 168–69.

CHAPTER ELEVEN

1. My knowledge of the New York Stock Exchange is based primarily on some ten days over three years spent in several programs of the NYSE's Educational Services Department under the direction of Murray M. Teitelbaum, to whom I remain very grateful. Also see Dalton 1993.

2. Also see Alchian and Allen 1972, 67–68.

3. There is much more on the distribution of resources in chapter 12.

4. The days of "the pit" are coming to an end as more and more futures contracts are made electronically. However, the functioning of the pit is easier to grasp and explain.

5. The description of the adjustment process in this and the preceding paragraph is simplified for the purpose of exposition. In fact, commodity prices change from moment to moment with changes in supply and demand, just like the prices of stocks.

6. It is just as wasteful to spend time, energy, and wealth economizing on things that are relatively abundant as it is to squander things that are relatively scarce.

CHAPTER TWELVE

1. See Backhouse and Medema (2009) for evidence of the pervasiveness of scarcity in modern economics. Appendix D elaborates modern economists' viewpoint and explains what is wrong with it.

2. Modern economists claim that there is such a goal. See appendix D.

3. Relative scarcity does not measure the relation between the absolute quantities of two or more goods. There is no necessary relation between the price of a good and the number of units that are produced each year. Goods with lower prices may be more or less greater in number than goods with higher prices. Automobiles are much more expensive than jet skis, but many more cars than jet skis are produced each year.

4. The following discussion divides the causes of an increase in relative scarcity between (1) Demand increases relative to supply and (2) Supply decreases relative to demand. This division is for the purposes of explanation only. An increase in demand relative to supply has the same effect as a decrease in supply relative to demand, and any relative change that fits under one heading can be rephrased to fit under the other.

5. For details, see pp. 187–88 above. It is also possible that the seller can increase his output with a change in unit cost. Part C below considers the connection of cost to relative scarcity.

6. Note 4 applies equally here for decreases in relative scarcity.

7. With the exception of those goods in fixed supply whose prices usually do not equate the quantity demanded to the quantity supplied. Nevertheless, the prices of such goods are the best measure possible of their relative scarcity.

8. This is true even though the consumer may have bought the product as the means to some further end, such as dinner. When a product is purchased by the final consumer, it passes outside the economic context, where everything has a price and is subject to purchase and sale at a profit. Outside that context, ends are personal and individual, not economic.

9. The Austrian School originated with Carl Menger, whom I saluted in chapter 2 (note 9). Böhm-Bawerk was Menger's student, and I have made important use of his principle that replaceable goods are valued at the price required to replace them.

10. The traditional name for this subject in economics is "the allocation of resources." Since collectivist ideology saturates the approach represented by that name, I do not use it.

11. Rent, royalties, and interest are other forms of income that I will not explain.

12. This is an approximation because for the most part, retail firms do not produce the goods they sell and, consequently, total revenue does not measure their output. Chapter 13 deals with this issue.

13. Evidently, the average rate in today's economy before taxes is about 9% (Browning and Zupan 2009, 536).

14. From this perspective, a recession every few years is a good thing for a free economy. Unneeded workers are fired, increasing the profits of the firms who employed them, and unprofitable firms go out of business. The human and nonhuman factors who lose their jobs in this process then find employment with businesses making profits, thereby increasing aggregate output.

15. This is not to deny that there are enormous spiritual benefits gained by people from living in a prosperous, growing economy. The value for one's personal happiness of a general cultural sense of optimism and confidence about the future can hardly be overestimated. This feeling about the future is not primarily a function of how well the economy is doing, but a good economy certainly helps. In addition, if the economy grows faster than the population, the average standard of living rises over time, which is an enormous gift to everyone from the economy's businessmen.

CHAPTER THIRTEEN

1. *Survey of Current Business* (April 2010), Table 1.1.5. Gross Domestic Product, p. D–3.

2. See note 1 above.

3. The national income accounts do not view intermediate services as sold for the last time because unlike business fixed investment, businesses use or use up intermediate services in the current period. Intermediate services count as costs in the current period, and businesses pay for them out of current sales receipts.

4. Income payments include interest to bond holders, rent to landlords, and royalties to authors, composers, and inventors, when these are private individuals. If they are businesses, then payments to them are counted in payments to other businesses.

5. A third component which we are ignoring is depreciation on plant and equipment. The standard approach is to eliminate depreciation by assuming that total revenue and total cost are net of depreciation—that is, we assume total cost does not include depreciation and we subtract depreciation from total revenue, so profit still equals total revenue minus total cost.

6. The fact that, according to this theory, almost all that value is created by businesses' workers, means that the labor theory is alive and well in the national income accounts.

7. When the final product is a service, like banking, it is treated the same as a good. The national income accountants take the price of the service as equal to the sum of all the value-added at all the stages of producing that service.

8. For several years in the 1970s, George Reisman and I were colleagues at St. John's University. I learned many things from Reisman, but by far the most important was something he said in a conversation about the national income accounts. "Firms do not produce value," he said. "They produce goods which *have* value." Forty years later, this is still the most illuminating thing anyone ev-

er has said to me about economics. I saw immediately that the orthodox view depended on intrinsic value, intrinsic value having played a major role in the dissertation I had just completed. To the best of my knowledge, however, Reisman did not do anything with this idea, and intrinsic value does not figure in his criticism of the national income accounts (Reisman 1998, 674–82).

9. These estimates could, should, and would be calculated by private, profit-making businesses if the government did not do it.

10. *Survey of Current Business* (April 2010), Table 1.12. National Income by Type of Income, p. D–16.

11. See note 10 above.

12. *Survey of Current Business* (April 2010). Table 1.1.5. Gross Domestic Product, p. D–3.

13. See note 12 above.

14. See note 12 above.

15. See note 10 above.

16. See note 10 above.

17. The revision of the national income accounts in the text brings down the entire Keynesian apparatus and virtually everything in modern macroeconomics. To see the consequences of this analysis, the reader should read the relevant chapters in *Capitalism* by George Reisman.

APPENDIX A

1. *Survey of Current Business*. "Gross-Domestic-Product-by-Industry Accounts: Value Added by Industry as a Percentage of Gross Domestic Product (Percent)." Release date May 25, 2010.

2. This point is touched on by Silberston 1970, 557.

3. See Cohen and Cyert 1965, 225–6, for exactly this point. Also see Hall and Hitch 1939, 21 and Blaug 1978, 415.

4. An example is the kinked demand curve analysis, famous among economists.

5. See Clower 1998 for an expression of grave skepticism about the direction of modern economics, including its mathematization, especially p. 403. Also see Mayer 1993.

6. Economists also apply this theory of price in contexts where it *is* completely inappropriate—to firms that are alleged to have "monopoly power"— that is, to any firm that is not a pure competitor. In other words, the economic theory of monopoly is applied to firms that have competitors. Thus, economists sometimes solve the problems associated with the theory of price for oligopolies by ignoring the problems and treating such firms as monopolies.

APPENDIX B

1. This is widely recognized. See High 2001 for a comprehensive review of all the aspects of competition obviated by pure competition (pp. xxvii-xl) and without which aspects pure competition is utterly desiccated.

2. See Baumol 1959, p. 6 for a closely related view.

APPENDIX C

1. Schumpeter (1954, 301) stresses that this paradox had been solved before, but this is the point at which the solution entered the thinking of most economists.

2. The additional unit is the standard context in economics for marginalism. It is much too narrow. The correct context is a change in condition, circumstances, or facts (pp. 299–300 below).

3. For those philistines, like Veblen (chapter 3, note 7), who claim they do not see any objective value to men of diamonds, jewelry, crystal goblets, fine china, silverware, etc.—aesthetically, the value is beauty; psychologically, the value is standards—that is, the self-value implied by having standards, as opposed to the brute who has none.

4. This is Böhm-Bawerk's idea again (1959, 182; 1892, 54, 57).

5. The interested reader can find the complete argument for this conclusion in any principles of economics text.

6. See chapter 4, pp. 77–83 above.

7. Appendix A (pp. 280–81 above).

8. Hall and Hitch (1939) were evidently the first to make this point, based on interviews with 38 businessmen. They set off a debate which continues to this day (Blinder and others 1998, 40). For example, see Early 1956, Jobber and Hooley 1987, Lanzillotti 1958, Lanzillotti 1964, Nowotny and Walther 1978, and Weston 1972. For a survey, see Silberston 1970. This debate is usually described as being between marginal cost pricing and full cost pricing. My theory is *not* full cost pricing.

9. Chapter 7 mentions and rejects this doctrine in three different places (pp. 124, 135, 137 above). Note 7 of that chapter (p. 323) shows the absurdity of marginal revenue product when applied to CEO compensation.

10. Mandler cites the first (1890) and second (1891) editions of Marshall, which are not readily available. The passage closest in content in the eighth (1920) edition is on page 337. It is likely that Marshall dropped this material from editions subsequent to the second, probably because he decided it was invalid.

APPENDIX E

1. The highest E_{AC} I am considering here is 0.5, which is in the middle of the inelastic range. If the E_{AC} is 0.5, a 10% increase in quantity causes a 5% increase in average cost (in an increasing cost industry). That seems like a very big change in cost to me. Consequently, I hypothesize that E_{AC} higher than 0.5 are unlikely within the range of output that firms normally produce. This is a subject, like many in this book, which calls for empirical research.

2. As we can observe in this last case, the effect on industry profits of changes in price can be unexpected. Price changes other than 5% and 10% give different results from those presented here.

EXEGESIS AND GLOSSARY

The fundamental concept of this book is *value*. Important subdivisions of that concept have two meanings which run concurrently throughout the book. This raises an obstacle to the book's clarity which this exegesis and glossary is designed to remedy. However, if the reader finds the discussion in the next four paragraphs confusing (which it well may be outside the context created by the book), please wait to read it until the end. The glossary of definitions, however, should still be helpful.

The *Oxford English Dictionary* gives fifteen definitions for the word value, seven as a noun and eight as a verb. Most of these fifteen meanings are subdivided two or three times, for a total of thirty-eight. Sixteen of these are identified as obsolete, which leaves twenty-two meanings for value which are currently in use, according to the OED. Twenty-two meanings are too many. They overwhelm the crow (Rand 1990, 62–63) and paralyze thought.

In this context, Ayn Rand's definition of value as "that which one acts to gain and/or keep" demonstrates again her ability to cut to the heart of an issue. This concept of value as a goal of action is the fundamental meaning of value. Everything else is built on this. The second meaning of value in this book presupposes Ayn Rand's definition. That second meaning is the ranking or standing or importance of the goals of action, the things that one acts to gain and/or keep. This is the concept of value as the ranking in a hierarchy of values. The second meaning of value is both a noun (the ranking) and a verb (to rank).

After twenty years of thinking about value, the following guidelines to its meaning are the best I can do. Usually when value appears as a plural, its meaning is a goal of action—for example, "The values of many young men are limited to their mothers, their dogs, and their girlfriends." (Thus, I use value(s) in the index when the meaning is goals of action.) When value is used as a verb, almost always it means ranking or to rank—for example, "They value their dogs more than their girlfriends." Monetary value is a price and means the ranking in the market's hierarchy of values—for example, "Spot is a mutt so his value is low." Thus, value as ranking in a hierarchy can refer to two very different types of hierarchy: first in the minds of human beings and second in the market via prices. Because they are so different, these two kinds of hierarchy are easy to distinguish according to the context in which they appear. Like every other concept, context is the decisive factor in determining the meaning of value.

The two meanings (1) goals of action and (2) the ranking of a goal, are shared by "value," "economic value," and "objective economic value." Other concepts of value are defined below which have only one meaning, at least for the purposes of this book. If the reader is in doubt about a meaning of value in the text, he can consult this glossary. Page references are to the pages in the text where the concept is explained, defined, or significantly elaborated. The order of the definitions is roughly hierarchical, starting with Ayn Rand's definition.

VALUE (AS A GOAL OF ACTION): This is the root concept. Used without a modifier, value has three meanings that are relevant for this book (pp. 34–35). As a goal of action, value means the things in existence that one acts to gain and/or keep (pp. 31–32).

VALUE (AS RANKING IN A HIERARCHY): the ranking of things in existence in a hierarchy of values (p. 34).

OBJECTIVE VALUE: something that one grasps as good for one's life, based on a rational understanding of the facts and evaluated by the standard of man's life on earth (p. 32).

NONOBJECTIVE VALUE: values that contradict either or both of the two foundations of objective value: (1) man's life as the standard and/or (2) reason as the faculty for grasping the means to that end (pp. 35–36). Nonobjective values are objective disvalues (see below).

SOCIALLY OBJECTIVE VALUE: the value of a good or service to the people who buy the good (pp. 99–100).

PHILOSOPHICALLY OBJECTIVE VALUE: the value of a good or service evaluated by the standard of "the best possible to man, i.e., by the criterion of the most rational mind possessing the greatest knowledge, in a given category, in a given period, and in a defined context..." (pp. 99–100).

ECONOMIC VALUE (AS A GOAL OF ACTION): values that are bought and sold. These are the goals of trade and exchange, that is, "goods and services." Values that are produced but not sold, such as the family dinner cooked by a homemaker, are not *economic* values (p. 24)

ECONOMIC VALUE (AS RANKING IN A HIERARCHY): a synonym for *market value*, the economic value of a good or service is its price, which gives its ranking in the market's hierarchy of values (pp. 150–51).

MARKET VALUE: the price at which a good or service is bought and sold (p. 24).

OBJECTIVE ECONOMIC VALUE (AS A GOAL OF ACTION): objective values that are bought and sold (p. 38), that is, economic values rationally appraised as good for one's life on the basis of the facts and the standard of man's life (p. 32).

OBJECTIVE ECONOMIC VALUE (AS RANKING IN A HIERARCHY): the price of a good or service created on the basis of a rational grasp of the economic facts (pp. 139–40, 150). Such a price is objective. The proposition that prices measure the objective economic value of goods and services is this book's theory of price.

OPTIONAL VALUES: values that are optional on the standard of man's life; they are not required to live, but they objectively support man's life (p. 35).

DISVALUE: something which has negative value and whose removal or elimination is a value, such as garbage, trash, and disease (p. 60).

NONOBJECTIVE PRICES: prices based on something other than the economic facts; these are equally subjective prices and arbitrary prices (p. 140).

The last two value concepts following are technical concepts in economics and are not indebted to Ayn Rand's concept of value.

PRESENT VALUE: the value today of a sum of money to be received some time in the future. Normally, the present value is less than the future value because a present sum can earn interest until the future time is reached (91, 117, 125).

VALUE ADDED: the total revenue of a business minus the cost of its purchases of goods and services from other businesses (p. 261). The value-added tax is widely used in Europe and popular with politicians there because it is invisible to consumers who pay it in higher prices of everything they buy.

REFERENCE LIST

Ackley, Gardner. 1978. *Macroeconomics: Theory and Policy*. New York: Macmillan.

Adams, Walter. 1977. "The Steel Industry." In *The Structure of American Industry*. ed. Walter Adams, 86-129. New York: Macmillan.

Alchian, Armen A. and William R. Allen. 1972. *University Economics*. 3rd ed. Belmont, CA: Wadsworth.

Alter, Max. 1990. *Carl Menger and the Origins of Austrian Economics*. Boulder, CO: Westview Press.

Andrews, P.W.S. 1964. *On Competition in Economic Theory*. London: Macmillan.

Arrow, Kenneth J. 1959. "Toward a Theory of Price Adjustment." In *The Allocation of Economic Resources*. ed. M. Abramovitz, 41-51. Stanford: Stanford University Press.

Backhouse, Roger E. and Steven G. Medema. 2009. "Retrospectives: On the Definition of Economics." *Journal of Economic Perspectives* (Winter): 221–33.

Baumol, William J. 1959. *Business Behavior, Value and Growth*. New York: Macmillan.

———. 2000. "What Marshall Didn't Know: On the Twentieth Century's Contributions to Economics." *Quarterly Journal of Economics* (February): 1-44.

Binswanger, Harry. 1992. "Life-Based Teleology and the Foundation of Ethics." *Monist* (January): 85–103.

Blaug, Mark. 1978. *Economic Theory in Retrospect*. 3rd ed. Cambridge: Cambridge University Press.

Blinder, Alan S., Elie R. D. Canetti, David E. Lebow, and Jeremy B. Rudd. 1998. *Asking About Prices*. New York: Russell Sage Foundation.

Böhm-Bawerk, Eugen von. 1959. *Positive Theory of Capital*. 2nd vol of *Capital and Interest* in 3 vols. trans George D. Huncke. South Holland, IL: Libertarian Press.

——— 1892. "Value, Cost, and Marginal Utility." trans George Reisman. *Quarterly Journal of Austrian Economics* (Fall 2002): 37-79.

Bronowski, J. 1973. *The Ascent of Man*. Boston: Little, Brown and Company.

Browning, Edgar K. and Mark A. Zupan. 2009. *Microeconomics: Theory & Applications*. 10th ed. John Wiley & Sons.

Buchanan, James M. 1969. *Cost and Choice*. Chicago: Markham Publishing Company.

———. 1982. "The Domain of Subjective Economics: Between Predictive Science and Moral Philosophy." In *Method, Process, and Austrian Economics*. ed. Israel M. Kirzner. pp. 7-20. Lexington, MA: D.C. Heath and Company.

Buechner, M. Northrup. 1971. *A Critical Exposition of Frank H. Knight's Conception of Capital and the Production Process*. unpublished doctoral dissertation, University of Virginia.

———. 1974. "Dog-Eat-Dog Competition." *The Freeman* (October): 614–26.

———. 1976. "Frank Knight on Capital as the Only Factor of Production," *Journal of Economic Issues* 10 (September): 598–617, reprinted in *Pioneers in Economics 37: Frank Knight (1885–1972), Henry Simons (1899–1946), Joseph Schumpeter (1883–1950)*. ed. Mark Blaug. 48–67. Aldershot, England: Edward Elgar, 1992.

———. 1981. "The Root of Terrorism." *Objectivist Forum* (October): 6–12.

———. 1982. "Ayn Rand and Economics." *Objectivist Forum* (August): 3–9.

Burczak, Theodore A. 1994. "The Postmodern Moments of F. A. Hayek's Economics." *Economics and Philosophy* (April): 31–58.

Cantillon, Richard. 1730(?) *Essai Sur La Nature Du Commerce En General*. ed. Henry Higgs. London: Frank Cass and Company, 1959.

Clower, Robert W. 1998. "Three Centuries of Demand and Supply." *Journal of the History of Economic Thought* (December): 397–410.

Coats, A. W. Bob. 2000. "Roundtable: The Progress of Heterodox Economics." *Journal of the History of Economic Thought* (June): 145–48.

Cohen, Kalman J. and Richard M. Cyert. 1965. *Theory of the Firm: Resources Allocation in a Market Economy*. Englewood Cliffs, NJ: Prentice-Hall.

Colander, David. 2000. "The Death of Neoclassical Economics." *Journal of the History of Economic Thought* (June): 127–43.

Colander, David, Richard P. F. Holt, and J. Barkley Rosser, Jr. 2004. *The Changing Face of Economics: Conversations with Cutting Edge Economists*. Ann Arbor: University of Michigan Press.

Cowin, Tyler and Randall Kroszner. 1987. "The Development of the New Monetary Economics." *Journal of Political Economy* 95 (June): 567–80.

Dalton, John M. 1993. *How the Stock Market Works*, 2nd ed. New York: New York Institute Of Finance.

Davis, Steven J., R. Jason Faberman, and John Haltiwanger. 2006. "The Flow Approach to Labor Markets: New Data Sources and Micro-Macro Links." *Journal of Economic Perspectives* (Summer): 3–26.

Dolan, Robert J. and Hermann Simon. 1996. *Power Pricing*. New York: The Free Press.

Earley, James S. 1956. "Marginal Policies of 'Excellently Managed' Companies." *American Economic Review* (March): 44–70.

Fisher, Franklin M. 1983. *Disequilibrium Foundations of Equilibrium Economics*. Cambridge: Cambridge University Press.

———. 1987. "Adjustment Process and Stability." In *The New Palgrave, A Dictionary of Economics*, vol. 1. 26–29. London: Macmillan.

Fog, Bjarke. 1960. *Industrial Pricing Policies: An Analysis of Pricing Policies of Danish Manufacturers*. Amsterdam: North-Holland Publishing Company.

Friedman, Milton. 1953. "The Methodology of Positive Economics" in *Essays in Positive Economics*. Chicago: The University of Chicago Press.

Friedman, Milton and Anna Jacobson Schwartz. 1963. *A Monetary History of the United States 1867–1960*. Princeton: Princeton University Press.

Fusfeld, Daniel R. 2000. "Comments on the Roundtable Discussion: The Progress of Heterodox Economics." *Journal of the History of Economic Thought* (June): 171–77.

Glasner, David. 1989. *Free Banking and Monetary Reform*. New York: Cambridge University Press.

Goldberg, Joel H. 1994. "Setting the Right Price for Your Practice." *Medical Economics* (August 22): 61–68.

Greenspan, Alan. 2007. *The Age of Turbulence*. New York: Penguin Press.

Guerrien, Bernard. 2002. "Once Again on Microeconomics." *post autistic economics review*. 16: (September).
1.http//www.btinternet.con/~pae_news/review/issue16.htm

Haddock, David D. and Fred S. McChesney. 1994. "Why Do Firms Contrive Shortages? The Economics of Intentional Mispricing." *Economic Inquiry* (October): 562–81.

Hahn, Frank. 1987. "Auctioneer." In *The New Palgrave, A Dictionary of Economics*, vol. 1. 136–38. London: Macmillan.

Hall, R. L. and C. J. Hitch. 1939. "Price Theory and Business Behavior." *Oxford Economic Papers* (May): 12–45.

Hand, D. Wade. 2001. *Reflection without Rules*. Cambridge University Press.

Haslett, D. W. 1990. "What Is Utility?" *Economics and Philosophy*. 65–94.

Hausman, Daniel M. and Michael S. McPherson. 1993. "Taking Ethics Seriously: Economics and Contemporary Moral Philosophy." *Journal of Economic Literature* (June): 671–731.

———. 1994. "Preferences, Belief, and Welfare." *American Economic Review* (Papers and Proceedings) (May): 396–400.

Harriman, David. 2010. *The Logical Leap: Induction in Physics*. New American Library.

Haynes, W. Warren. 1962. *Pricing Decisions in Small Business*. Lexington: University of Kentucky Press.

Heilbroner, Robert L. 1988. *Behind The Veil of Economics*. New York: W. W. Norton & Company.

Hessen, Robert. 1975. *Steel Titan*. New York: Oxford University Press.

Heyne, Paul. 1997. *The Economic Way of Thinking*. Upper Saddle River, NJ: Prentice Hall.

High, Jack, ed. 2001. *Competition*. Northampton, MA: Edward Elgar.

Howitt, Peter. 2002. "Looking Inside the Labor Market: A Review Article." *Journal of Economic Literature*. (March): 125–38.

Hume, David. (1739 & 1740). *A Treatise of Human Nature*. Garden City, New York:Dolphin Books (Doubleday & Company), 1961.

Jain, Chaman L. and Igor M. Tomic. 1995. *Essentials of Monetary and Fiscal Economics*. Flushing, NY: Graceway Publishing Company.

Janssen, Maarten C. W. 1993. *Microfoundations: A Critical Inquiry*. New York: Routledge.

Jevons, W. Stanley. 1871. *The Theory of Political Economy*. 5th ed. New York: Augustus M. Kelley, 1957.

Jobber, David and Graham Hooley. 1987. "Pricing Behavior in UK Manufacturing and Service Industries." *Managerial and Decision Economics*. 167–71.

Kaldor, Nicholas. 1937. "Annual Survey on Economic Theory: The Recent Controversy on the Theory of Capital." *Econometrica* (July), reprinted in *Essays on Value and Distribution*. 153–91. The Free Press of Glencoe, Illinois, 1960.

Kaplan, A. D. H., Joel B. Dirlam, and Robert F. Lanzillotti. 1958. *Pricing in Big Business: A Case Approach*. Washington, DC: The Brookings Institution.

Knight, Frank H. 1935. "The Ricardian Theory of Production and Distribution," *Canadian Journal of Economic and Political Science* (February and May), reprinted in *On The History And Method Of Economics*. 33–88. Chicago: University of Chicago Press (Phoenix Books), 1963.

——— 1936. "The Quantity of Capital and the Rate of Interest I," *Journal of Political Economy* (August): 433–63.

Kohler, Heinz. 1990. *Intermediate Microeconomics*. 3rd ed. United States of America: Scott Foresman and Company.

Kotler, P. L. Fahey and S. Jatusripitak. 1985. *The New Competition*. Englewood Cliffs, NJ: Prentice Hall.

Krueger, Anne O. 1974. "The Political Economy of the Rent-Seeking Society," *American Economic Review* (June): 291–303.

Kurtz, David L. 2008. *Boone & Kurtz, Contemporary Marketing*. 13th ed. United States: South-Western Cengage Learning.

Lanzillotti, Robert F. 1958. "Pricing Objectives in Large Companies." *American Economic Review* (December): 921–40.

———. 1964. *Pricing, Production, and Marketing Policies of Small Manufacturers*. Pullman, WA: Washington State University Press.

Mandler, Michael. 1999. *Dilemmas in Economic Theory*. New York: Oxford University Press.

Marshall, Alfred. 1920. *Principles of Economics*. 8th ed. Philadelphia: Porcupine Press.

Mas-Colell, Andreu. 1980. "Noncooperative Approaches to the Theory of Perfect Competition: Presentation." *Journal of Economic Theory* 22:121–135.

Mas-Collel, Andreu, Michael D. Whinston, and Jerry R. Green. 1995. *Microeconomic Theory*. New York: Oxford University Press.

Mayer, Thomas. 1993. *Truth versus Precision in Economics*. Brookfield, Vermont: Edward Elgar.

Menger, Carl. 1871. *Principles of Economics*. trans. James Dingwall and Bert F. Hoselitz. New York: New York University Press, 1976.

Mill, John Stuart. 1848. *Principles of Political Economy*. Fairfield, NJ: Augustus M. Kelley, 1987.

Mises, Ludwig von. 1949. *Human Action*. 3rd ed rev. Chicago: Henry Regnery Company, 1966.

Monroe, Kent B. 1979. *Pricing: Making Profitable Decisions*. New York: McGraw-Hill.

Montgomery, Michael R. 1994. "Fully Inarticulate Model Economics: or Does Math Equal Macro?" *Journal of Post Keynesian Economics* (Fall): 45–68.

Myerson, Roger B. 1999. "Nash Equilibrium and the History of Economic Theory." *Journal of Economic Literature* (September): 1067–82.

Nowotny, Ewald and Herbert Walther. 1978. "The Kinked Demand Curve— Some Empirical Observations." *Kyklos* 31:53–67.

Peikoff, Leonard. 1982. *The Ominous Parallels*. New York: Stein and Day.

———. 1991. *Objectivism: The Philosophy of Ayn Rand*. New York: Dutton.

Popper, Karl R. 1934. *The Logic of Scientific Discovery*. New York: Routledge, 1959.

Prescott, Edward C. 1986."Theory Ahead of Business Cycle Measurement." Federal Reserve Bank of Minneapolis *Quarterly Review* (Fall): 9–22.

Pribram, Karl. 1983. *A History of Economic Reasoning*. Baltimore: Johns Hopkins University Press.

Rand, Ayn. 1943. *The Fountainhead*. New York: Bobbs-Merrill Company.

———. 1957. *Atlas Shrugged*. New York: Random House.

———. 1961. *For the New Intellectual*. New York: Random House.

———. 1964. *The Virtue of Selfishness*. New York: New American Library.

———. 1966. *Capitalism: The Unknown Ideal*. New York: New American Library.

———. 1967. *Introduction to Objectivist Epistemology*. expanded 2nd ed. NAL Books, 1990.

———. 1969. *The Romantic Manifesto*. New York: World Publishing Company.

———. 1971. *The New Left: The Anti-Industrial Revolution*. New York: New American Library (Signet Book).

———. 1982. *Philosophy: Who Needs It*. New York: Bobbs-Merrill Company.

———. 1988. *The Voice of Reason*. New York: New American Library.

———. 2009. *Objectively Speaking: Ayn Rand Interviewed*. eds. Marlene Podritske and Peter Schwartz. New York: Lexington Books.

Ayn Rand's Marginalia. 1995. ed. Robert Mayhew. New Milford, CT: Second Renaissance Books.

Reisman, George. 1998. *Capitalism*. Ottawa, IL: Jameson Books.

Renehan, Edward J., Jr. 2007. *Commodore: The Life of Cornelius Vanderbilt*. New York: Basic Books.

Ricardo, David. 1821. *On the Principles of Political Economy and Taxation*. ed. Sraffa. Cambridge, England: Cambridge University Press, 1951.

Sargent, Thomas J. and Neil Wallace. 1982. "The Real Bills Doctrine Versus the Quantity Theory of Money: A Reconsideration." *Journal of Political Economy.* (June):1212–36.

Schumpeter, Joseph A. 1954. *History of Economic Analysis.* New York: Oxford University Press.

Scitovsky, Tibor. 1971. *Welfare and Competition.* rev ed. Homewood, IL: Richard D. Irwin.

_____. 1995. "The Meaning, Nature and Source of Value in Economics." In *Economic Theory and Reality.* 197–208. Brookfield, VT: Edward Elgar.

Selgin, George A. 1988. *The Theory of Free Banking: Money Supply under Competitive Note Issue.* Totowa, NJ: Rowan and Littlefield.

Silberston, Aubrey. 1970. "Surveys of Applied Economics: Price Behavior of Firms." *Economic Journal* (September): 511–82.

Sinclair, Stuart. 1993. "A Guide to Global Pricing," *Journal of Business Strategy* (May/June): 16–19.

Smith, Adam 1776. *The Wealth of Nations.* Glasgow ed. Indianapolis: Liberty Classics, 1981.

Sraffa, Piero. 1926. "The Laws of Returns under Competitive Conditions." *Economic Journal* (December): 535–50.

Stigler, George J. and Gary S. Becker. 1977. "De Gustibus Non Est Disputandum." *American Economic Review* (March): 76–90.

Thweatt, William O. 1983. "Origins of the Terminology 'Supply and Demand.'" *Scottish Journal of Political Economy.* (November): 287–94.

Tracinski, Robert. 1999. "Liberty and Morality: Alexis de Tocqueville's *Democracy in America.*" *The Intellectual Activist* (February): 15–23.

Vaughn, Karen I. 1982. "Subjectivism, Predictability, and Creativity: Comment on Buchanan." In *Method, Process, and Austrian Economics.* ed. Israel M. Kirzner. 21–29. Lexington, MA: D.C. Heath and Company.

Weston, J. Fred. 1972. "Pricing Behavior of Large Firms." *Western Economic Journal* (March): 1–18.

Winkler, John K. 1940. *Five and Ten.* rev 1957. New York: Bantam Books.

Woods, Thomas E. Jr. 2009. *Meltdown.* Washington, DC: Regnery.

INDEX

In the index, page references for "value," "economic value," and " objective economic value" are subdivided "as goals of action" and "as ranking in a hierarchy." For an explanation, see the "Exegesis and Glossary" (pp. 333–36). Also, in many instances, "firm" or "firms" has been substituted for "businessmen" or "businesses" to economize on space (see pp. 92–93).

evaluation of the theory, 146–50
fundamental fact of, 173
negotiated prices, 94, 121–25
relation to market prices, 146
relative scarcity and, 242–43
sealed bid prices, 95, 125–28
someone sets the price, 97–110
summary statement, 88–89, 150–52, 238
three facts affecting prices, 97–98
underlying principle of, 201–2
wage rates, 134–38, 243
theory of price
importance of, 39–41
key theory of economics, 10
modern economics' conception, 279
the theory modern economics' does not have, 321n2(chap. 5)
theory of wages and salaries
CEO compensation, 168–70
facts affecting, 134–37
moral justification for, 254–55
role in creating wages of:
addition to total revenue, 137
relative scarcity, 166–68, 242, 243
supply and demand, 166–67, 167–68
value of workers' production, 205
worker markets, 160–70
how wages fall, 165–66
how wages rise, 164–65
market demand for workers, 161–62, 163
market supply of workers, 162
worker pools, 163–64
decreases in supply, 324n11
increases in supply, 324n12
three meanings of value, 34–35
Tocqueville, Alexis De, 119
total cost
calculation of profit and, 98

explanation of, 75
not always obvious, 321n1(chap. 6)
equals objective economic value of factors used and used up, 251
of an industry, 325n9
of producing less is less, 181, 185, 313, 325n8
relation to contractor's bid, 127
required relation to total revenue, 101, 103, 104, 247, 296
total income (in NIPA), 257
total revenue
calculation of profit and, 98
equals total objective economic value produced, 251
required relation to total cost, 101, 103, 104, 247, 296
total spending (in NIPA), 257
based on intrinsic value, 263–65
based on objective value, 267–70
equals spending on final products, 259–63
effects of intrinsic value, 269
total variable costs
of producing less is less, 74
to whom and for what, 32, 265–66
tripartite division, 9, 25–28

underpriced (stock), 221
understanding versus prediction, 291
unemployment rate (when it is meaningful), 23–24
unit costs, 75
role in price setting, 101–4
structure of, 104–7
U. S. Steel, 90, 141
utility
in opportunity cost doctrine, 54
Jevons' view, 86–87
meaning in modern economics, 30

value(s) (as goals of action)
action "for the sake of" a, 130